The
Montessori
Controversy

John Chattin-McNichols, Ph.D.

SEATTLE UNIVERSITY

&

THE MONTESSORI EDUCATION INSTITUTE OF THE PACIFIC NORTHWEST

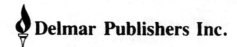
Delmar Publishers Inc.

NOTICE TO THE READER

Cover Design: Nancy Gworek
Cover Photos Courtesy of: Top: Seattle University & Estate of E. M. Standing
                             Bottom: John Chattin-McNichols

Delmar Staff
  Administrative Editor: Jay Whitney
  Editing Supervisor: Marlene McHugh Pratt
  Project Editor: Andrea Edwards Myers
  Production Coordinator: Teresa Luterbach
  Design Supervisor: Susan C. Mathews

For more information, address Delmar Publishers Inc.
3 Columbia Circle, Box 15-015
Albany, New York 12212-5015

Copyright © 1998 by Delmar Publishers

Printed in the United States of America
Published simultaneously in Canada
by Nelson Canada,
a division of the Thomson Corporation

Library of Congress Cataloging-in-Publication Data
Chattin-McNichols, John
    The Montessori controversy / John Chattin-McNichols
      p. cm.
    Includes bibliographical references and index

    1. Montessori method of education. I. Title.
LB775.M8C54 1998   90-19319
372.12'92--dc20   CIP
      ISBN-13: 978-0-8273-4517-1
      ISBN-10: 0-8273-4517-8

TABLE OF CONTENTS

FOREWORD

The renaissance of the philosophy and practices known as the "Montessori Method" began in the United States in the late 1950's. Driven by a handful of zealous educators and philosophers and supported by a slightly larger group of American parents, the movement spread rapidly from teacher training centers on the East Coast, Midwest, and Southern California to private schools serving middle and upper income families.

A first public school program was established in the late 1960's, but not until the development of the "magnet school" concept in the mid 1970's did Montessori come into its own in certain large public school districts throughout the country.

Whether in the private or public sector, however, the movement has been characterized by the enthusiasm, dedication, and "workaholism" of teachers, administrators, and parents of the children involved. The prodigious tasks of starting schools, teaching children, training teachers, and growing from preschool classes to elementary to secondary and back to infant and toddler childcare centers left little time or energy for studying outcomes.

By the 1980's, it was becoming clear that Montessori education could well fade again from America's educational arena if its advocates failed to conduct research regarding the nature and efficacy of current Montessori practices and the impact of Montessori upon the development of children throughout the U.S.

One of the clearest advocates for the need for research has been Dr. John Chattin-McNichols. He began publishing research on Montessori in 1981 and since then has contributed more than twenty articles to professional magazines and journals.

His significant activities have included looking at early research on Montessori in new ways in order to help contradict misconceptions about the practice of the method. He has been particularly interested in bringing points of view from outside the Montessori community to effect greater understanding and common benefit. For the past four years he has co-directed a program to train teachers how to conduct research in their own classrooms.

Dr. Chattin-McNichols' book is a major addition to the literature in early childhood education. It answers the most-asked questions about Montessori within and outside of the Montessori community. Indeed, everyone interested in planning curriculum based on the best knowledge of research, theory, and practice should find *The Montessori Controversy* an invaluable resource.

Bretta Weiss, National Director, American Montessori Society

PREFACE

Why a Book on Montessori?

This book on Montessori education represents the first mainstream American book on Montessori in more than a decade. Its goal is to examine Montessori in the context of current theory and practice in child development and early childhood education.

Montessori is in a unique position as a model (and a movement) in early childhood today. It continues to grow in popularity, and in scope. For example, new teacher education programs now prepare Montessori teachers for working with infants through high school age students. Public Montessori schools are now found in many areas of the country. These programs exist in well over 100 school districts, and some of them serve 600 or more students. They offer a bewildering array of services for preschool age students through seventh and eighth graders. Public school Montessori educators have a newspaper and a well-attended national conference. Montessori continues to be very strong as a model for private preschools, and to a lesser extent, elementary schools. In many areas of the country, one-third or more of all preschools claim some sort of Montessori affiliation.

To make matters worse for the early childhood educator who wants to provide fair coverage of Montessori, there is a remarkable array of Montessori organizations, each with claims of representing the best possible Montessori model. Information on Montessori in general is typically quite hard to come by; many Montessori organizations assume that anyone with a serious interest in Montessori will be able to take Montessori training, a commitment (usually) of a year's study which many of us are unable to undertake. Many find Montessori's writings, while inspiring, difficult to translate into contemporary terms: at times, she seems to be advocating a very behaviorist practice, and the next minute, what she writes about seems like Summerhill, A.S. Neil's classic free school. This book lays out the basics of Montessori, both the theory and actual classroom practices, explaining the terms and concepts unique to Montessori.

Some writers on Montessori have chosen to comment on Montessori's original writings, rather than focusing on current practices in American schools today. While this has the advantage of certain authenticity, it neglects the changes that have come about in Montessori practice since 1907. I have chosen to draw heavily on my own Montessori teaching experience and my 12 years as a Montessori teacher educator and supervisor of Montessori teachers. This book does reflect the wide diversity that characterizes American Montessori today. The politics of Montessori--at least the major issues and camps -- are discussed rather than ignored, preparing the reader for the diversity she will see in actual Montessori classrooms.

The research on Montessori is more extensive than many early childhood educators realize. Much of it, however, is in sources that are relatively difficult to locate. This book critically summarizes all available research to date.

This book and the *Instructor's Guide* should allow an early childhood educator who is not a Montessori teacher to cover Montessori in an Early Childhood Education course, such as a "Programs" or "Introduction to ECE" course or a "Current Issues" course. The book could also be used in a Child Development, Philosophy of Education, or Curriculum & Instruction course.

Preface

Plan of the Book

The *Instructor's Guide* and the chapter introductions and summaries should be helpful to both instructors and students in organizing their use of the book. The *Instructor's Guide* allows expansion of the material covered, including suggestions for films or videotapes, formats for observation, and a national list of contact people for finding Montessori schools to observe. An annotated bibliography is provided for assigning or suggesting further reading, especially for graduate students. Many instructors have found that just allowing students to conduct a few structured observations in Montessori classrooms is enough to raise so many good discussion topics that time does not allow all of them to be covered.

The book can be divided into three parts. Chapters 1 through 5 are concerned with the basic concepts of Montessori. The first chapter presents a framework to understand the multiple meanings that have come to be associated with the word "Montessori." Terms unique to Montessori, her philosophy and theory are covered in the next chapters. Clearing up common misunderstandings about Montessori is important enough to have an entire chapter (Chapter 2) devoted to it.

The ideas of Montessori's philosophy are presented and then extended into Montessori practice. An important goal of this section is to make readers see how the practice in Montessori classrooms comes from Montessori's theories and her values; that is, to see the unity of Montessori theory and practice, rather than to focus on isolated practices that seem to be at odds with other models.

In the next five chapters, content areas in the Montessori classroom are examined in some detail. The Practical Life or everyday living chapter (Chapter 6) gives a rationale for these exercises, and compares and contrasts this area to the role play or dress-up area in traditional nursery schools. A short section in this chapter discusses the role of practical life for older students, including the use of computers in the Montessori classroom.

In Chapter 7, the sensorial materials are discussed. This chapter begins the discussion of Piaget's theories and the relationship of Piaget and Montessori, both in theory and in actual classroom practices. The many opportunities for classification and seriation available to Montessori children are presented, as well as the more limited opportunities for conservation activities. The chapter uses the content area to deepen the reader's understanding of certain key Montessori concepts, using materials as examples. This content area is often misunderstood, and this detailed chapter discusses how Montessori practices can be seen in comparison to other models.

The mathematics chapter uses the wonderful Montessori math manipulatives to expand the discussion of several Montessori concepts. The chapter discusses the whole notion of the role of manipulatives for the learning of young children, and Montessori's pioneering role in this area. In a detailed example from elementary math materials, the Montessori concept of abstraction and of how materials should be related to the concepts they are designed to teach is presented.

In Chapter 9, the theory and practices of the Montessori language curriculum area are presented. This chapter begins with a review of language acquisition theories, and compares current thought to Montessori's ideas as presented in her book, *The Absorbent*

Mind. The materials and presentations of the language area are discussed, with special attention being given to the teaching of reading. The relation of the Montessori approach to current practices, especially emergent literacy and whole language approaches, is discussed.

The final chapter of the middle part of the book discusses Montessori Geography, History, and Social Studies materials in the elementary classroom. This and the choice of examples in the Math chapter are attempts to counterbalance the stereotype that Montessori is only for preschool age children. In this chapter, an example is chosen that contrasts strongly with traditional elementary school practices. Not only the materials that would be involved in teaching this to children, but also the rationale for the Montessori practices are explained in detail.

The final section of the book (Chapters 11-15) can be thought of as a "special topics" section. The discussion of Piaget begun in the sensorial curriculum chapter is taken up again in detail in Chapter 11. In addition to a discussion of Piaget and other writers such as David Elkind who have written on Piaget and Montessori, the detailed discussion of Montessori by constructivist researcher Rheta DeVries in her latest book is examined at length. One of the most controversial areas, Montessori's ideas on fantasy and role play, was felt to be so important that Chapter 12 is focused on this topic. This chapter begins with clarifying what Montessori actually said. Research on actual classroom practices is used to examine the critical question of whether Montessori's writings still describe what really goes on in classrooms today.

In Chapter 13, the research on classroom processes in Montessori is presented. In this section, we are able to use several studies to look at what actually goes on in Montessori classrooms. This chapter introduces some of the problems with the research base on Montessori so far. This critical review is continued in Chapter 14, a longer chapter in which outcome research on Montessori is presented. The results are grouped by cognitive, academic, motor, and other headings, to make it easier to grasp the overall results of the review. Each subarea is summarized, and the chapter summary at the end covers the findings in each area, the weaknesses in the research base, and crucial future directions for Montessori research.

A final chapter discusses the wide variety of new trends and issues in Montessori. The public schools movement is discussed, as is the re-emergence of a Montessori-based religious education movement. A variety of other issues and topics is presented, from attempts to achieve federal recognition for Montessori teacher education programs, to the Teacher's Research Network. In the appendices, additional resources are presented, in addition to an index and list of references. These include a long translation of definitions of key Montessori terms, a list of suppliers of Montessori materials, and Montessori teacher education centers.

To sum up, this book is designed to allow detailed coverage of the complex phenomenon that is the Montessori movement, and, with the *Instructor's Guide*, to allow the instructor to include this area in her class.

ACKNOWLEDGMENTS

This book is dedicated to Gregory and David

I would like to thank a long list of people who helped this book come to completion. My wife and children must receive first mention, for putting up with many hours of extra work. The staff, parents, and children of Woodinville Montessori School and West Seattle Montessori School were very gracious in allowing me to take photos in their environments. I would also like to thank Greg Nelson, a fellow Montessorian, Teacher-Researcher, and friend, for his careful reading of the manuscript. Many Montessori teachers and teacher educators have helped me grow in understanding Montessori; I would like to mention Dr. Peggy Loeffler, Joy Turner, Dottie Feldman, Lorna Terhune, Dr. Rae Rosen, Eileen Buerman, and the other members of the Elementary Task Force of the Teacher Education Committee as a group that was particularly good at helping ourselves think things out.

JCM
Seattle, 1991

John Chattin-McNichols, Ph.D., took his Montessori training at the International Center for Montessori Studies (Association Montessori International) in Bergamo, Italy, in 1970/71, where his instructors and examiners included Mario Montessori, the son of Maria Montessori. Dr. Chattin-McNichols received his baccalaureate degree in Psychology from UCLA; his doctorate is in Child Development and Early Education from Stanford University. He taught Developmental Psychology at Purdue University before coming to Seattle University to conduct an American Montessori Society affiliated Montessori teacher education program in 1979. In 1987/88, he taught at the University of the West Indies, St. Augustine, Republic of Trinidad and Tobago as a Fulbright Scholar. He is currently an Associate Professor at Seattle University, directs the Montessori Education Institute of the Pacific Northwest, and is a member of the Board of the American Montessori Society.

CHAPTER 1
What Is Montessori?

Chapter Goals: In this chapter, you will learn:
- Four possible meanings of the word "Montessori."
- A three-part structure for examining the Montessori method.
- Some basic concepts in Montessori theory and practice.

As a former Montessori teacher and now as a Montessori teacher educator, I'm always being asked to give a clear and detailed outline of Montessori--usually during the last 15 seconds of an elevator ride, or at a party with music blaring.

One of the reasons it's so difficult to explain Montessori is the number of topics that could be considered. There are some **people**, one in particular, who have that last name; there are a number of **books** by and about Dr. Montessori and her work; there are a number of **organizations**, such as schools, training centers, and societies or associations; and finally, there is the Montessori **method**, what it is that goes on (or should go on) in Montessori schools. Any one of these is hard to cover adequately in the elevator. A year's study is usually considered the right length of time for a person to learn enough about Montessori to begin "doing Montessori" in a classroom. But let's break the topic into these four areas and outline what there is to be discussed in each one.

First, the **people**: Dr. Maria Montessori (1870-1953) was Italy's first woman doctor of medicine, an extraordinary person by anyone's standards. She founded the first Montessori school (*Casa dei Bambini*, or Children's House) in Rome, in 1907. The two best biographies of her life are excellent introductions to her work: E. M. Standing's *Maria Montessori; Her Life and Work* is less critical, but contains more information on the actual method. Rita Kramer's *Maria Montessori; A Biography*, is more recent and more concerned with Montessori in her other roles--feminist, social reformer, etc.

Dr. Montessori's son, Mario Montessori, was, until his death in 1981, the lifetime head of the Association of Montessori Internationale (AMI), the organization that she founded in 1929 to carry on her work. Maria Montessori's grandson, Dr. Mario Montessori, Jr., is a psychologist less directly concerned with the running of the AMI and Montessori schools.

Secondly, there are a number of **books** by and about Dr. Montessori and her work, in addition to the two biographies already mentioned.

The following by Montessori are recommended in addition to the biographies:
The Montessori Method (Montessori, 1967, Shocken Books)

1

The Absorbent Mind (Montessori, Delta, 1967)
From Childhood to Adolescence (Montessori, Shocken, 1973)

A much larger reading list can be found in the publications list of the American Montessori Society, 150 5th Ave, New York 10011. The AMS is one of several **organizations** whose primary role is the spread of information about Montessori and her methods. The oldest is the AMI; their international headquarters is in Amsterdam (AMI, Koninginneweg 161, 1075 CN, Amsterdam, The Netherlands). They publish *Communications* and can provide a list of AMI affiliated schools and accredited training centers here and abroad. The AMI has approximately 400 affiliated schools in the U.S., and many more around the world. Currently, AMI operates 14 training programs in the United States, including an elementary Montessori program in Washington D.C., and infant and toddler training in Houston. NAMTA, the North American Montessori Teachers Association, is also aligned with the AMI. NAMTA publishes the *Quarterly* (a journal), a series of pamphlets for parents titled *Montessori Talks to Parents,* and operates a media service. Their address is 11424 Bellflower Road, N.E., Cleveland, Ohio, 44106.

The other major organizations in the United States, mentioned above, are the American Montessori Society, founded in 1960 and the National Center for Montessori Education, a newer organization. The Society has over 45 affiliated training programs across the country, and provides services to members, including sale of books and Montessori materials. American Montessori Society teacher eduction programs are accredited by a separate organization, the Accreditation Council for Childhood Education Specialist Schools (ACCESS). The AMS publishes *Montessori Life* (formerly called *The Constructive Triangle*), a quarterly journal. The NCME publishes the *Reporter*, and has some 15 teacher education programs associated with it nationwide.

Insofar as schools are concerned, independent schools (those not affiliated with any organization) probably outnumber all the schools affiliated with all organizations put together. While many unaffiliated schools are excellent, **there is no legal way to prevent any unscrupulous person from labeling any early childhood program "Montessori."** In any metropolitan area, there are a few schools so labeled, without trained teachers, Montessori materials, or the faintest idea of Montessori methods. More consumer awareness on the part of the parents is the only answer to this problem. The same situation exists with Montessori teacher education programs, and expensive, insubstantial, "quickie" programs frustrate many well-meaning students each year.

I have included a pair of pie charts to show the distribution of Montessori schools in the U.S. by affiliation and age level of children served (Figures 1-1 and 1-2).

In looking at schools in my area and around the country, by far the most common type of school is one that serves 3- to 6-year-olds, and is unaffiliated with any national Montessori organization. The AMS records show that it affiliates the largest number of schools, some 400 to 750 annually. Newer Montessori organizations also affiliate schools, although the standards for affiliation may not be as stringent, or the affiliation program may not be reinforced with periodic on-site school visits.

The most common Montessori school is still the traditional grouping of 3-, 4-, and 5-year-olds that Montessori first worked with. As more training programs become available for working with other age groups, these are beginning to increase. With new schools opening to serve older children, and existing schools adding on elementary programs, the 6-9 and 9-12 levels of Montessori are probably growing at least as quickly as the 3-6 level.

Figure 1-1

Distribution of Montessori Schools by Affiliation

From 1989 Survey, Seattle, N = 69

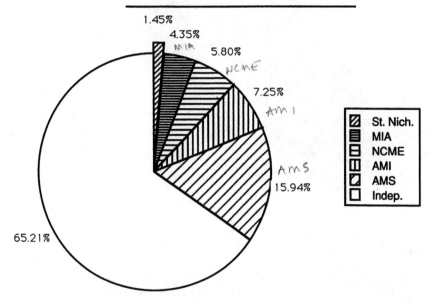

One important component of growth in elementary Montessori is the public Montessori schools; approximately 50 districts in the U.S. have some sort of Montessori program. These are usually elementary programs, and some, such as the Dallas Independent School District and Buffalo, N.Y. programs, continue beyond grade 6. Secondary programs are still few and far between, although this is an area that many schools are planning for. The recent availability of Montessori teacher education programs for this level should be an impetus for further growth here.

Programs dealing with children younger than three are also enjoying a growth surge, due again in part to the fact that training in Montessori methods for this age level is now available at several locations around the country. The dramatic growth in this area is also partly the result of demographics: the new baby boomlet and the large numbers of families seeking high quality programs for their children have certainly contributed to this growth.

In describing the various parts of the Montessori **method**, I have divided the information into three levels (Figure 1-3). The first level is that of theory and philosophy, the background of Montessori's ideas which are the rationale for her model of education. Montessori had a clear theory of development, primarily a constructivist theory similar to Piaget's. This area contains her theory of 4 planes (or stages) of development, her idea of sensitive periods, and so on.

Figure 1-2

Distribution of Montessori Schools by Age Ranges

From 1989 Survey, Seattle, N = 69

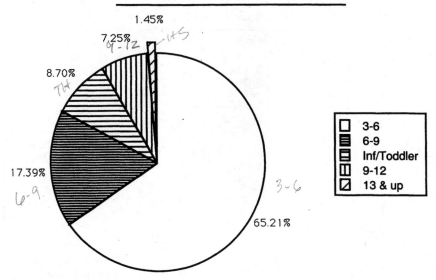

Another important area in Montessori's theory and philosophy is the area of child learning. This includes her ideas on the importance of manipulative materials, of isolation of difficulties, the importance of concentration, her ideas on reinforcement, and so on. In the area of reinforcement, for example, her ideas anticipated the concept of "competence motivation," the notion that children can be motivated to work through a desire to become better at a skill, without external rewards such as praise from adults.

A final key part of Montessori's theories concerns the goals of education. Every philosophy of education must include this. Montessori sought to develop independence, responsibility, and respect for others. The source of the information at this level of theory and philosophy is Montessori's writings and also the lectures on Montessori theory that are a part of any good Montessori teacher education program.

The ideas of Montessori at this top level (theory and philosophy) determine the content of the next level, the Montessori model. The model level contains the information on the ideal Montessori classroom. One key area here is Montessori's ideas on the environment. This includes macro-environment (classroom design, furniture, shelf height, for example) and the micro-environment (the Montessori materials). Another important area is the teacher. Teacher behaviors are specified in this, the model level. A final area of the model concerns Montessori's ideas on appropriate behavior for the child: the expectations that are reasonable for a teacher to hold.

Figure 1-3
Montessori Theory, Model, and Practice

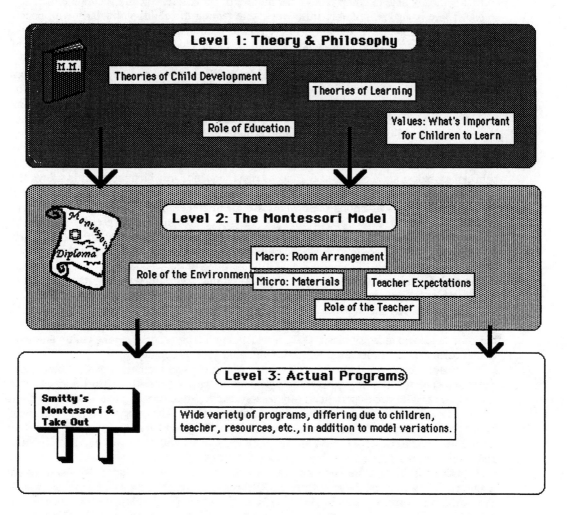

Let's examine how theory (on the top level) influences model practices on the second level. In the top level, we have Montessori's ideas on the child's power of memory. Montessori claimed that each sensory experience of the child left a trace, a record in the child's subconscious mind. The subconscious for Montessori, then, was a great storeroom of these memories, which were constantly being processed, examined for similarities, and so on (see Chapter 16 in *The Absorbent Mind*).

In the model level, this idea results in an emphasis on presenting a great deal of information to the child, and a reduced emphasis on testing. Montessori preprimary classrooms have been criticized for offering the child math activities beyond what the young child is typically able to comprehend, for the use of long, scientifically accurate terms, and so on. There is also remarkably little work with testing the child, particularly with pencil and paper assessments. If the child really retains memories of his or her sensory experiences, and if that knowledge does not need to be in the child's conscious memory to be of use, then these aspects of the Montessori model make sense.

Another example of a practice derived from this theory of memory (which behaviorists would reject out of hand) is the concept of "indirect preparation." The majority of the activities that are undertaken with the Montessori materials have an indirect aim in addition to their more obvious direct aim. In placing knobbed cylinders back into their corresponding holes, the child is perfecting her eye-hand coordination and fine motor control. Piagetian child psychologists would also attach importance to the fact that the child is seriating the cylinders according to size, and establishing a one-to-one correspondence between cylinders and holes. But the left to right sequence in which the child is shown the materials (which is often mimicked by the child), the fact that there are ten cylinders, and the size of the cylinder knobs themselves are all indirect preparations. The left to right sequence is a preparation for reading, the 10 pieces are an indirect preparation for the decimal system, and the pencil-thickness of the knobs, as well as the modified pencil grip by which the child is shown to grasp the cylinders, are all examples of indirect aims.

Another example of indirect preparation is found in the wonderful puzzle maps of the continents. Each large wooden puzzle map is sawn into pieces representing the countries of the continent. North America, for example, shows Alaska, Canada, the U.S.A., Mexico, and the Central American states. The logical place for the peg for picking up the USA piece would be at the balance point, geographically somewhere near Kansas, perhaps. But the knob is located at Washington D.C., unbalancing the piece, drawing the child's attention to that particular city or location which is important for this country.

A story (of the kind that are common at Montessori gatherings) provides some anecdotal evidence for the long-term effects of experience with the Montessori maps. I was riding in a car with two experienced Montessori teacher educators and one Montessori child grown to adolescence, the son of one of the Montessorians. The other was telling a story of how she used to try to test her daughter's knowledge of geography in early grade school by asking her questions. Apparently, all the daughter's work with the maps had been in vain; she couldn't or wouldn't answer her mother's questions.

On a trip home from her first year of college, however, she was full of complaints about her fellow students in an anthropology class: they didn't know where anything was in the world! The instructor kept having to refer to maps to show the class the locations he was describing. The mother questioned the daughter, and she appeared, after all this time, to have a clear "map" available to her. The Montessorian in the car was describing how the daughter would look into the air in front of her and point to locations, much as an experienced pianist can move his hands down in front of himself and hear the resulting chord.

In describing this, the Montessorian happened to quote her daughter saying," Well, of course, I can see South America, it's the big orange piece right be-". And then she was cut off by the teenager in the front seat, who, we thought, hadn't been paying attention to the conversation at all. He said, without even appearing to think about it, "Orange!? No, South America is red!" (Actually, the color was changed, so that they both remembered correctly, given when they were in Montessori schools.) So, at least in some cases, the work with the Montessori puzzle maps can make a strong impression that stays with a child for a long time.

A child in a 3-6-year-old classroom concentrates on producing his own map.

Another goal or value that Montessori espouses is the development of children's sense of responsibility for their own learning. In the Montessori model, one of the teacher behaviors that has caused some criticism is the much more subdued use of praise, in comparison to traditional nursery school teachers. Montessori wanted the child to develop a sense of satisfaction from a job well done, not from the value that the teacher placed on it. The praise that is offered in Montessori classrooms is typically focussed on redirecting the child's attention back to the completed work, rather than to the child himself. You might hear,"You've put all the pieces in correctly? Good job!", but seldom,"Such a good boy!" If the child is "Such a good boy!" for putting a puzzle together correctly, is he bad when he can't? In reality, of course, every Montessori teacher does dole out both positive and negative feedback to her students; the difference is in emphasis and degree.

There are certainly many more examples that could be given to show how the theory of Montessori is carried out by the model. Montessori's sensitive period for language, for example, is behind the availability of Montessori language materials, such as the sandpaper letters, movable alphabets, object and label matching games, etc. But let's move on now to the level of the program.

Programs are implementations of the models; programs have actual children and teachers in them. Thus, they are much more variable than models. Programs differ as a result of teacher variables, class composition, and other factors. The best way to learn about the variety of Montessori programs is through observation.

In practical terms, you don't need to know a great deal about Montessori to make a quick assessment of the classroom. First, make sure that the environment is safe, clean, and that the room size and teacher-child ratio are appropriate (your state or county will have guidelines in these areas). The most important clue to the quality of the Montessori environment is the activity of the children. If the majority of the class seems busily involved in purposeful activity, and most of the activity is individually chosen, rather than teacher chosen, you probably have found a program that is implementing Montessori successfully. For this to happen, the environment will need to have a certain degree of order, a large number of shelves should be filled with attractive materials, and the teacher should have imposed a certain amount of structure.

Some of the materials from the suppliers of Montessori materials are easy to spot: things like a tower of pink cubes; long red and blue rods; golden beads for units, tens, hundreds, and thousands; and sandpaper letters. Things harder to see are the teacher's background and Montessori teacher preparation course, and the quality of the support provided by the administration of the school. But these things can sometimes be found out through careful questions.

The program is, then, the result of one teacher's interpretation of the Montessori model in which she has been trained. That model is derived from Montessori's ideas, both those written in books and those given primarily in training programs.

So, these three levels make up the Montessori method, from theory to practice. And these three levels of the Montessori method leave out the person, the books, and the organizations that are also "Montessori." One of the purposes of this chapter and this scheme of organizing knowledge of things Montessori is to enable you to put the remaining contents of this book and future information on Montessori into some kind of comprehensive framework.

Summary: In this chapter, the persons, books, organizations, and methods linked with "Montessori" are discussed. The ideas that all Montessori schools are the same, or that they serve only preschool children were shown to be incorrect (if common) misunderstandings. The Montessori method is examined on the level of philosophy/theory, models, and actual programs. Montessori terms are introduced, such as her concept of "sensitive periods" for learning. Her idea of the subconscious, and the concept of "indirect preparation" are discussed as an example of how Montessori's ideas on development and learning affect the model.

CHAPTER 2
Some Common Misconceptions

Chapter Goals: In this chapter, you will learn:
- Ten of the most common misconceptions about the Montessori method.
- The concept of "structure" in looking at early childhood programs, and how this concept applies to Montessori programs.

As we have seen, "Montessori" can refer to a person, books, organizations, or the Montessori method. And the method itself can be discussed on the level of theory, the model, or actual classrooms of children. One of the reasons that Montessori has had slow acceptance in this country is the amount of misinformation that exists. For example, many people think that all Montessori schools are the same--they assume that the name is copyrighted, or even that Montessori is a chain like the national child care center chains that have recently sprung up. In fact, there is a great deal of variation among Montessori schools, and some are not really Montessori at all, but no one can prevent them from using Montessori's name. In this chapter, we'll examine some of the other common misconceptions about Montessori.

MONTESSORI: JUST FOR SPECIAL LEARNERS?

There are several reasons why people may have these misconceptions. First, Montessori **did** begin her work with children in the State Orthophrenic School in Rome. The classification of these children as retarded was very likely incorrect. Probably they included children with a wide range of problems, almost certainly including language delays, other communication disorders, autism, severe learning and behavior disorders, and other disabilities as well as retardation. But Montessori's *Casa dei Bambini*, in which the method evolved, was designed for normal children of the working class parents in the poor San Lorenzo district of Rome.

Another reason that people might think Montessori schools are just for special needs children (especially learning-disabled or gifted learners) is because the methods used in Montessori schools are so similar to those used with both of these kinds of learners. For example, the use of concrete materials, and the availability of materials in many sense modalities--sight, hearing, touch, even smell and taste-- are considered very appropriate educational techniques for learning-disabled students. The idea that a child might have moved very far ahead in one area--say, math-- and still be below other children his age in other areas is very much a part of both the Montessori method and good programs for gifted children.

The way in which a Montessori teacher might show a young child how to scrub a table would seem preposterous to many adults. The way in which all the tools (water, soap, brush, etc.) are laid out in the order in which they'll be needed, the emphasis that the teacher puts on giving a clear example in her movements, and so on, seem ridiculous for teaching a task we take for granted. But this "task analysis," breaking down the parts of a more complex job into manageable bits, is also a teaching technique that's very successful with special learners.

In Montessori classrooms, this step-by-step method lets very young children do a good job with tasks that would otherwise be too much for them. It's important to note that these tasks are ones that appeal to the children, that **they** think are important, such as table washing, not tasks that we think might be important, such as doing a math worksheet. Another secret that Montessori discovered was that children are very attentive to whether or not they have done a good job. They know when their table is clean, and when it still has a soap film. Your surreptitious cleaning up after they have cleaned up gives them a clear message that they can't really do it yet. And so the <u>isolation of difficulty</u> that Montessori talks about, that seems so laborious and unnecessary, and is similar to the careful breaking down of tasks in special education, is a very important part of how the Montessori method lets children succeed at the tasks they have chosen.

A final reason that people may link Montessori with gifted or learning-disabled students is the fact that many of the children in elementary Montessori schools may be one or the other or both. The classrooms I have taught in have had children whose intelligence and academic skills were above the norm. Many of the parents who choose to spend the private school tuition to send their children to elementary Montessori schools do so not because they have discovered the wonders of Montessori but because they felt that their child was not reaching his or her potential in the previous school placement. So Montessori schools in some areas have acquired a grapevine reputation of schools well- suited to deal with gifted or learning-disabled children.

MONTESSORI FULL-DAY?

Montessori's first program in Rome was a preschool in terms of the age group, which was from 2 1/2 to 7. But it was a child care center in that it ran for a full day, from 8 in the morning until 4 or 5 in the afternoon. The majority of the Montessori schools in the United States (as we saw in Chapter 1) are in fact preschools, rather than elementary or infant/ toddler programs.

But all of these levels exist in the United States today, and there are training programs for Montessori teachers for infant and toddler levels, through elementary and even secondary Montessori. Most larger cities will have at least a few classes for 6-9 year olds and perhaps a 9-12 class and an infant and toddler program. Secondary programs are still quite rare.

The issue of child care and Montessori is a touchy one. Many Montessori schools have decided to provide only the 3 hour or so preschool program, typically nine to noon or one to four. Parents who need additional care for their children are forced to look for a second program close to the Montessori school. At the Montessori school my older son attended, one nearby woman provided a high-quality child care situation for the Montessori kids for years and years.

Sometimes, however, administrators in a Montessori school decide that they are going to meet the parents' need for full-time child care. This is certainly a reasonable decision, and can make economic sense from both sides. The problem comes when administrators or program directors don't think the program through. For example, I have seen schools with very good Montessori programs running in the morning-- the teacher is qualified and experienced, the shelves are full of materials, and the classroom hums with purposeful activity. Then lunchtime arrives. The teacher goes home, shelves are covered with sheets, or the children are herded into another room, the TV comes out, and the administrator's teenage daughter becomes the primary caregiver. This is not attending to Montessori's cardinal principle of respect for the child!

Children at an Indian Montessori school in the 1950's work outside. Courtesy Seattle University and Estate of E.M. Standing.

It is equally inappropriate to expect 3-6 year olds to live for eight hours in the same environment in exactly the same way as the children who are there for only three hours. A full-day Montessori program should be carefully planned as a full-day program, with attention to the child's needs. There are many such programs in the country today. A good pamphlet on this is "Montessori All Day" by Celma Pinho Perry, available from the American Montessori Society.

Basically, the full-day Montessori programs that I think are the best have several things in common. A very common characteristic is expanded offerings in the Practical Life area. This area is discussed in detail in a later chapter, but it concerns the daily life activities of young children, and includes personal hygiene, cleaning, and food preparation activities along with the prerequisite skills for these, such as pouring, spooning, and so on. It is a large set of activities, which should be at a range of difficulty to challenge every child, but with no obvious "academic" component. This emphasis reduces the amount of time that children spend on more cognitive materials such as puzzles, math work, or language materials. There is the sense that these activities in the other parts of the day, such as nap time, recess, art, stories, or music are important. Lunch and snack are ideal times for integrating Practical Life activities into the real work of the classroom. The lunch tables and chairs can be cleaned, the tablecloth cleaned and ironed, places set with real china and glass (not plastic) glasses. Children love to arrange flowers in small vases. Lunchboxes are opened and food and drinks put onto plates and into glasses. One school in Seattle (The Niche) has the children make the candles that go on the table.

The area of Practical Life also includes the subarea of Grace and Courtesy, which includes lessons on things such as placement of silverware, ways to ask that the milk be passed, and so on. If lessons like these seem very strange to you, consider the following: Isn't it very typical of our demands of the child to expect him or her to know certain things, but not to take the time to teach them? How often do parents say things like,"Argh! Stop slamming the door!" or "Your nose is running!" (I include myself in this group)? But how few parents explain how to close the door quietly, or where the tissues are, what is expected, and how to dispose of the used tissue? In Montessori schools we find that children are very interested in things like how to arrange the silverware; it's as important to them as the way to make numerals, or the names of flowers.

To return to our topic of full-day programs, there are a small but growing number of Montessori schools that have made the decision to create and run a carefully planned Children's House, in which Montessori principles are carefully followed. If you need full-time care for your child, they are worth searching out.

MONTESSORI: A CULT?

Montessori supporters can seem this way, sometimes, especially at conferences! Montessorians certainly have their own jargon. Unfortunately, this serves to keep those not familiar with Montessori terms at a distance. Also unfortunate is the fact that some Montessorians feel no need to keep up on developments in the broader fields of early childhood education and child development. They feel that they have learned everything they need to know about their preschool or primary grades program and the development of children during their Montessori training. Also, one of the common ways that Montessori teacher educators make a concept clear is to contrast Montessori practices with those in traditional nursery school or in the home. While this is a handy teaching device[1], if used to excess it can lead to an "us vs. them" mentality in Montessori teachers.

While the small amount of research on Montessori that has been done is quite supportive, many Montessori teachers do not have this information readily available. In fact, many of the goals of Montessori education are not easily researched, such as long time effects on the child's model of the world, respect for others, and so on. This means that Montessori teachers must rely on anecdotal evidence or their intuition that Montessori really works. This can leave Montessori teachers somewhat defensive, especially when other early childhood educators start asking questions in jargon **they** don't understand.

Although there is certainly a lack of understanding between Montessorians and other early childhood educators, Montessori is not a cult. There is tremendous diversity in the Montessori community, for one thing, and there is certainly no attempt to recruit non-believers into the fold, other than by the methods common to any particular school of thought or educational philosophy. Despite the miscommunications, Montessori teachers have a great deal in common with other early childhood teachers. It's one of my hopes that this book will help to reduce the misunderstandings on both sides.

ARE MONTESSORI SCHOOLS RELIGIOUS?

This is another misconception that has had a great deal of staying power because of the half-truths it contains. Montessori herself was raised as a Catholic and both she and her followers, such as E.M. Standing, have written and spoken about the religious education of children. Montessori's *The Mass Explained to Children* (New York, Sheed and Ward, 1933), and Standing's *The Child in the Church* (Notre Dame, Indiana, Fides Publishing, 1964), are examples. Another source of this confusion is the fact that many of the early Montessori schools in the "second wave" of American Montessori that began in the late 1950's were Catholic. The most influential of these was the Whitby School, in Greenwich, Connecticut, founded by Nancy McCormick Rambush, which was later the "cradle" of the American Montessori Society.

Despite these early links between Montessori and Catholicism, the majority of Montessori schools are not aligned with any religious group. The public Montessori programs cannot be, and only a few private school administrators want to limit their market by choosing a particular religious orientation for their school. Of the religious Montessori schools that I am familiar with, the majority are Protestant or, to borrow C.S. Lewis' phrase, merely Christian, rather than Catholic. Other religious organizations have also found benefits in the Montessori method. The American Sikhs and various Islamic communities, for example, have shown an interest in Montessori.

The other fact that can lead to the misunderstanding of a link between Montessori and Catholicism is the high percentage of Catholic colleges and universities with Montessori teacher education programs. This is partially explained by the historical links described above, partially explained by the small total number of university-based programs, and partially explained by Sr. Christina Trudeau, who is now working on beginning a fourth college-based Montessori program! The trend toward non-Catholic universities operating

---

[1] I am occasionally guilty of this myself...

Montessori teacher education program is evidenced by the newer programs at Cleveland State University, and N.Y.U.

Parochial school systems are very infrequently adopters of the Montessori method. Whether this is due to a misunderstanding of Montessori's ideas on discipline, a reluctance to tamper with their success as the largest nonpublic school system, the concern over the high cost of materials and teacher education, or some other factor, is unclear.

MONTESSORI IS ONLY FOR THE RICH (OR POOR!)

It is interesting that both of these criticisms get leveled at Montessori schools. Montessori's first *Casa dei Bambini* was designed for the children of low income workers in the San Lorenzo district of Rome. But the second American Montessori movement that began in the late 1950's was primarily a private preschool movement. This means that Montessori schools are dependent on tuition and that they will be found primarily in middle income areas. This is an unfortunate economic fact of life, rather than a limitation at the model level.

Private and public Montessori schools today serve children from a wide range of economic and cultural backgrounds. These children are preparing and enjoying snack as one of their choices.

Certainly there are some programs that provide a Montessori experience for lower income children. The 100 or so public school districts with Montessori programs are the largest example. Some Headstart programs describe themselves as "Montessori" or

"Montessori-oriented." Many programs offer scholarships or try to ensure in other ways that the Montessori schools are not enclaves of middle class children. The unfortunate fact remains, however, that Montessori is most often available at private schools, and that the tuition fees of these schools put them beyond the reach of many families.

Before we blame either Montessori or greedy private school owners, we need to consider some facts. Most private preschools or elementary schools run on a very tight budget, educating children at a cost per pupil well below that of the public schools. It is certainly not the case that Montessori teachers are overpaid! While there are undoubtedly schools (including Montessori schools) that charge a very high tuition and do not provide a good educational experience, the competitive nature of private education in this country is such that these schools often find themselves with lowered enrollments. The costs of running a Montessori school--rooms, materials, supplies, salaries, insurance, and so on--demand a certain level of tuition. Attempts to increase tuition to make large profits for the owner will often cause parents to move their children to another private school eager for their business.

The real candidates for blame are the public programs that provide services to children from low income families--the Headstarts, the laboratory schools, and other funded programs. Why are virtually none of these programs Montessori? Some of the historical reasons for this are discussed in the next chapter.

TOO STRUCTURED OR TOO FREE?

If some people claim the programs are too structured and rigid, and others say they are too unstructured, perhaps Montessorians are doing something right after all! Let's examine how people could have come to these impressions.

The first important fact to remember is that rigidity and structure are relative terms. If Montessori programs are seen as too rigid or over-structured, this must be in contrast to other programs, or perhaps the home environment.

These criticisms come about at least partially from the ambiguity of these terms. "Structure," in particular, can refer to the lessons given, narrowness of work allowed with the materials, restriction of a child's choices, or even the building the class is housed in! In discussing this impression of rigidity and over-structuring with a number of people who feel this way about Montessori programs, I have found that almost all of them have based their opinions on one of three aspects of Montessori practice.

First, many people react very negatively to the structure they see in various Montessori presentations. This is a common problem with teachers-in-training: "Why must I memorize 17 steps to teach a child how to scrub a table!?" The structure is seen in both the layout of the materials and in the very exacting standards required of the Montessori teacher. My response to this is that, first of all, they assume that the child perceives this same level of structure in a layout or a presentation, which may not be true. The child's perception is simply of being shown a clear, step-by-step way to do something. The reason for the extra effort in structuring the presentation so carefully is to increase the chances of success for the child.

The layout of materials, for example, is done for a reason, like the neat organization of a surgeon's or a dentist's tools on a tray would serve. As far as whether or not teachers need the detailed structure of Montessori presentations, I leave this to your observations of traditional nursery school teachers' and parents' lessons to their children. Montessori gave some examples of traditional teacher's lessons that are still as painfully current today as they were when she wrote them; see, for example *Discovery of the Child*, pages 153-154. Montessori writes about a teacher who wants to teach young children about the colors red and blue, and uses objects in the room to demonstrate these colors. Unfortunately, the teacher's presentation is fast, full of rhetorical questions and other excess words that, Montessori would claim, distract the child from the simple linking of one color to one name. So, the structure in the layout and in the teacher's lessons is more work for the teacher, but this structure has the important goal of clarity and ease of learning for the child.

What about another meaning for structure--the restriction of a child's choice (to particular materials in the classroom) or structuring the way a child uses the material? The words "Montessori teacher" seem to conjure up a picture, for some people, of a teacher waiting to swoop down on a child using a material incorrectly and either correct him sternly or whisk it away. This stereotype is so common among people that I can only conclude that either people are confusing the elaborate details required in the teacher's presentation with the expectations that a teacher has for every child, or some people have seen some very bad Montessori programs held up to them as examples of "real Montessori." On the model level, Montessori's position about interfering with the child is very clear. No justification exists for intervening when a child is concentrating on work with a material; this concentration is in fact the goal of the whole method--teacher, environment, and materials. I would hope that no well-trained Montessori teacher would interrupt a working child. Even the necessary interruptions, such as for a snack, can be minimized through self-service snack arrangements.

What about teachers intervening too often when children don't appear to be concentrating on a material? One of the most important tools of the teacher, according to Montessori, is observation. In *The Montessori Method*, (p. 108), she writes about the importance of the teacher noticing "whether the child interests himself in the object, how he is interested in it, for how long..." She warns against trying to "provoke" the child to be interested in something not inherently or naturally interesting to him. If the child shows no interest, Montessori says, the teacher should be warned against insisting (by repeating the lesson) and against making the child feel that he has made a mistake.

The teacher may certainly intervene if the child is in danger of hurting himself or another child, or damaging the materials or the classroom. The real question concerns the occasion when the child is using the materials in a non-destructive way unrelated to their purpose.

For example, the broad stair materials are designed to give the child experience with length and width and height. Many free form building activities with these materials would support this growth. Using the stair as a sword would not, even if the child is not endangering or disturbing others. Space fortresses built with the broad stairs are a borderline decision. The additional information needed by a teacher to make a decision in a case like this would include: the child's level of concentration, her mastery of dimension knowledge given by the materials, the child's self-esteem, her interests in other areas, alternative building materials available, and so on.

In any case, the intervention is to be given in the form of a suggestion, either redirecting activity to a different use of the material or toward another material. No competent Montessori teacher would punish a child for inappropriate, non-destructive work--although perhaps they would intervene to redirect. And although there are certainly teachers who are too quick to intervene and redirect, the richness of the Montessori environment makes it likely that the child will be able to find another activity to meet his needs.

This brings us to the definition of structure as a control or limitation on the child's choices. Many teachers in Montessori classrooms feel that a child must have had a short demonstration lesson with a material before he can work with it alone; other teachers are content if the child has observed a lesson given to another child or group of children. All good Montessori teachers would observe a child's work with a material she has taken before deciding that the child should be re-directed. Montessori teachers generally work very hard to make sure that each child has many activities to choose from. This is done by introducing new materials to them as quickly as is appropriate. Also, especially at the beginning of a new school year, materials are provided that need no introduction--Lego™ blocks, simple puzzles, etc.

The Montessori method is quite structured in the demands it places on the teacher for the creation of a rich, stimulating, but orderly environment. It also demands very structured activities of her in maintaining the ground rules, introducing materials to the children, and displaying high expectations of the children's ability to learn independently. These structures in teacher behavior and environment make the freedom of the children possible.

Without these limits, license rather than freedom exists. The child who is not given clear ground rules and evidence that these will be enforced impartially will spend large amounts of time exploring the relationship between his behavior and the consequences applied by the teacher and the environment. One can almost hear the child thinking in such cases, "Sometimes running in the class results in intervention, sometimes not. I wonder if shouting while running would change the likelihood of intervention," and so on.

As to whether Montessori children can do whatever they want, I think that an observation of any good Montessori classroom would clear up this misconception quickly. Certainly, the children have a great deal of freedom, as we have discussed. But their choices have limits, set both by the teacher and the environment. The research evidence on what children learn in the much freer atmosphere of the Montessori classroom seems to indicate that they do at least as well as children in other programs.

WHAT ABOUT ART AND CREATIVITY ?

The idea that Montessori children are less creative, that they are stifled because their preschool environment lacks a dress-up area, is important enough to merit its own chapter. In brief, Montessori was opposed to several very specific kinds of fantasy for children under six, particularly teacher-directed fantasy in the Froebellian tradition. The link between the role play or dress-up corner and creativity is an intuitive one that is not supported by findings of reduced creativity in Montessori children.

All Montessori schools should have (and the majority of them do have) art programs appropriate to the age and interests of the children they serve. There is an interest in skill development, and a good sense of sequence in art skills and art activities.

Children in a 3-6 year old class color together.

The fact that there is an ongoing interest in art in Montessori schools can be seen by observing at a good school and from the following list of articles and books:

The earliest articles are by Jenny Merrill in *The Kindergarten-Primary Magazine* (2 in 1910).

Around the Child: Articles by three people (1964, 1969/70, and 1967) on art and handicrafts. Article from Maria Montessori on free expression, reprinted from an AMI document, 1960.

The Constructive Triangle (AMS) Numerous articles on art, including twelve by Jo Wood Savoye, from 1970 through 1975, one by Howard Ginger on photography (1982), and a comprehensive 1982 article by Joy Turner. Also, the earlier AMS *Bulletin* has an article by Lucia Pearce in 1965.

Communications (AMI) has had articles, such as one from the <u>Bulletin</u> of the English Montessori Society by Deidre Maton, and one by Varnas from 1937, reprinted in 1977.

Lena Gitter has written on Montessori and art for the *Bulletin of Art Therapy* (1962, 1964, 1968); *Children's House* (1967); *Academic Therapy* (1972); and *Journal for Special Educators of the Mentally Retarded* (1973).

Nell Weginer's book, *Guidelines for Art Activities in the Montessori Classroom*, is from the Montessori Development Foundation and distributed through Nienhuis.

My two favorites are the *Constructive Triangle* article by Joy Turner and Nell Weginer's book.

One of the things that you <u>shouldn't</u> find in a Montessori classroom is a focus on product rather than process, or a teacher who produces her model and then holds it up as the exemplar for the children to imitate.

TOO MUCH (NOT ENOUGH?) ACADEMICS?

Again, it seems strange that two (opposing) criticisms are frequently made of Montessori schools--both too much and too little in the way of academic work such as reading and math. I think that the purposeful, ordered, yet not teacher-directed activity of a good Montessori classroom answers most people's concern that Montessori children can "do whatever they want. " Chapter 13 summarizes what we know from the research on what Montessori children actually do in their classrooms.

The criticism that Montessori schools push children too far, too fast, is unfortunately true for some Montessori schools, although it is the furthest thing possible from the Montessori model. That is, it is very clear in both Montessori's writings and in the information presented in a good Montessori teacher education program that the Montessori model is based on the individual needs and capabilities of each child. Montessori's dictum,"Follow the child," speaks for itself. But in almost every city, you may find what I have called "clipboard Montessori," in which a Montessori teacher may descend on a child to suggest that he or she now choose some math or reading work.

The fact is that many Montessori schools serve middle class and upper class families. Increasingly, these families see preschools as a necessary first step in a child's education, or even as a prerequisite to acceptance at the "best" private elementary schools. In far too many cases, administrators and teachers have given in to parent pressure to produce graduates of Montessori classrooms who are all at a high level of competence in reading and math skills. Many children will have these skills as a result of their own choices in the classroom. And the Montessori materials are quite successful at allowing children to learn even if the teacher has chosen the materials, not the child. But this force-feeding of children to bring them up to a certain standard by a certain age is clearly in contrast to Montessori's most central ideas.

NOT ENOUGH PARENT PARTICIPATION?

A good Montessori school should encourage observations and have a planned program of parent involvement in the school. There should be regular opportunities for observation and regular reporting (either written or oral) on the child's progress at least two or three times per year. Observation may be limited for good reasons; for example, many teachers would rather not have the parents in the classroom during the first few weeks of the school year, because the younger children may be having a hard time, and the presence of the parent may make the separation more difficult. Also, it's a very good idea for the school to inform parents about proper behavior in the classroom. Most parents are just fine, watching quietly and asking any questions they may have later, when the teacher is free. Some parents can't seem to resist walking around, following their child, or even interrupting other children to ask them about their work, praise them, or pat their heads. Needless to say, this is not welcomed by Montessori teachers. Other times, parents observing in my class discussed their children and others, in loud voices right in the classroom. Another parent, without bothering to ask, brought a live duck to school under her arm to share... Guidelines should be brief and specify what parents should and should not do.

I would warn parents away from any school that has an observation policy that limits observations severely, prohibits them during the beginning of the school year (after the first few weeks), or in any way seeks to prevent parents from observing their child at school. In a normalized class, a quiet observer should not be a distraction.

Parent participation in the classroom is usually a good idea, and many good Montessori schools make use of parent skills. Parents can share their ethnic and cultural heritages with projects such as cooking; they can share a job or a hobby, and so on. Some schools, however, have had a bad experience with a parent who has tried to "take over" a classroom, or one with a "marvelous new way" of teaching math or reading. Some schools feel that parents will not have the time or interest to participate. And some schools feel that the time and energy required to orchestrate a parent participation program is not worth it. This is a shame, since at least one study in this area has shown higher parent satisfaction with programs that have parent participation (Ross, unpublished Masters' thesis, University of Washington, 1983).

In summary, Montessori schools vary greatly in their provision for parent observation, education about Montessori, and classroom participation. Parents should find a school that suits their needs. No school should deny parents the right to observe their child easily and often.

MONTESSORI IS OUT OF DATE

The idea that a program as old as Montessori "should have changed" is based on the knowledge that we have learned a great deal in the fields of child development and early childhood education since the beginnings of the Montessori method. The most important fact for people to know in response to this question is that certain parts of the Montessori method <u>have</u> changed. For example, the Practical Life curriculum area should reflect the real world, in particular the culture or cultures of the children in the classroom. Practical Life in Japan includes silk scarf tying, which is not on the shelf in Cleveland.

There have also been other changes in Montessori since the beginning of Montessori schools. Almost all of the materials and activities on the shelves in the Language area, both in three to six and elementary classrooms, have been developed by Montessorians, rather than by Montessori. The "root" materials are still there: the Metal Insets, the Sandpaper Letters, and the Movable Alphabet, but especially in English, much more had to be created. This area continues to grow and develop. The best Montessori schools and teacher education programs are true to Montessori's empirical traditions; they are constantly making small changes and adjustments and carefully observing the children's reactions.

The elementary Montessori material was developed by a number of people. Montessori herself, of course, created materials and activities, but so did Mario Montessori and teacher trainers at this level, especially at the International Center for Montessori Studies in Bergamo, Italy. This curriculum continues to grow and change. For example, the science curriculum is constantly being revised, with new findings in physics and earth science, and with taxonomy changes in the life sciences. More infrequently, changes are made for pedagogic reasons; see Pamela Lanaro's article on classification development in the *Constructive Triangle* for some ways in which a better understanding of the child's development can affect the materials used.

Many U.S. Montessori elementary schools are making use of computers, a material that certainly was not an option in Montessori's day! Most of these schools have made a careful study of the possible uses of computers and have attempted to find software and computer uses that are consistent with Montessori's approach. For example, many schools have chosen to use the programming language Logo, seeing similarities in the educational philosophy of Logo creator Seymour Papert and Montessori. (For more information on this area, see three articles in the *Constructive Triangle* by myself and by Larry Campbell, and Peter Gebhart-Seele's book *Computers in the Montessori Classroom*.)

Still, a great deal of what Montessori describes in her books can be seen in contemporary classrooms. Why hasn't this changed or been brought up to date? The answer is that it is still as "up to date" as it was when Montessori developed it. The Sensorial curriculum still attracts children and still provides them with a rich, graded-difficulty environment in which to practice matching, seriating, and classifying activities. Montessori's ideas of environment, teacher behaviors and expectations, and so on still result in happy, self-motivated, and independent children. In many respects, early childhood education took decades to catch up to Montessori! This is discussed in more detail in Chapter 3.

Summary: In this chapter, ten of the most common misconceptions about Montessori and the Montessori method were discussed. The Montessori method was seen to be in use with a broad range of children, not just the middle class, the gifted, the learning disabled, or in Catholic or other religious schools. In discussing how some Montessori schools serve children as a full-day program, some distinctions among Montessori programs were brought up. In discussing several misconceptions, the clear separation of Montessori from the mainstream of early childhood education was considered; the historical reasons for this are discussed in Chapter 3. In that and other chapters, the notion that Montessori is out of date is addressed in detail.

The concept of structure in early childhood education programs was discussed in some detail. People mean many things by "structure"; Montessori has been criticized for both too much and too little structure. All programs offer the child some structure through the physical layout, the time schedule, and the teacher's rules and expectations. The structure of the Montessori method may be seen in the detail with which each teacher is expected to show a Montessori material, and in the high expectations for control and initiative that Montessori teachers bring to the classroom. This is balanced by the child's choice of activities, both a larger number than in many other preschools, and over a greater part of the day. The rules the teacher enforces have the effect of allowing children the freedom to concentrate on the task they have chosen.

The freedom to choose one's work is also discussed in relation to the misconception that Montessori schools are academic hothouses, pushing children as far and as fast in academic subjects as possible. The role of parents in a Montessori school is discussed, and the importance of a good parent education and participation program is presented. The chapter also discusses the role of art in the Montessori classroom and the idea of creativity; this concept is covered more fully in Chapter 12.

CHAPTER 3
Why Hasn't Anyone Told Me About This Before? A History of the American Montessori Movement

Chapter Goals: In this chapter, you will learn:
- The historical reasons why Montessori failed in the first American Montessori movement.
- Several reasons why educators and psychologists in the early 1900's rejected Montessori's theories and why many now accept them.

At any non-Montessori early childhood conference, there are meals, cocktail hours, or other chances for participants and presenters to mingle. One of the first questions that comes up is,"And where are you working?", or "What are you doing?". The reaction from many early childhood educators to Montessorians is a little like what might be expected at a doctor's convention when someone announces a strong interest in Patagonian herbal cures. As Arlo Guthrie says in the the song *Alice's Restaurant:* "They all moved away from me on the bench..."

Why is there this reaction?

There is a certain amount of "in-group" behavior among Montessorians. They have their own special jargon, their own set of jokes, their own conferences, and so on, all of which are perfectly natural phenomena for specialists in any area. The fact is, however, that many Montessori teachers and even some of the leaders in Montessori education have not made very great efforts in breaking through this barrier of specialized jargon to reach other groups, such as traditional preschool or elementary school teachers, parents, or researchers. Unfortunately, there is a kind of smugness in some Montessori teachers. Their training in the Montessori method has given them the tools and the understanding to work successfully with children; those without this understanding are unable to grasp what they do. Why attempt to explain to others, who will be unable to understand and are likely to deride what they can't understand? Even in the teachers who have no trace of this smugness, there is a natural focus of the teacher on her own classroom.

For whatever reason, there is a perception on the part of traditional early childhood teachers, public school teachers, and even many parents, that Montessori teachers consider themselves superior, and that they feel that no real explanation (short of the Montessori training itself) can bridge the gap. It's a little like the responses of psychoanalytic therapists to criticisms from behaviorists and others in the beginnings of psychotherapy. If someone criticized psychoanalysis, the first question asked was, "Well, who did he work with for his own psychoanalysis?" Whatever the answer, a raised eyebrow or a knowing shrug made it clear that the critic had deep-seated problems that were behind his doubts about psycho-analysis.

This perceived superiority of we-Montessorians-have-all-the-answers is a tremendously unfortunate attitude, since it isolates Montessorians from others devoting their lives to children, and restricts greatly the spread of Montessori's very worthwhile ideas.

On the other hand, there is a perception on the part of those involved in the Montessori movement that there is a tremendous ignorance about Montessori on the part of the public, teachers, and even professors of early childhood education. Some Montessorians go so far as ·to describe this as a willful ignorance. Try this test to see if this is a correct perception:

Choose a university, either a famous one, or a local college that offers Masters or Doctoral level programs in Early Childhood Education. Call the School or College of Education on the telephone, and ask the secretary to speak to the chair or program coordinator in early childhood. When you actually get a faculty member on the telephone, ask three things: What text is used in the introductory course in early childhood (often with a title like "Programs in Early Childhood")? Then ask if the University offers any courses in Montessori education, or what the professor thinks of the Montessori method in general. When you have noted the reply, ask about the professor's own knowledge in that area: has she or he read any books by Montessori? Ever observed in a Montessori school? (You might ask this as if you were seeking a recommendation for observing yourself.) Is there any research available that speaks to whether or not the Montessori method works?

This girl is preparing a snack in a 6-9 classroom. Why do so many early childhood experts fail to mention elementary Montessori programs?

The results of these interrogations are not uniform, but they reveal a pattern that is quite consistent. The exceptions to the pattern are the dozen or so universities that have Montessori teacher education program themselves or some chance connection, such as a professor who is a Montessori parent. The textbooks used will be found in almost every case to have **only historical** references to Montessori and Montessori schools, as if these no longer existed or were too few in number to merit consideration. The professor will typical admit to a lack of detailed familiarity with the Montessori method, but will also typically recommend against it in favor of "more modern" programs, or "programs that allow for more creativity." The professor may or may not have read any of Montessori's books, has been to one or two Montessori classrooms in his or her lifetime, and is typically unable to suggest a single piece of research on Montessori. (Take a look at the bibliography from Chapters 13 and 14 to see what's been missed!)

One explanation for this might be that it only happens at second rate universities. I urge you to test this yourself. I have found it to be true at universities that are considered first rate by almost everyone's standard. Another possible explanation is that the number of Montessori schools in the country is actually so small, or the Montessori method so out of date, that it really does not merit inclusion in textbooks or knowledge on the part of early childhood education leaders. The question of the validity of the Montessori method is taken up in this book, primarily in Chapters 13 and 14. The question that remains, then, is the extent of Montessori schools in the United States.

Although no precise figures are available, some data is available. Washington state surveyed those providing services to 3- and 4- year-olds in a large study in 1980 (Quill & Chattin-McNichols). The 875 programs that responded were broken down into categories, such as licensed and unlicensed child care, church-based child care centers, and private preschools, with and without child care. The qualifications of the staff members were assessed in the survey. Of the private preschools that responded in this comprehensive survey, almost 43% reported that they had someone on staff with Montessori teacher preparation. Eliminating programs that were not fully Montessori would seem to leave well over a third of the private preschools Montessori schools or at least Montessori oriented. Since this survey was not limited to the urban or middle class areas of Washington, and since Washington is fairly representative, there is no reason to suppose that this percentage is different in other states.

Figures collected by the Accreditation Council for Childhood Education Specialist Schools (ACCESS) for their proposal to the Department of Education indicate that between 8,000 and 10,000 people belong to Montessori organizations in the United States. While this does not come close to the membership of the National Association for the Education of Young Children (NAEYC), it is still a substantial number for an early childhood professional group for a specific sub-area such as Montessori.

Another indicator of the national interest in Montessori is the conferences. The Montessori track at the NAEYC National Convention has been a part of the program for years now, and is typically well-attended. National conventions of the various Montessori groups are limited by the competition among the groups, but often draw 400 to 800 participants to 5 or 6 national meetings yearly.

Support for Montessori in public schools varies with budgets and other changes in public opinion, but by most counts there are some fifty districts in the U.S. with publicly supported programs, and others in Canada. Some of these have been in operation for a long time and are well-known and desirable options in the districts, such as Milwaukee and Cincinnati. Others are very large programs, some of which even extend Montessori to the junior high grades, such as Dallas and Buffalo. Programs seem to be created slightly faster than they disappear, at least based on the last survey that addresses this issue (Chattin-

McNichols, 1983). These figures do not justify the total disregard of the Montessori method in textbooks or in the minds of the leaders of early childhood education in this country. The problem is actually even more widespread. Where are the laboratory schools for Montessori, either university based, or supported by governments or foundations? Where are the research studies coming from?

In education, with Masters' students always looking for topics for their thesis research, some very obscure topics have received a great deal of research. The research on Montessori is being done almost exclusively by Montessorians--no one else is interested. Where are the HeadStart programs, the United Way funded child care programs with Montessori programs? There is, in fact, an almost complete lack of communication between Montessorians and other educators.

Figure 3-1

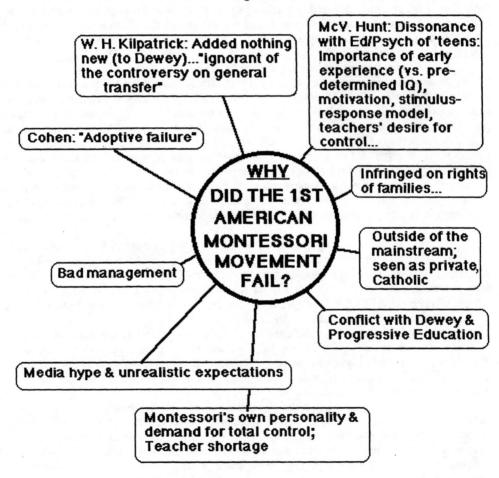

What are the reasons for this? There is a separate "pyramid" of Montessori education, separate from the mainstream of early childhood education in the United States. The leaders in Early Childhood Education are the persons in large research universities, federal and state agencies, and large school districts. If the information on Montessori that these leaders received is as limited as the coverage in current textbooks, it's no wonder that they are not training others below them on the pyramid to understand and appreciate Montessori.

The question remains, however: How did Montessori come to be so separate from the rest of early education? There are a number of historical reasons for this separation. Some of the most important are shown in Figure 3-1.

Montessori's success came shortly after her first school opened in 1907. Soon after there were two other schools, and a steady stream of visitors (Appelbaum, 1971). While Montessori was preparing herself for the opening of her first school, the United States was experiencing a great increase of interest in early childhood education in general. The forces of the kindergarten movement were everywhere, and states were adding kindergartens as an optional program more and more frequently. This was to continue until anti-German prejudice reduced this in World War I. The quality of the nursery schools and their number were being increased as a result of the beginnings of the child study movement and the social reforms that went along with it.

The first mention of Montessori in the United States is the five articles by Jenny B. Merrill, Ph.D., in the *Kindergarten-Primary Magazine* (December, 1909). These were based on Dr. Merrill's talks with Baroness Franchetti, rather than on direct observation in Rome. Although the articles were encouraging of more observation of what Montessori had created, the differences between the Montessori classrooms and the kindergartens was one of the main points of the article. In particular, the reading and writing of the preschoolers was commented on, and contrasted to the kindergarten practice.

S.S. McClure was the publisher of the popular *McClures Magazine.* He describes in his autobiography how he sent Miss Josephine Tozier to write on the new Montessori schools:

> *...I commissioned Miss Tozier to write an article on the Montessori method of teaching young children. Every important article that appears in <u>McClure's Magazine</u> is always submitted to persons who have special knowledge of the subject treated upon, for criticism and suggestion. When Miss Tozier's article was completed, it was carefully compared with Mme. Montessori's book--then untranslated--by the English critic, Mr. William Archer, who assured me that it adequately represented Mme. Montessori's theories. Before the article was published it was submitted to several authorities on kindergarten and pedagogy in the United States. These experts, I found, greatly differed in their estimates of Montessori's methods. Some of them were very antagonistic in their attitude, and declared that, because Mme. Montessori recognized and valued the work of great educators of the past, there was nothing new about her method.*
>
> (From Applebaum, 1971)

Notice that there was already controversy about Montessori, even in the total absence of detailed information about what the program was and with no idea of the short-or long-term value of Montessori school experience.

Tozier's article was long, and a relatively complete discussion of Montessori, including a photograph of a young girl writing at a blackboard. But in a sense, the direction of American Montessori was already being set, even at this early period. The main emphasis of the article was the early reading and writing skills of the young children. The caption of the photograph reads,"ONE OF MARIA MONTESSORI'S PUPILS WRITING FROM DICTATION AT THE BLACKBOARD. THE AVERAGE CHILD OF FOUR LEARNS TO WRITE IN SIX WEEKS BY THE MONTESSORI METHOD." Four pages of the article dealt with reading and writing.

In October, 1911, less than six months after the Tozier article, Miss Anne George opened the first Montessori school in America in Tarrytown, New York. In her description of this school for the June, 1912, issue of *McClures,* Miss George describes one of the main differences between her school and the Roman *Casae*: the American school drew its students from "cultured families, whose greatest ambition it was to give their children everything possible in the way of education and rational enjoyment." A few months earlier, In April, 1912, the first edition of *The Montessori Method* sold out in four days.

Soon after this, a pattern of problems between Montessori herself and those attempting to spread her method in the United States began to emerge. McClure, along with Miss George and others founded the Montessori American Committee in 1912. They published information about the committee in *McClure's*. Montessori responded with a telegram, in which she stated that she was angry with this announcement and that it was contrary to what she had agreed.

Despite these problems, it was this group that helped to organize the first International Training Course in Rome. Of the 100 students who came, 67 were Americans. One of the most famous early adherents was Mrs. Alexander Graham Bell. With a teacher named Roberta Fletcher, she opened a school in Nova Scotia, and then another one in Washington D.C. The pressure from parents caused this school to move to its own quarters, a house at 1840 Kalorama Road in Washington, in 1913. The Montessori Education Association was begun in 1913, with Mrs. Bell as President.

Two schools opened in New York, one in 1913 and one in 1914, and other Montessori societies were started, such as the New England Montessori Association. (For more detail on the early history of Montessori in America, see Phyllis Applebaum's excellent 1971 doctoral dissertation,"The Growth of the Montessori Movement in the United States, 1909-1970.") Again, the character of American Montessori was set; an early report on a meeting of the New England group stated that, "all shades of opinion are represented in the Association, from radical Montessorians, who would abolish kindergartens, to those who believe in combining the two systems by using the Montessori material at a stated time in the regular kindergarten program" (Ellis, 1913, cited in Appelbaum, 1971).

From the very beginnings of the Montessori movement in America, then, several aspects of the American response to Montessori were set: the insistence of the educational establishment, whether at colleges or in the leadership of the new kindergarten movement, to comment on Montessori, often without any real information on her method. Second, there was a clear privatization of Montessori, a focus on the use of her ideas by the middle and upper classes. This focus came from the overemphasis (compared with Montessori's original ideas) of the academic focus of the program, and particularly its success in teaching reading.

Another key problem was the variety of ways in which Montessori's ideas were implemented, rather than the acceptance of Montessori as a complete system, which was more the case in Europe, and was certainly what Montessori herself expected, even demanded. Very central to this problem was the control of teacher preparation.

Figure 3-2

The Rise and Fall of the First American Montessori Movement

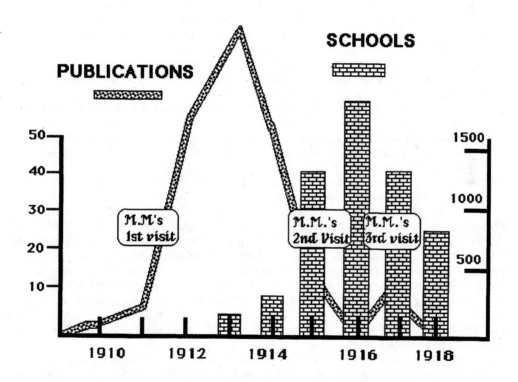

As early as 1912, there was controversy over a Montessori course offered in New York by a Myron Scudder, advertised as the most comprehensive offered outside of Rome. Montessori asserted that only her own courses constituted valid Montessori teacher preparation. Montessori also began to resent the books that were written about her work by others; she complained about Dorothy Canfield Fisher's book in a letter to the London *Times* in 1914.

The tale of Montessori's possibilities for success in America in the late teens of this century -- her successful lecture tours, her links with promoter S.S. McClure and the Bells-- and the subsequent failure of the movement by as early as 1925, is still a painful memory to Montessori advocates who have studied this period. Some idea of the rapid rise and fall can be seen in Figure 3-2.

The issues outlined above--poor or uncomprehending reception by the educational leadership, adaptation of her methods in a variety of ways, a focus on academics by demanding middle class parents, and a flood of "trainers" and authors eager to capitalize on Montessori--all contributed to the rapid downfall. No doubt, Montessori's own personality, her distrust of McClure, and so on, helped the rapid loss of interest. But J. McVicker Hunt, in his introduction to a new edition of *The Montessori Method*, claims that a **mismatch** existed between the educational and psychological leaders of the day and Montessori. He stated that six important areas of disagreement existed between Montessori and then-current thinking:

- The importance of schooling for three and four year olds.
- The belief in a fixed level of intelligence, unchangeable by experiences.
- A belief in predetermined development and the certainty that any training before age 8 or so would not transfer to useful learning.
- The belief that all behavior had to be motivated; it was also assumed that all or most motivation was instinctive, such as from hunger or comfort-seeking drives.
- A focus on the response, not the child's experience: "Fifth, the belief that the response side of the reflex arc is the one essential in education... The stream (of C. Lloyd Morgan's and Thorndyke's work and ideas) flowed on into the behavioristic revolt which replaced *consciousness* with *behavior* as the subject-matter of psychology..." (Hunt, 1967).
- The unwillingness of teachers to relinquish control of the classroom and to move out of center stage.

We can see from Hunt's analysis the major differences that existed between Montessori's ideas and the dominant theories in education and psychology in this country in the early part of this century. In terms of the effects of environment (vs. heredity), the mutability of intellect, motivation, the role of the senses in learning and development, and the focus on observable, testable behavior, Montessori was completely out of step. This was so much the case that Kilpatrick's 1914 book-length criticism, *The Montessori System Examined* was taken by most professionals for the last word--in fact the only word needed. If Columbia's "million dollar professor" and colleague of John Dewey's, William Heard Kilpatrick, saw nothing new or of interest in Montessori, that settled it for most educational leaders in this country.

The million dollar question is, why haven't these same leaders noticed that theories in these same areas have changed and now are much more in line with what Montessori had proposed? Her language is still the same, and can still be interpreted as representing out of date thinking. But most of the mismatches between Montessori and "current theory" have evaporated--and this has happened through advances in current theory, **not** through changes in Montessori's ideas.

Let's consider the relative importance of the environment on growth, and the whole question of the mutability of children's intellect. While there are a variety of theoretical positions held today, it is clear that almost all of the major theories allow the environment an important role in the child's development. The volume *Sensitive Periods in Development* (Bornstein , 1987[Lawrence Erlbaum Associates]) presents a wide range of evidence supporting not only the centrality of the environment, but the idea of sensitivities to particular environmental stimuli at particular developmental phases. Not only has Montessori's insistence on the importance of the environment been found to be correct, the way in which she says the child learns from the environment is very similar to current Piagetian and cognitive science theories.

Briefly, Montessori felt that the child was qualitatively different from the adult, and that his thinking and learning processes went through several discrete stages. In each stage, there are different sensitive periods, and each stage necessitates a different form of learning experience. Montessori felt that the three to six year old child was possessed of an absorbent mind, and that he learned through the manipulation of his environment.

When we talk of the child learning, we realize that we have come around to Montessori's view on the ability of the young child to learn, and that we have at least partially rejected the radical behaviorist view that would claim that only experiences which produce changes in behavior can be said to be learning experiences for the child. Montessori gave the child credit for his ability to learn indirectly, through observation of other children working.

Another central affirmation of Montessori's ideas comes from recent ideas (such as White's) of motivation separate from drives or reinforcement. (See Seattle Montessori teacher Laurie Ross' excellent article on this in the 1982 AMS *Constructive Triangle* magazine.) Montessori talks about children working to perfect themselves, about children's attraction to activities that are just at the edge of their competence. This is very similar to the "competence motivation" described by White and others.

As far as the desires for teachers to maintain control over their classrooms, discipline is certainly as popular a topic as it ever was, and various systems of education that promise more effective control, more on-task behavior, and higher scores on achievement tests are more popular than ever. The increasing demand for accountability in schools, and the mandated individualization of programs for special education students has led to an increasing dependency on a behaviorist model, and to narrowing of goals for higher scores on national tests. In this atmosphere, avoidance of Montessori is still strong, and for obvious reasons. Fortunately, the thinking-skills movement and other forces are beginning to rebel against this narrowing of the role of American education, and it is time for Montessori's ideas to be given their first real test.

That will come about only as Montessorians realize that they must do more than teach their own classrooms, that they must document what they do and show whether or not it is effective. It will also require the mainstream of education to be willing to give Montessori a fair test. And both sides must approach this with open minds, a desire to communicate across different orientations and jargons, and an understanding that both groups have the best interests of the child at heart.

Summary: In this chapter, the history of Montessori's visits to America in the early 20th century was presented, including the many problems she had with American Montessori promoters. The separation of Montessori from the mainstream of education which began then is still found to be very much with us; the reader is given several tests that she can apply to prove this. Six differences between Montessori's ideas and then-current education and psychology are presented, from J. McVicker Hunt's work.

CHAPTER 4
Montessori Theory and Philosophy

Chapter Goals: In this chapter, you will learn:
- The influences of Rousseau on Montessori.
- The influences of Locke on Montessori.
- The influences of Itard and Seguin on Montessori.
- What is Montessori's model of the mind, and of the stages of development?
- How does Montessori philosophy shape the role of the teacher?

In this chapter I'll begin to examine Montessori's philosophies and theories in more detail. To begin with, let's consider Montessori's borrowing from the ideas of Rousseau, Locke, and others. The relationship of Montessori's thought to that of Jean Piaget will require a separate chapter.

> *From Lecture 1 (Given April 5th) by **Dr. Maria Montessori**, in the International Montessori Course given in 1921. These notes by E. M. Standing. © 1988 by the Estate of E. M. Standing, Seattle University.*

> *To liberate the child we must reform the environment, and reform the world. This is a necessity if we are to have life at its highest development. A fine work of research and observation is required in order to give that which is necessary to the development of life.*
>
> *Liberty does not consist solely in the breaking of chains, but in creating a new form of life. Thus, if we desire to liberate the child it is not enough to remove the pressure of the teacher. The child is not merely enslaved by a position or a person, he is held in bondage by an unsuitable environment. The new school must be absolutely suitable to the minutest detail, to the developing soul.*
>
> ***Not only is it desirable that a new pedagogy be developed, but a new science.*** *(My emphasis-JCM) Under these changed conditions, not only will the child be liberated from his ills, but he*

will reveal to us those secrets of his nature which before were unknown.

We shall learn that discipline develops spontaneously, force and strength of character will show itself as a natural development, and the love of work will spring up and manifest itself as a natural consequence of free development.

Then shall we behold the new man, more strong, more industrious, more sure of himself than his predecessors.

The child, developing in freedom, gives us promise of the strong man of whom we have need, and for whom we wait. Then will come forth the truly free man, who works harder than the slave works, who is free and yet more disciplined than the slave, one who is guided by his intelligence, one guarded by his reason.

Liberty is not synonymous with the mere bursting of bonds, but, represents a power to reconstruct and to solve the manifold problems which confront mankind today.

INFLUENCES: ROUSSEAU

Perhaps because of her statements about the inherent goodness of the child, Montessori's philosophy is often assumed to derive primarily from Rousseau. Many of Montessori's ideas are like those of Rousseau. Certainly her conception of the child as basically or inherently good, and as a lover of work are similar to ideas in Emile. Another similarity is Rousseau's notion of controlling the child by making use of natural consequences.

This idea of natural consequences, that the child learns best by experiencing the results of his or her own actions, is central in Montessori's concept of discipline.[1] An equally important use of this concept of "natural" or "logical" consequences is embodied in the design of Montessori materials and their use in the classes. This is the Montessori concept of control of error. Almost every piece or set of apparatus that the child learns to manipulate has some built-in feature whereby the child can tell, on completing his work, whether or not he has done so correctly. The knobbed cylinders, for example, are fitted into a block in a certain order; the child who has placed a cylinder into a hole too big for it will finish the exercise with a cylinder that will fit into no available hole. In constructing the tower out of

---

[1] The work by Driekurs (*Children the Challenge*, New York: Hawthorne, Dutton, 1964; *Encouraging Children to Learn: The Encouragement Process*. ((with Don Dinkmeyer)) Englewood Cliffs, NJ: Prentice Hall, 1963; *Logical Consequences: A Handbook of Discipline* ((with Loren Grey)), New York: Meredith Press, 1968) in this area expands on the notion of natural and logical consequences. Driekurs' viewpoint is based on Adlerian ideas and Carl Rogers' work in nondirective therapy. Driekurs' work is regularly a part of the reading of Montessori teachers (in courses that make use of readings other than Montessori) and recommended as reading for parents at many Montessori schools. The practical applications of Driekurs' ideas are a frequent topic at workshops for working Montessori teachers.

cubes, if the child places a cube out of order, the likelihood of the tower falling over is much greater.

At a more general level, both Rousseau and Montessori recognize childhood as an important period, and hope for the modification of society through changing child-rearing and educational practices. (Rather than, for example, radical social change through revolution.) Furthermore, they both see the **environment** around the child, both physical and social, as the method of choice for change, rather than direct tuition or other more traditional methods of teaching.

Lastly, there is something of the same flavor in Rousseau's and Montessori's approach to education. Rousseau puts forth the isolated dyad of the father and son as an educational ideal and suggests Defoe's *Robinson Crusoe* as the principle text that Emile should use. Montessori training encourages teachers to see their classrooms as miniature societies, with equal rights among children and the benevolent non-interference of the directress as efforts in this direction. The small scale of the physical environment also contributes to the effect of making the classroom seem a separate environment, a "Casa dei Bambini" (Children's House). [1]

INFLUENCES: LOCKE

Although Rousseau and Locke are often presented as opposing educational philosophers, Montessori's philosophy also has several features that seem Lockean. For example, Montessori's emphasis on the "education of the senses" seems derived directly from the Lockean model of the mind. Locke felt that the mind of a child at birth was like an empty cabinet or room, and that sensory experiences were what filled it up. These sense experiences were the source of what he called "simple ideas," such as hot-cold, rough-smooth, and the colors.

Locke felt that all children (except for mental defectives) had almost equal capacities for receiving these sense impressions and thus forming the simple ideas. These ideas were then transformed and built upon by other (not well specified) cognitive capacities and formed "complex ideas." All other ideas that people have, according to Locke's theory, are the result of the recombinations and modifications of these simple ideas. Locke further theorized that the main reason for individual differences in cognitive functioning, language, and so on, was due to the impoverishment of the lower classes in experiences providing the simple ideas, rather than in the cognitive mechanisms for transforming these into complex ideas.

Locke thus stressed the importance of early experience, and suggested that some homes did not provide all that young children needed. This is a position with which many of the founders of Headstart would feel right at home. It is also reflected in Montessori's thought. The sensorial area in particular, as we will see, can be seen as responding to Locke's notions of allowing the child to experience simple ideas.

---

1 Practices described by social learning theorists confirm the effectiveness of the Montessori idea of stressing the differences in environment if we expect the child to behave differently in the Children's House than he may behave elsewhere. This giving of cues is a common practice. In Montessori the cues are both overt reminders by the teacher ("We don't run inside") and covert cues, through the "differentness" of the Montessori environment.

Locke and Montessori also agreed on the importance of an **orderly** exposure to these sense experiences. The labels that are applied to these experiments are critical, both theorists felt, to the development of later cognitive capacities. Montessori went further in her assertions that the orderliness of the child's preschool environment would determine not just the contents but the arrangement and orderliness of the child's mind.

INFLUENCES: ITARD AND SEGUIN

From Lecture 2 (Given April 7th) by Dr. Maria Montessori, in the International Montessori Course given in 1921. These notes by E. M. Standing. © 1988 by the Estate of E. M. Standing, Seattle University.

...Itard himself lays the first stone for a new concept of pedagogy. In fact all his work with the deaf and semi-deaf was simply a preparation for that work which he accomplished in association with the individual who was destined to render Itard famous. We know Itard dedicated himself for nine years to the education of an idiot child without obtaining satisfactory results. But he succeeded in laying down the first lines for the building up of an educational system which could be briefly described as follows:

That in order to recall and fix the vagrant attention of the idiot children, it was first necessary to find graded stimuli for all the senses as it had been necessary in the case of the deaf mutes to find graded stimuli attract the attention to sound.

But Itard did not obtain much success and he did not write a book upon this obscure work.

It was Seguin who gathered up this humble inheritance, which had proved so humble and discouraging, and he sought for 40 years to apply these principles, applying them to more and more varied subjects and experiments.

We may sum up Seguin's work thus, " The experiments with the graded stimuli for all the senses remain as experiences showing success, but it is found that we must do some things further in order to obtain success with the deficient child. We must educate the movements." If the movements of an individual are disorganized and uncontrolled, we cannot attract or fix the attention. It is necessary first to obtain muscular control and Seguin, by very patient work, obtained some success.

For example, he takes an excited and agitated child and holds him in his arms or between his knees for a whole hour, and he repeats this form of treatment every day until he succeeds in quieting the disordered movements. And when order has succeeded disorder, Seguin considers it a fact of fundamental importance, as the deciding factor as to whether the individual can or cannot be saved....

According to Seguin, it comes about only in one form, and depends upon whether the child is able to accomplish a movement having an intelligent purpose. In connection with this phenomenon Seguin tells the following anecdote:

A deficient child of rich parents had a little bow and arrow, and one day he was discovered shooting at all the portraits of his ancestors. His parents were horrified, but Seguin said, "Your child is saved, he has performed an action having a definite purpose."

After such a purposeful action, it is found that .. . .presentation of the gradation of stimuli, when attention can be fixed, mental training is possible.

Undoubtedly this is a contribution of new principles in pedagogy. How many discussions have been held by the philosophers concerning theories of sensorial education without any thought of a preparation which leads up to a definite mental training? And moreover, such discussions have been upon abstractions emanating from their own thoughts, neither have they realized that there is a starting point at which one may judge whether a person can be saved or [is] irretrievably lost.

That which I have done is to apply, more or less, the same principles to the education of the normal child. But in applying these principles to the education of the normal child the same results do not come, and we sum up the differences very briefly. Not only is there to be found in the normal child an expansion and power of application which is not possible to the deficient child, but we perceive that the normal child and deficient are on different planes.

The two most commonly cited influences on Montessori's thought (and the ones she herself credited) are Itard and Seguin. Itard's *Wild Boy of Aveyon* provided Montessori with a dramatic confirmation of the importance of the young child's environment. Seguin's pioneering work with handicapped children provided Montessori with more direct help in her early years in the State Orthophrenic school. She used many of the materials Seguin had developed, notably the grooved letters that were later to become the sandpaper letters, and a pair of boards for teaching number concepts, which are still called Seguin boards in many Montessori teacher education programs. These boards allow the numerals eleven through nineteen to be constructed by the child by sliding a wooden numeral "1" in over the numeral "10". Thus, the idea that "11" is composed of ten and one, rather than two ones is shown graphically to the child. In the Montessori sequence of activities, additional work with beads precedes this work with symbols, thus making this concept even more concrete.

Montessori also drew on the work of Italian philosopher Fantappie, and on philosophical concepts of Sir Percy Nunn and Bergson, notably his concept of *élan vitale*.

In summary, then, it is fair to say that Montessori was an eclectic borrower. But the primary borrowing of materials seems to have been from Seguin. The way in which she borrowed from all others shows much more in her writings, especially in the construction of theories to explain why her system worked.

MONTESSORI'S CONCEPT OF THE MIND

Some of Montessori's most important contributions have become such a part of our understanding of children that they sound like truisms today; but when she first presented them, they were a radical departure from the ideas of both the public and the experts. For example, the notion that the mind of the child is quite different from that of the adult, and that the child will go through a predictable series of changes, is something that almost all child psychologists, educators, and lay persons would accept today. (There are still a few radical behaviorists out there who would disagree, of course.) Montessori's observations of these changes led her to a description of these stages that is remarkably similar to Jean Piaget's. But she went on to suggest that, since the mind of the child was different from time to time in the child's life, the educational system must respond to these differences. That is, the structure and content of education should be determined by the child's needs, not by what society thinks is appropriate for children to know, and that this will change through the course of childhood. That suggestion remains controversial to the present day.

An important idea here is the Montessori concept of the Four Planes of Development. Montessori divided the years from birth through age 24 into four six-year periods. Two of the periods are active periods of tremendous growth: early childhood (0-6) and adolescence (12-18). The other two periods are relatively calm periods of consolidation: middle childhood (6-12) and early adulthood (18-24). Like any other stage theorist, Montessori stressed that these ages are approximate; only the sequence of the stages remains invariant.

The period of infancy and early childhood was a period of such great and diverse learning that the powers of the infant astonished Montessori, as they have done so many students of the young child. Montessori felt that this was the period of the greatest learning potential in the entire human developmental cycle. This was the time of the "absorbent mind." She uses the example of the absorption of language or languages in the home to show the power of the child. Her ideas on language development are spelled out in more detail in the chapter on Language Curriculum, but for Montessori, the success of the very young child at mastering the complexities of language was proof of the existence of **sensitive periods** in the child.

A sensitive period is a window in the development of the person. It is a genetic component, available to all humans regardless of cultural background. The use of the sensitive period is what will vary from culture to culture, family to family, even child to child within the same family. The sensitive period for language is a potential for language acquisition. The language or languages acquired will depend on the child's experiences with her environment.

Many other sensitive periods are described by Montessori, the majority of them coming in the 3-6 period. For example, there is a sensitivity to order in the environment, beginning at or a little before age two. Montessori observed children becoming upset when things were moved from their accustomed places. She also saw the child's developing skill at moving through the environment. For Montessori, these two sensitive periods were linked together; the child's perceptions of order were connected to his ability to move through the environment in increasingly varied ways.

She also commented on the child's love at this time of tiny objects. As is the case with each of these sensitive periods, Montessori was not content merely to observe characteristics like this in children. Everything that she saw was used to modify the environment or the teacher's behavior in the Montessori classroom.

Montessori subdivided the first six years into a period of unconscious (0-3) absorption of the environment and a period of conscious (3-6) absorption. The child in this first period is one who is not conscious at all in the same way that older children and adults are, but rather is driven by impulses coming directly from his unconscious mind. If you have ever had the opportunity to observe in a Montessori toddler environment, and watched how a child of eighteen months chooses something to do from the shelf, you can see what Montessori meant. Their minds work very differently from the mind of a preschool aged child. A normal four year old might scan a shelf or set of shelves, looking for what she wants to work with. I had a child in one class who came early one day and lined up ten sets of Montessori materials in a long row leading away from her mat. As she stood contemplating this with her hands on her hips, she said,"There! That will be my work for today."

A toddler, on the other hand, walks into the class with "big eyes," perhaps not even focussing on anything, as far as an adult observer can tell. In wandering past a shelf, his hands might reach out and take something from a shelf, perhaps without even turning to see what it is his hand has grabbed. Sometime later, the toddler might look down to see what he has in his hands, and after a moment of astonishment, choose to work with it. Montessori, it seems to me, was right on target when she called this a period of unconscious absorbency.

Montessori also wrote about sensitive periods in the older child. For example, the child in the 6-12 period is sensitive to imagination. Although he is no longer as strongly pushed toward his own development (by hormé, as mentioned in Appendix A), any lesson that strikes his imagination will strongly motivate him. The child in the 3-6 period is primarily concerned with the development of her own skills, her own self. Thus, she will spend a good deal of time in the Sensorial and Practical Life areas, learning how to order things in various sense dimensions and how to manage many things about her own life. She is thus content for the most part to remain in the classroom: her focus is inward. The elementary child has finished that stage of development (which is very similar across all cultures), and now wants to absorb the particular culture of his own group. This is the time in the Montessori curriculum for a great number of lessons and experiences in history, geography, and the sciences, which Montessori grouped together as the Cultural Subjects.

In her later writings, particularly in a book titled *From Childhood to Adolescence* and two pamphlets, *Erdkinder* and *Functions of the University*, Montessori set out her ideas on the later two periods. The third period of 12-18 is a time of great physical and psychological growth, which has more in common with the 0-6 period than with the 6-12 period which just precedes it. The child is growing and changing rapidly, and the physical and psychological changes of puberty occur. The task of the young person at this stage, according to Montessori, is to construct himself as a social being, to put himself in relation to various parts of the culture that he has learned about in the previous period. To facilitate this development, Montessori has a controversial suggestion (once more!) for secondary education: the Erdkinder.

This German word means "Earth children." What Montessori had in mind was a period of one to three years in close contact with the Earth, and fairly far away from heavy academic pressures. The children were, first of all, to be separated from parents in a boarding school environment. This would help them make necessary steps toward independence. The boarding school might be a small hostel, situated in the countryside; rather than classwork in math, languages, and science, the students would run the hostel themselves as a business. They would do all of the tasks, from a truck garden producing food to be served, to laundry and bookkeeping.

Montessori's rationale for this seems to be based at least in part on her anthropological background. Almost every society has one or more important ceremonies marking the movement of persons from childhood into adulthood. The hunting tribe may send a young boy out to make his first solo hunt; some Native American nations send young people out to have their magic dream, in order to find out what their totemic animal will be. The Hopi of the American Southwest have the visit from the kachinas. These fearsomely dressed "monsters" come to the village and, amidst loud wails and beating of pans, take the young candidate away to the desert for a few days. In the desert, the cosmology of the Hopi nation is revealed, and many other secrets, along with the fact that the kachinas are his uncles. The candidate returns as a full adult, aware of the knowledge of the group. His life is permanently changed by the experience and everyone relates to him in a different fashion.[2]

Montessori felt that contemporary Western society had reduced the markers for the transition to adulthood. Religious ceremonies, such as Confirmation or Bar Mitzvah no longer hold dramatic significance for many young people. Even when they do, the rest of the society is so large and heterogeneous that almost no one at school, for example, would relate to a person differently after undergoing such a ceremony. In small towns 50 years ago, high school graduation was perhaps such a marker, in that it was a large and important ceremony and everyone in town knew which side of this marker a person was on. But in most schools today, graduation has been devalued, both because of the general push toward postsecondary education, and the unrelatedness of high school graduation to work: you don't usually get a raise or recognition at your job at a fast food restaurant because you are a graduate.

Montessori felt that these ceremonies of transition were important because they signified to everyone, but especially to the young person himself, that he could do the essential things required for adulthood in his own culture. Her design for the Erdkinder, then, centered around preparing the young people for the real world of contemporary society: the world of work and the responsibilities associated with living apart from the parents. Her design also recognized something that every junior high school and high school teacher knows, that students at this age pay a lot of attention to interpersonal relationships, both same sex and across the sexes. By acknowledging this rather than ignoring it, and by developing a system that responded to the very real needs of people at this period, Montessori hoped, again, to maximize the potential of each person.

Consider as another example the mandatory service required of young people in Scandinavian countries. One of the requirements of this service is that it be done in a location removed from home.

If Montessori's concentration on areas other than academics (when American students are typically working on grades and requirements for college admission) seems absurd, ask yourself if you ever knew any very bright, very knowledgeable people in high school who never amounted to much because of personality or motivational problems. You might also think about our rising teenage suicide rate.

---

[2] I have advocated this Hopi method for Doctoral dissertation oral examinations for some time now, beginning with my own, but so far without success.

Montessori's goal for her Erdkinder was to produce students who would get a number of personal and social milestones out of the way in a supportive environment. The academic work done by the average 9-12-year-old in a Montessori upper elementary environment will have brought her, in many cases, up to or beyond typical American high school levels in some subject areas. Then, at the university, the Erdkinder graduates will be able to make better use of the resources offered, rather than being merely a student identification number on a conveyor belt towards graduation. Can you imagine (or remember) the 19 year old sophomore sitting in a dorm room, trying to decide on a major? The major is supposed to be determined by the course of work the student will pursue, perhaps for decades after graduation-- and this sophomore may never have experienced satisfaction at doing a job that used any major part of her skills and abilities.

Figure 4-1

Montessori's Idea of the Human Mind

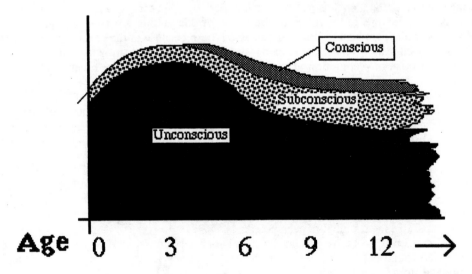

To summarize the four planes of education: Montessori saw dramatic differences in the growing person, and organized these into four stages. In addition, she saw special "windows of opportunity" for growth, the sensitive periods. Her educational method is built on the idea that education must be developed to meet the specific needs and sensitivities of each age. [3]

THE MIND: THREE LEVELS

Another central idea in Montessori's thought is the role of the subconscious mind. As can be seen in Figure 4-1, Montessori divided the mind into three parts.

The unconscious part of the mind is, for Montessori, the largest and the most important. The unconscious level of the mind is the location of *mneme* and *horme´*, described in Appendix A. Thus, most of the motivations of people, especially young children, come from the unconscious. The sensitive periods are also felt to be on the unconscious level.

One aspect of Montessori's theories combines the notion of the unconscious mind with the idea of sensitive periods. When a developing person enters a sensitive period and changes a potential (a nebula) into a new skill or ability, components of that skill reach down to the unconscious. Montessori says that Mankind creates new instincts from the environmental stimuli around him. Language is one of Montessori's favorite examples of a sensitive period. In this case, Montessori implies that the language or languages learned during the sensitive period for language will have far-reaching effects, not only on our conscious mind. How many colors are there in the spectrum between yellow and blue? The answer is dependent on language.

Montessori also hypothesized a subconscious layer to the human mind. This is a layer in which all sense experiences are stored. She used the since-discarded term *engram* to describe a "memory trace," laid down in the subconscious by each sensory experience. In the chart, I have shown this subconscious layer of the mind as possibly even extending backwards to before birth. We now know that the unborn fetus can sense, at the very least, light and vibrations.

These subconscious memory traces are not always able to be called up into consciousness; otherwise we would all have a perfect memory. But a number of pieces of evidence seem to indicate that some model like Montessori's may be needed to explain the complexity of human memory. For example, numerous studies in human memory have shown that many kinds of information, once forgotten, are re-learned in a shorter period of time the second time. Also, the ability of people to remember things in great detail under hypnosis suggests that more is remembered than can be easily recalled in the conscious mind.

For Montessori, the memory traces stored in the subconscious are active, constantly being processed. The way our mind can come up with new answers after a period when the conscious mind is turned off (as in sleep) was proof of this for Montessori.

---

[3]This is in contrast to an educational philosophy that works backwards from a given goal to determine curriculum. For example, exam-based systems may start from the premise that a certain amount must be known by a certain age, when a national examination will be given. Since the exam content and age of examinees is known, the curriculum is then divided up so that the ideal child will have mastered all the content needed by the right age. This method ignores the developmental readiness of learners for particular content.

This idea--that experiences are retained deep in the mind, that these experiences are "put together," and that the resulting new idea can emerge into the conscious mind--is behind several aspects of the Montessori model. The focus on having the child experience the material, rather than on weekly tests, is an example. The whole concept of **indirect preparation**, the preparing of the child for later skills and concepts, is based on this notion of the subconscious mind.

The conscious mind, for Montessori, is the smallest of the three parts. Consciousness emerges around age three; the mind of the toddler and the infant is so different from ours that it cannot be said to be conscious in the same way.

ENTROPY AND SYNTROPY

In the final chart, two ways of explaining the world are shown. The phenomena of the real world are seen by many people to be the result of causes. These causes have other causes, and so on. This causal system is governed by entropy. Entropy is a term from physics; it means that systems have a tendency to "run down"; that is, to move to a state of less energy and less organization. For example, think about wood burned in a fire. The cellular structure and chemical composition of wood is very complex; the ashes at the end of the fire are simply carbon dust. Energy has been lost, released from the wood as heat during the fire. Or, think about a glass pushed off a table. The energy of the glass is higher when it is up on the table ("potential energy"). It is then converted to kinetic energy as the glass falls, and the energy breaks the glass and is lost when the glass's pieces come to rest. The glass has also obviously gone from more organized to less organized.

The Italian philosopher Fantappie felt that this system--of causes and entropy--was a good description of most of the world, but that certain parts of the world, especially living things, were not well explained by these concepts. For example, consider a seed. It actually moves in the opposite direction of entropy; it takes sunlight, mineral, and water, which are relatively unorganized, and organizes them into a much more organized plant. The same is true for any living creature, such as a human: what we take in from the outside world (food, air, water, etc.) is organized into a very complex organism, which has more energy as an adult than as a fertilized egg.

These living systems are also, according to Fantappie, not operating under a cause and effect model. What causes a tree to grow? Certainly, many things are needed (water, sunlight, a seed, and minerals), but none of these cause the tree to grow in the same way that a push causes a glass to fall off a table and break. What causes a human being to grow and develop, to organize food into an adult human body? Fantappie said that living systems were better described as moving toward goals, toward final development, rather than being simply or mechanistically caused. That is, a tree or a person is moving toward a goal of development, being pulled toward this goal, rather than being pushed from behind by a simple cause. That is, living things behaved teleologically, moving toward a goal, rather than causally. Instead of being governed by entropy, they were governed by syntropy. Syntropy was Fantappie's new phrase for the opposite of entropy, moving towards a state of more organization and more energy.

Montessori took Fantappie's distinction to heart and applied it to education. She felt that traditional education was clearly based on the causal model. The teacher saw herself as the cause of learning in the children; she talked or wrote on the blackboard and directly caused learning in the children. Montessori felt that since children were living and therefore teleological beings, the Montessori teacher should not think of herself as a cause of learning in children. The children are moving towards their goals; the teacher, like the gardener, doesn't cause growth or learning, but merely provides what is needed and removes obstacles to growth.[4]

Figure 4-2

Montessori's Application of Fantappie's Philosophy to Education

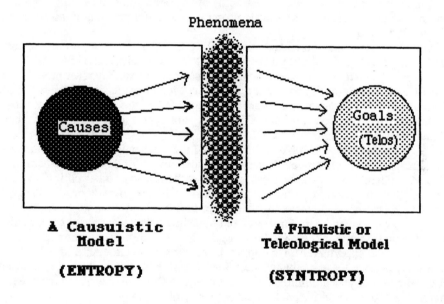

Phenomena

A Causuistic Model

(ENTROPY)

A Finalistic or Teleological Model

(SYNTROPY)

A FINAL PRINCIPLE: RESPECT FOR THE CHILD

The task I have set myself now seems like an impossible one; how can anyone summarize Montessori's rich and complex philosophy into a single chapter, when she herself couldn't express it all in year-long training programs and the more than 20 books she wrote?

---

[4] See also Montessori's concept of the Center and the Periphery, in Standing's biography, *Maria Montessori: Her Life and Work*, pages 234-239.

As we come to the end of this chapter, I have chosen the over-arching theme of respect for the child to bring together a number of important parts of Montessori's ideas.

The most obvious element signifying respect for the child is the child-sized environment. Although universal in early childhood education today, this was a new idea when Montessori proposed it. It will remain an enduring tribute to her concern for children.

Respect for the child is also evident in Montessori's ideas of how children should be motivated to work in the classroom. The teacher must not be seen as the rewarder of behavior. This position puts Montessori in direct opposition with the behaviorists and the programs, such as DISTAR, which they have designed. Part of this stems from Montessori's notion of the child's drive to master himself and his environment. Montessori felt that even very young learners must learn the joy and satisfaction from their own work well completed. This learning of internal rewarding, rather than a dependency on teacher rewards, is perhaps one explanation for the extraordinary staying power of a year or two of Montessori experience (See Chapter 14 for research on the long-term effects of Montessori). Teachers working in elementary Montessori classrooms often comment on how long it takes children from traditional school classrooms to stop coming to them for praise or punishment on every bit of work they do.

Montessori operationalized this fine idea of self-motivation and self-reward rather than leaving it as an abstract ideal for teachers to try to implement somehow. One of the most revealing descriptions of good Montessori materials is that they must provide a "motive for activity." That is, a very important part of the Montessori teacher's job is to make sure that things in the environment do attract the children in her class to work. This trusting that the child's choices (from a carefully selected range of opportunities) are best for her is also an example of respect for the child.

Montessori also emphasized the role of the teacher in creating an atmosphere of mutual respect in the classroom. The "ground rules" of a Montessori classroom protect the rights of children to work on their chosen work without having other children step on their work or otherwise interfere. One of the reasons for the use of mats or small rugs, even in carpeted classrooms, is to ensure that the rest of the class knows where a person's work area is. If you have seen an intent three-year-old threading his way carefully across a floor covered with rugs, you would realize how deeply this idea impresses young children. There must also be the opportunity for group work and for socialization, and the best Montessori classrooms provide these in abundance. But the luxury of being allowed to concentrate is not often given to young children in our society, and this must be raised as an example of what makes Montessori different from other preschool programs.

Montessori's idea of respect for the child, then, can be seen in a number of places: respect for the child's ability to work, for his need to concentrate, for his ability to absorb information, and for his choice of work that will most benefit him. We owe the child the respect shown by a clean, orderly, attractive, and child-scaled environment. We need to respect the child's particular developmental stage, and not try to teach him with chalk-and-talk lessons more suitable for adults. Even such minor considerations as speaking to a child at her own eye-level, rather than looming over her, are examples of Montessori's principle of respect for the child.

A final consideration is Montessori's strong commitment to peace education, as can be seen in her book "Education and Peace," in numerous lectures, and in the thrust of the international movement for educating world citizens.[5] (It was not by chance that Mussolini closed all Montessori schools, or that her books were burned in Nazi Germany.) Montessori's position was that of almost all intellectuals of her day, an almost unbelieving horror at the rise of Facism and the horrors that it wreaked on the countries of Europe and the minds of the world. She wrote about her new education creating a new man, specifically a man incapable of repeating such a disaster. The respect that each child learns to have for others must grow into a respect for all people, everywhere in the world. This idea is specifically (and brilliantly) built into the structure of the elementary social studies curriculum, as we will see in a later chapter.

> *From Lecture 26 (Given June 23rd) by Dr. Maria Montessori, in the International Montessori Course given in 1913. These notes by E. M. Standing. © 1988 by the Estate of E.M.Standing, Seattle University.*

(Emphasis is mine throughout-JCM)

...Before passing on to the practical work I should like to sum up some of the ideas which we have been discussing. In the natural psychic development one finds two periods, the first which is the primitive period, and which is also the creative period. I will give an example: the very young child begins to walk; he feels an irresistible impulse which impels him to do so. We could not hold back the child from walking, and if we did it would be a form of violence and would have serious effects on his motor development.

The child begins to speak because his development leads him to do so. The child does not develop because he wishes to utilize these developments. The child does not reason in this way: "Because I wish to walk from here to there I will begin to develop my capacity for walking in order to do so." He does not say, "I wish to develop language so that I shall be able to ask for food when I am hungry." No. We have first the development, and it is only in a subsequent period that the human individual utilizes this development.

*Thus when the child has developed the power of walking where he pleases, and when he has developed the power of speaking, he says that which he desires to utter. There is then a whole period when the child does exercises without any purpose except the purpose of the doing of the exercises in themselves; and this form of exercise requires great effort on the part of the child. One sees that the child is very active when he wishes to begin to walk himself. We must consider this principle not only in connection with these primitive activities of the child, but we must **consider it as a***

---

[5] See, e.g., Turner's fine paper, "Child Discipline and World Peace", ED 304 226, 1988

general principle underlying all development during the whole of childhood.

One of the errors of the established method of education is that it only takes into consideration the utilization of the things which are developed. For instance, it is considered useless to develop writing in the child before the child is able to utilize this accomplishment, and it seems only necessary to develop it when he is about to use it. When, in my method of education, I laid down this principle of the development in itself as the fundamental basis of all, an objection was raised that there would be difficulty in making the social application of these things which have been developed, because man must develop these capacities for utilization. For instance, it was said,"If you merely think of the development itself, how will these children be able to pass their examinations and do their required work?"; because it would seem that they should in some way be prepared directly for this utilization.

Objectors spoke as though the two principles, the one of development and the other of utilization were entirely separate one from the other, as though it were necessary to make a choice between the two. Whereas, the more perfect the development, the better it can be utilized. If one examines this idea profoundly, experimenting with the children, one will find that the whole question of utilization lies in this fact of development.

Once we have studied the question in this way, we immediately see the logic of it. Looking back to the very first development in the child, we have the proof in nature herself. It is evident that the child in order to be able to utilize his capacity of walking must first develop the power to walk; and before he can utilize his language, before he can use it to express his feelings and ideas, he must develop his language. There is no dualism in the first periods.

That first primitive activity, that almost irresistible activity, is due to the impulse of development. Thus, little by little, as the child develops his reasoning power he also develops the capacity for the utilization of this development: the two things go along side by side; he utilizes this development of the power of reasoning as his reasoning power develops.

The fact of culture or learning must always be acquired with a certain technique, that is, they have to be given in a certain way. For instance, if the older children of seven or eight are to write compositions, it is absolutely essential that they should first learn to write. Thus, we feel the necessity of developing what we call the elements of culture or learning. The ordinary methods recognize this principle of development in relation to learning. But instead of recognizing the development of the child, they take into consideration the development of the period of culture, during the period when it cannot really be recognized. For instance, when they taught children these little strokes or lines for writing it was evident that these marks would not be used for writing, but they served to prepare for this future learning. Progress in development was considered in regard to the cultural subject matter rather than with regard to the child himself.

It would appear that ordinary methods consider it sufficient to have these graded periods for learning the different subjects, in order to teach certain subjects to the children. If, instead, we consider the development of the child himself and if in considering this development we do not take into consideration the purpose of this development of culture, but only the development of the child himself, then we shall find ourselves facing a very radical change in the concepts of education. This change would not be noted externally, perhaps, because we also teach the same things; we teach the alphabet, reading and writing, arithmetic and grammar; therefore it might seem as if this were the same as any other method. But we use all this apparatus merely as a means for the development of the child himself and not in order to teach him certain things. Here we have come to this fundamental difference between the two concepts.

We may say that the great difference lies in the life, vivacity, interest, and joy which the child shows in doing the work and also in the facility and precocity with which he learns. To enable us to follow the development of the child we try to find and follow the impulse of the child. We are trying to cultivate and give exercises which strengthen these inner energies. For this reason, instead of logically teaching certain things, we expose in the adapted environment certain stimuli and allow the child to choose.

Summary: In this chapter, the influences of several thinkers on Montessori were examined. From Rousseau, she took the notion of the classroom as a community, and of the importance of freedom for the child. From Locke, she took the idea of the importance of early experiences, of learning through the senses, and the importance of order. Itard and Seguin were very influential on Montessori's actual practices; many of the materials were similar to those developed by these two pioneers.

Montessori's ideas of the unconscious, subconscious, and conscious parts of the mind underlie many aspects of the model she developed. The unconscious is seen as the seat of drives, including the drive that motivates children to learn at the edge of their experience and competence. The ability of the subconscious to store all sense experiences, and to coordinate these experiences into new learning is behind Montessori's emphasis on the child's own interaction with the material, and her concept of indirect preparation.

Montessori's stage theory of development proposes, as do Piagetian theorists, a fixed sequence of stages, each qualitatively different than the others. This theory has implications for the way learning is fostered at each age. Finally, Montessori's ideas about the active nature of learning suggest a model in which the teacher does not directly cause learning in students, but rather prepares the environment and removes impediments to learning.

Reading loft in a Montessori 3-6 class.

CHAPTER 5
The Montessori Model

Chapter Goals: In this chapter, you will learn:
- The role of the environment in the Montessori model, including a comparison with the traditional preschool environment.
- Basic ideas concerning the uses of the Montessori materials.
- The role of the Montessori teacher, the materials, and the other children as co-educators in the Montessori class.
- When does a Montessori teacher intervene?
- The Montessori concept of normalization through work.

As discussed in the first chapter, one way to break up all of the information about Montessori method is to separate the <u>model</u> (the ideal program) from the <u>program</u> (actual classrooms). In this chapter, the basic aspects of the Montessori model are presented.

The model is in the "middle" of the outline presented earlier; it is derived from Montessori's ideas on the theory/ philosophy level and guides practices in actual classrooms on the lowest level (See Figure 1-3). One of the goals of this chapter is to help the reader see how the elements of the Montessori model are dependent on the higher level of philosophy. For example, the heavy reliance on active manipulation in the model is derived from Montessori's ideas of the active nature of learning in the young child. The model can be further broken down into three main areas: environment, materials, and teacher behaviors and expectations.

ENVIRONMENT

I hope that the reader will have had the opportunity to observe in several Montessori environments, and in other early childhood classrooms as well. These observations will help a great deal in understanding the differences and the similarities that exist between Montessori classrooms and traditional nursery schools. In most of the comparisons that follow, I will compare and contrast Montessori with traditional/developmental nursery school programs, rather than behaviorally oriented, direct whole group teaching approaches such as DISTAR.

Information on the Montessori models is available in Montessori's own books, in the work of others about her schools, and from Montessori teacher preparation courses. Important books on the Montessori model include Montessori's *Spontaneous Activity In Education, The Discovery of the Child.* and *From Childhood to Adolescence*; E.M. Standing's

Maria Montessori: Her Life and Work and *Revolution in Education*; Mario Montessori, Jr.'s *Education for Human Development;* Anne Neubert's *Montessori: A Way of Learning*, as well as numerous articles by Montessori and others. Information on the traditional nursery school model is likewise available from a variety of sources, including materials from the National Association for the Education of Young Children (NAEYC), observations (especially at laboratory schools) and books such as those shown in the bibliography at the end of this chapter.

It's important for the reader to realize that there is a large and in some cases widening gap between the Montessori model given by Montessori herself, the model set forth in others' books and in various teacher preparation programs, and in the model that can be inferred from observations in programs. The divergence of these models is different in various content areas; for example, wide diversity exists in the proposed role of open-ended materials such as blocks, whereas little divergence is seen in areas such as the Sensorial or math curricula. In this book, the model described represents the author's own viewpoint of the best Montessori models.

Let's begin then, with some similarities between Montessori and traditional or developmental classrooms. All sources agree that the environment must, first of all, be a safe place for children, from shielding of wall outlets to adequate and sanitary toileting facilities. The size of the room should also be appropriate for the number of children. Typical state regulations require 35 square feet for the child. Since often bathroom and hallway space are taken into this count, Montessori classrooms are typically 500 to 900 square feet. Some traditional/developmental programs, especially laboratory schools such as Stanford's Bing Nursery School, use large environments, more children, and more teachers. Montessori classrooms typically contain 20-25 children, one teacher, and one aide.

A typical classroom in either model would include both carpeted and non-carpeted areas. The Montessori classroom area of Practical Life (or Daily Living) is often on a hard surface floor, to facilitate cleaning up after spills. This is considered to be an appropriate children's activity and is demonstrated to the children. In a traditional classroom also, messier activities such as a water table, sand or cornmeal table, or easels for painting are on the hard surface flooring. Toilet arrangements would vary widely but should be accessible, allow some privacy, and facilitate supervision. Although wide variation exists, both models support food preparation activities and snacks as a part of the day. The Montessori model appears to encourage the set up of a snack area and individual snack "breaks," limited perhaps by the number of chairs, rather than a group snack.

The model Montessori classroom typically contains four areas for four sets of materials: Practical Life, Sensorial, Math, and Language. The model also provides for an area for science and social studies materials, called either "cultural subjects" or "cosmic education."[1] These materials include both discovery table areas and more typically Montessori materials such as puzzle maps, the cabinet of leaf shapes, etc. There is also an art area, an area for removal and storage of coats and shoes, a snack preparation area (typically in the Practical Life area) and storage areas for both teacher and child.

---

[1] Highly recommended is a published dissertation on Montessori's cosmic education by Sr. Christine Trudeau, which is available from the director of the Montessori Teacher Education Program at Chaminade University in Honolulu, Hawaii.

In each of the curriculum areas (Practical Life, Sensorial, Math, Art, Language, and Cultural Subjects) there are some common features. First, materials are displayed on low open shelves, accessible to the child. Each area is also set apart by some arrangement of the room, such as placement of the shelves, change in floor covering, and so on. Finally, the room is arranged so that the materials on the shelves can be taken out by the child and moved to an appropriate work area easily.

There are also child-sized tables and chairs, usually a mix of individual tables and 2–, 4–, or 6-child tables. A teacher's desk or table is common, but is used as a storage area rather than a location for delivery of direct whole group instruction. Indeed, the classroom is obviously not designed to facilitate long periods of direct whole group instruction. The tables and chairs are scattered through the room, not aligned in rows. The number of chairs is often smaller than the number of children present and the tables and chairs are not aligned to the teacher's desk.

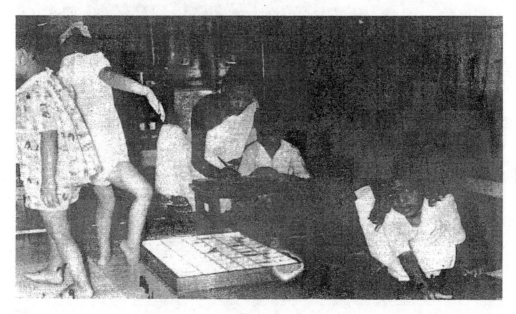

Children at an Indian Montessori school in the 1950's at work. What similarities and differences can be seen between this and a contemporary American Montessori classroom? Courtesy Seattle University and Estate of E.M. Standing.

There is also a line on the floor in a central location, usually in a circle or elliptical shape, perhaps an inch wide. This serves for the Montessori exercise of walking on the line, a large motor activity that can be combined with music. Although not strongly supported in written descriptions of the Montessori model, this line is also often used for whole class activities such as stories, songs, or whole-group instruction. In the photos, you can see some of these characteristics.

To contrast this with traditional classrooms, first consider the differences in areas. Typical traditional classrooms are divided in a variety of ways, but most of them have a role play, dress-up, or housekeeping area. This may include a variety of materials for playing house, or store, and costumes for dress-up play. A block area with unit blocks is also typical, as is a small motor area that would include a variety of activities such as bead stringing, parquetry blocks, puzzles, construction materials such as Legos^{TM}, etc. Water tables for water play and sand or cornmeal tables are also common.

There is also usually a larger portion of the space devoted to Art. There may be discovery tables with materials set out for exploration, learning centers such as a tape recorder with earphones, and so on.

These children in an American Montessori 6-9 classroom are working together on math.

The absence of the role play/dress-up/housekeeping area in the Montessori classroom is one of the most obvious differences. Advocates of traditional nursery school models point to the interest of the children in this area, the opportunity for language use, and the theorized link between role play, creativity and social development. In Montessori's writings, her main attack on fantasy is on <u>teacher</u>-directed fantasy, as is commonly seen in Froebelian kindergarten programs. Montessori gives the example of a teacher who builds a "village" with unit blocks and then gallops a "horse" (an identical block) around.

Montessori also cautioned against a too-early introduction of fantasy and fairy tales arguing that the child's development of imagination needs real objects and realistic stories for maximum development. This position is in contrast with traditional views and with Bruno Bettelheim's view in "The Uses of Enchantment." Dr. Bettelheim theorizes that fairy tales are important to young children for passing on culturally important themes and types.

While Montessori's writings are not nearly so opposed to fantasy and role play activities as supposed, the practice in schools is not to include a role play or dress-up area. Montessori children, however, do have the Practical Life area, in which to perform a variety of "grown up" skills. The primary differences here are that the materials in the Practical Life area are usually child-sized and breakable, rather than doll-sized and unbreakable. Most observations in the Practical Life area reveal some fantasy play being engaged in. Our knowledge about the effects of early childhood programs is general; little information is available on the effects of this one aspect of a model on children's growth and development. Research evidence on creativity in Montessori children indicates possible lower scores in creativity in terms of picture elaboration and higher scores on divergent production. See Chapter 9 for more detailed information on some recent research on fantasy in Montessori classrooms and where it occurs.

Children's interest in water play is at least partially met by pouring activities in the Practical Life area. Hands, table, dish and clothes washing, as well as food preparation, are typical Montessori Practical Life activities that involve water.

The availability of unit blocks for building is another clear difference between traditional/developmental and Montessori programs. A variety of materials in the Sensorial area are used by children for building and stacking, however.

It is important to clear up the mistaken notion that none of the Montessori material is open-ended, that all have only one right way to be used. It is certainly the case that each Montessori teacher learns a limited set of particular presentations for each of the traditional Montessori materials. It is also true that children are typically required to see the teacher's short (one- to three- minute) lesson on the use of a material before they are free to take it from the shelf to work with it. And teachers do intervene when materials are used destructively. It is not the case, however, that children are prohibited from experimenting with the materials. More information on this is presented in the section on teachers later in this chapter.

MATERIALS

> *Notes from E.M. Standing from Dr. Montessori's 1921 course. Lecture 14, given 5th May. Copyright © 1989, E..M.Standing and Seattle University.*
> *(Emphasis by the author)*

I will sum up briefly what I have said regarding the use of the material. First of all, let us consider the presentation of the material, which consists in using it in the precise way when placed for the first time in front of the child. In this particular case it consists in the displacing and replacing of certain objects. Sometimes the correct presentation of material requires the preparation of the individual. For instance, the preparation of the fingers for the tactile exercise, or the temporary impeding of some other sense, such as the sight, may be required. Sometimes it is necessary to demonstrate a cer-

tain mode of procedure in the presentation, such as the lightness of the hand in touching surfaces and the almost imperceptible movement of the hands when weighing the baric tablets.

All this is in relation to the mode of presentation of the material, and now what shall we call the presentation itself? **It would not be suitable to call it a lesson, especially as we have said that we must avoid teaching as commonly understood, so that the child will not have the idea that he must merely imitate that which the teacher is doing. But as it is necessary to give this presentation a name, we will call it an initiation.**

So the teacher initiates the child, and it is almost as though she gives him a key to the secret of this modification or development of himself of which he is in need. We do not in effect teach him anything in the presentation; we are merely placing his feet upon the path which will lead him to his goal, which is perfection. *In order that this material will have the desired effect, that the child shall be stimulated to the exercise, it is necessary that the teacher should know the technique of correct presentation.*

The first thing to say about the Montessori materials (besides how beautiful and expensive they are!) is that they are **manipulatives for the child, not teaching aids for the teacher**. Thus, in many kindergarten classes, there is a large globe that the teacher may use from time to time to illustrate a point. In the Montessori classroom, there are small globes that are used--held, turned, studied, and matched with flat maps--by the child. The teacher's role is merely to introduce the child to the material and to indicate some of the possibilities of the material, to call the child's attention, through modeling, to certain interesting aspects of the material. The work with the materials is the child's job.[1]

One of the goals of the Montessori method is to have each child reach her full potential; one of the primary mechanisms to do this is to allow each child to choose an activity from the dozens offered in the classroom. Montessori's rationale for this was that only the child really knows exactly what interests him, and that we can rely on the child's drive to work at the boundary of his learning to keep him moving on to new things. Aside from the enormous faith in the child that this idea represents, it places a great deal of responsibility on the teacher, in particular on her design of the environment and the diversity of the materials she offers. Thus, the teacher's role is quite indirect--a good deal of her work is done before the child enters the classroom.

---

[1] Other examples of teacher aids are pull-down map charts, blackboards and overhead projectors, and any other objects that are used at the front of the classroom, manipulated by the teacher. Manipulatives, on the other hand, which would include things like geo-boards and Cuisinaire rods in addition to Montessori materials, are used primarily by individual children.

Both the environment (such as low, open shelves) and the materials are crucial in allowing for the degree of independence that characterizes a good Montessori classroom. One of the most important characteristics of many materials is that they are **self-correcting**; that is, the teacher does not need to be there with the child to tell her whether she has gotten it right. The materials themselves will tell a child whether they are being used in a correct way. (Note: I said **a** correct way, not **the** correct way.)

Some of the materials, such as the knobbed cylinders, will only work one way-- any other way of putting them into their holes will not work. Other materials, such as the cube tower and the broad stair, have many ways of being used, all of which have in common an awareness of their graduated size. These materials, then, have themes, such as size differences in one, two, or three dimensions, and are mid-way between open- and closed-ended materials.

The Montessori teacher during the actual classroom day spends her time moving around the classroom. She may stop to give a short lesson, move to correct a disturbance or restate ground rules, or observe a child at work. Research on the process aspect of Montessori teaching is reported in Chapter 13. One fact bears mentioning here: in a large study of the processes of different models, Montessori teachers spent less time correcting inappropriate behavior and disciplining than did teachers in traditional nursery school models (see Miller and Dyer, 1975).

The fact of self-correcting materials is partially responsible for the degree of independence that can be seen in Montessori classrooms. If the teacher had to correct every activity that goes on, there is no way she could allow each child to choose his own work. This use of self-correcting materials makes for a classroom atmosphere that is very different from the traditional nursery school, and radically different from the traditional elementary school. Rather than answers to math or spelling problems being the closely guarded secret of the teacher, a variety of materials with the answers is available in the classroom. The focus has shifted from getting the right answer to using the correct process. Children work busily with materials to determine the answers and then get the control sheets, a calculator, etc., to check themselves. This has the effect of placing the emphasis on process rather than on the correct answers, which can be a disadvantage to learning, especially to learning problem solving skills. It also frees the teacher from her role as the sole dispenser of correct information. This has a number of effects.

One effect of making the teacher **one** source (rather than the **only** source) of information in elementary Montessori classrooms, is to free her up from constant correcting, enabling her to do more individual and small group lessons, and more observing of students. As we'll see in Chapter 13, this actually does happen. The control of error idea also makes the evaluation of the student's work more separate from the teacher's opinion. Have you ever corrected a student's composition and had the student tell you that you just didn't understand what he or she meant? When the correction comes from a neutral source, these problems seem to be reduced.

Another characteristic of the materials is what Montessori called the isolation of difficulty. In the Sensorial area, the children work with a wide range of materials that have a common theme. Each material is constant on all but one sense dimension, such as color, shape, etc. An example would be the red rods, which are all red and two centimeters square in cross section, but vary in length from ten to one hundred centimeters. Color tablets are small rectangles of wood with plastic handles, which vary only in color. Small metal bottles are full of water of varying temperatures. This isolation of difficulty is a central idea in Montessori's conception of materials design. [1]

This isolation of difficulty concept has another aspect that has resulted in some confusion-- and negative feelings--about Montessori preschools from traditional nursery school teachers. This has to do with how these materials in the Sensorial area are used. The basic principle is that the objects to teach a particular sense mode must vary regularly in that mode and be identical in all other respects. Color, for example, should not be taught with colored objects (cars, trucks, etc.) but with the color tablets, which have no other purpose. Montessori felt that the isolation of "redness," warmth, or length was more important than the familiarity of red trucks, warm soup, etc.. She saves this learning for later explorations of the child's environment. While this makes sense from both the Lockean/Montessori and behaviorist perspective, it makes Montessorians seem anti-toy, a criticism that draws strength from the misunderstood Montessori position on fantasy and dramatic play.

A final consideration about the Montessori materials is the idea of abstraction. Montessori felt strongly that abstract concepts, such as the decimal system of numeration, the sound-symbol system that is reading, and even basic taxonomy of plants and animals could all be learned by children six years old and under, through the use of concrete manipulative materials. A more detailed example of the passage to abstraction is given in the chapter on Math.

THE TEACHER AND EXPECTATIONS

The Montessori "teacher": I have used this more typical title, rather than the word "directress," favored by Montessori, or the now popular "guide," which arose from the sense that "directress" was too descriptive of someone authoritatively directing children. Even with the familiar title of teacher, it should be clear by now that what this person does in a Montessori classroom is a new role, one radically different from more well-known roles in relation to children: babysitter, parent, friend, primary grades teacher, or traditional preschool teacher. Veteran Montessori teacher educators at conferences sometimes argue about whether most of our problem students, the ones who have such a hard time adjusting to this new role, are those who have been previously successful as a traditional teacher in either preschools or early primary grades. What are some of the ways in which the Montessori teacher role differs from other more familiar roles?

One thing that is hard for many of the people who would be Montessori teachers is that the role includes very little teaching of the class of children as a whole. The vision we all have of the teacher, standing before the blackboard and giving a good lesson to the whole class, is very seldom a part of what Montessori teachers do. Group times typically take up only 20 to 40 minutes in a 2 1/2 to 3 1/2 hour day. These group times include a number of activities, such as announcements, discussions on what children have done or will do, seeing who is absent, updating a calendar or weather chart, songs, fingerplays, and stories. A short

---

[1] Although it probably came to Montessori from Lockean sources modified by Itard and Seguin, our appreciation of how these materials actually facilitate child learning is best explained by Jean Piaget. The Sensorial material, and the work of classifying and seriating that they allow the child to undertake are discussed in Chapter 7.

group lesson may also be included, but this does not happen every day, and should take less than five minutes. If Montessori teachers are going to be true to the idea of tailoring lessons to each individual child's needs, then very few lessons can be presented to a normal group of 3- to 6-year-olds, since it's very unlikely that everyone in the group will be ready for any single lesson.

Group lessons are used more frequently at the beginning of the year, to introduce (or reintroduce, for the experienced children) some of the basic materials. For example, the presentation on getting a rug or mat to work on may be shown to the entire class. Other common group presentations in the 3-6 class include carrying a tray, hygiene lessons such as nose-blowing and bathroom and lunch procedures, and basic Sensorial and Practical Life presentations.

Another thing that is difficult for beginning Montessori teachers to accept is the fact that although their Montessori teacher education program has filled their minds to overflowing with presentations (demonstrations of materials to be given to individuals or small groups), they will not spend most of their time doing this! More of their time is spent in moving around the room, observing children, intervening when necessary, reinforcing ground rules, suggesting work to children who have already been shown how to use it, noting changes that should be made in the environment and materials, and, generally, maintaining an overview of the classroom. Presentations to individuals can only be given, as experienced Montessori teachers will tell you, when chaos is not reigning over the rest of the room! That is why the typical Montessori presentation is so short, a mere introduction to the material.

Although it may be short, it should never be hurried or imprecise. Nor should the teacher give the child she is with the feeling that she is only partly "there" for him, even though she may be longing to stand up and deal with a growing problem on the other side of the room. One teacher developed the bad habit of giving her presentations in a position like a football player before the snap of the ball, down on one knee and one foot with one hand resting on the floor, ready to leap up to the next person at any moment. Needless to say, the children were much more interested in seeing when she would leap up than in attending to the presentation.

Before we move on to discuss the presentation in more detail, Figure 5-1 may help to illustrate the difference between Montessori and traditional teaching.

In the traditional teaching model (as was discussed in Chapter 4 as a causal model), the primary direction of influence among the three parts is from the teacher to the child. This is the direction that learning is supposed to follow. Materials and the environment are seen as of secondary importance; their role is primarily to support the teacher's instruction. Thus in the diagram of the traditional model, the heaviest arrow comes from the teacher to the child. A lighter curved arrow shows that the teacher (not the child) uses the materials and to a lesser extent the environment, to deliver instruction.

Figure 5-1

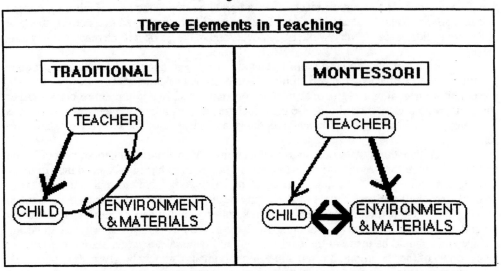

In the Montessori half of the diagram, the heaviest line is a two way arrow indicating interaction between the child and the environment. A heavy line between teacher and environment and materials shows the importance of the teacher's role as developer and maintainer of the learning environment. She must organize the environment and in some cases create materials for the class of children. A light arrow shows that the teacher still has some responsibility for teaching the child directly.

To move on now to the presentations, the format common to many presentations is the three period lesson. First, the new information is introduced: "This is /b/."[1] The child is typically shown two or three new objects at a time; some recent research conducted by Montessori teachers in their classrooms seems to indicate that two is more appropriate for four year olds.

Then the child is given a chance to respond non-verbally, typically with a pointing or giving response: "Show me the /b/" In this second period, the child is asked about the objects in a specific order different than the order in which they were presented. If objects were presented in the order 1,2,3, then the pointing response in the second period is in the order 3,1,2. That is, the most recent first, followed by the first object, and then the most difficult middle object last, when it is the only one left. This part of standard Montessori practice has been confirmed as an appropriate practice in studies of the short-term memory recency-primacy effect. That is, in tests of memory, the most easily recalled item is the one most recently heard--number 3 in our example. The next most easily recalled is the item at the beginning of the list, number 1 (hence the name-- recency-primacy). The most difficult items to recall are those in the middle of the list. This one is made easy, since it is now the only one left.

---

[1] As discussed in the chapter on Language curriculum, the Montessori model makes use of phonetic values for teaching about letters, not their names. Thus, /b/ rather than "bee."

The second period is not limited to a few moments, as the teacher's initial presentation in the first period is. The child may work for quite a long time without being asked to associate the new names with the new objects. Remember that the second period is a non-verbal test. Finally, the child will be ready to produce the new names in relation to the new objects. This final third period is also conducted in the 3-1-2 order.

Only after this third period would the child extend his learning to other examples of the concept. For example, at this time, the teacher would begin discussing words that the child knows that begin with the sound /b/, and so on. In the Sensorial area, this is the time at which the red cars, red trucks, and red sweaters are brought into the lesson. So it isn't the case that Montessori teachers never try to make the lessons relate to the real world of the child. Rather, the Montessori teacher isolates the concept and ascertains the child's understanding before moving on to applications of the idea. This is similar to Piaget's ideas of the learning process as a balance between assimilation and accommodation. It's also a very fertile area for more research.

At the risk of making readers think (incorrectly) that this is what the child is expected to know, I reproduce here a presentation write-up from a Montessori teacher's album.

First Presentation of the Noun (Noun Game)

Age: 4 & up

Prerequisites: Good oral language background; most sandpaper letters; understanding of what a word is; some decoding of three letter phonetic words (pink level), including some word building with movable alphabets, ideally labeling of the farm objects.

Materials: Paper (either small slips or a roll of adding machine paper tape in a holder to allow slips to be torn off) and black felt marking pen; the farm or another small set of small, well-known objects. Montessori never intended that the farm would be the only set like this ever to be used in Montessori classrooms. Also, there are certainly less expensive farm sets available than the one from Nienhuis.

Presentation: (Individual or small group)
   1. Invite the child(ren)
   2. Recall the name of the set--the farm or whatever set you are using.
   3. Ask the child(ren) the names of 5 to 9 objects in the sets. As each one is named, write the name down carefully on the slip of paper with the pen. Use the same letters as the sandpaper letters and movable alphabets that the child has been exposed to.
   4. Each child is allowed to "read" the word from the paper after they have told you what to write. Give the slip

to the child, ask him what it says, and then ask him to put it next to the object it names.

5. As you proceed, begin to refer to the slip as a noun. Say things such as, *"Now John, what is this? Yes, a pig. Let me write the noun for you."* and *"Where will you put this noun?"*

6. When you have finished labeling all of the objects, gather the slips together as a column. Say, *"These words are all names of things on the farm. These words are nouns. Can you say the word noun?"*

7. Offer the children the opportunity to read and re-place the slips, or to copy them down on a chalkboard or their own slips of paper.

Variations: Later lessons will extend this concept with the "Bring me--" game, and the introduction of the noun symbol.

Extensions: The making of classroom noun lists, use of the noun symbol, noun family chart, etc., are not usually introduced until later in the sequence.

Points of Interest: 1) Seeing the familiar objects' names turned into written words 2) The first idea of word classes (parts of speech).

Control of Error: The teacher checks to be sure of correct matching of words to objects. If for some reason a child with poor initial sounds background gets included in the lesson, choose objects which have all different initial sounds.

Direct Aims: Introduction to the noun; the idea that words are in groups by functions, and that name words are nouns.

Indirect Aims: Additional experience with the relation between oral and written language; preparation for further work with the noun and other parts of speech.

So Montessori teachers maintain the environment and materials; they keep order in the classroom, and they give short presentations to individuals and small groups. They also have whole class times, with talking, songs, and stories. Of all of these activities, the one on which the general public and non-Montessori early educators seem the most misinformed has to do with intervention in the classroom.

Intervention is called for by a number of possible behaviors in the Montessori class-room. No one thinks that it is inappropriate to intervene in the case of danger to children, and the data from my study of when Montessori teachers intervene confirms that Montessori teachers from four countries and all major Montessori training organizations are quite consistent.[1] (See Figure 5-2.) In the following charts, the likelihood of teachers to intervene (self-reported) is compared across four different Montessori training (teacher education) traditions: AMI, AMS, NCME, and all other groups together. These organizations were discussed in Chapter 1.

Figure 5-2

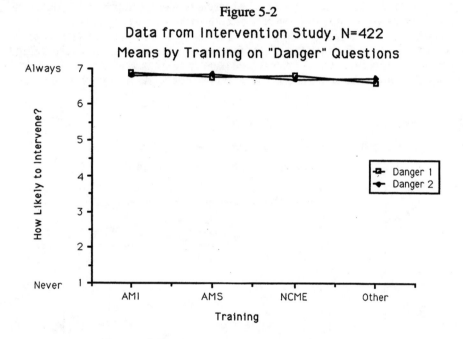

Data from Intervention Study, N=422
Means by Training on "Danger" Questions

As you can see, the study showed that Montessori teachers from a wide variety of training traditions were in quite strong agreement about intervention when there was a danger to a child, as in the example given in one question-- a child begins to use the number rods as swords. The questionnaire is shown at the end of this chapter.

---

[1] This study was still in the data collection and analysis stage at press time for this book. The study was based on a questionnaire describing two dozen situations, and a scale of 1 (Never intervene) to 7 (Always intervene). Montessori teachers from AMI, AMS, St. Nicholas, the National Center for Montessori Education, the London Montessori Centre, and the Caribbean Montessori Society completed the questionnaire, from Trinidad (N=30), Haiti (N=9), Canada (N=21) and the USA (N=362). The letter N stands for the Number of respondents. Please write to me at Seattle University for more information.

The area where the most misinformation exists is in intervention when no child is in danger. There are many possible times for such intervention: disruption in the class-room, fantasy play with Montessori materials, errors of fact (such as misidentification of col-ors, spelling errors, errors in addition), and errors in the use of Montessori materials, such as mistakes in seriating or classifying with the Sensorial materials. When to intervene, and when to do more observing is a critical decision that Montessori teachers must learn to make. The intervention study reveals quite a bit about when Montessori teachers say they do and do not intervene.

In Figure 5-3, several questions about disruption are shown. The lines are the different questions (Q 27, Q 22, etc.) that asked teachers about disruption. As you can see, Montessori teachers are relatively intolerant of children's disruptive activities. There was also some variation in the responses to the different questions. The questionnaire is shown at the end of this chapter, so that you can look at the questions the teachers were responding to. Training traditions affect some of the means, and country of origin is almost always a signifi-cant influence. Haitian teachers, in particular, brook little or no disruption in their class-rooms.

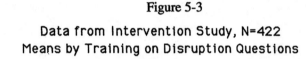

Figure 5-3

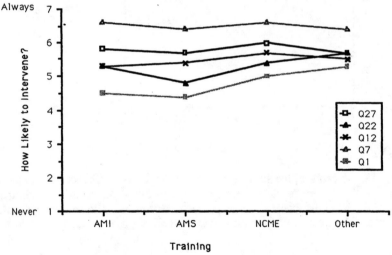

One of the most interesting areas is intervention when children make a mistake in putting cylinders in order or in classifying things into groups. These seriating and classifying errors are important to study because Piagetian theory would predict that little learning would take place in these areas if the child is kept from making mistakes through teacher intervention. It is precisely from experiencing his own errors that the child learns. Correction of errors in factual matters is also important; Montessori clearly says that children's invented spellings should be let go in the interests of expression, but can Montessori teachers keep their hands off?

Figure 5-4

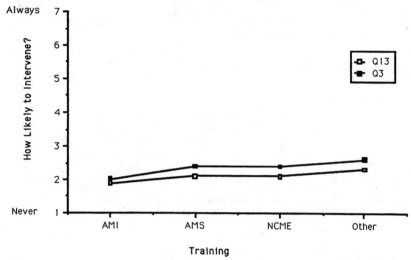

Data from Intervention Study, N=422
Means by Training on Classification Errors

Figure 5-5

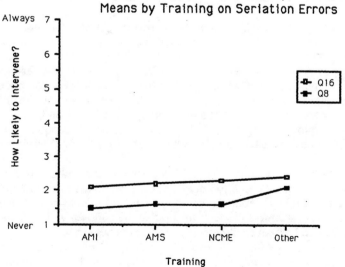

Data from Intervention Study, N=422
Means by Training on Seriation Errors

Figure 5-6

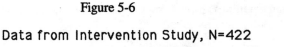

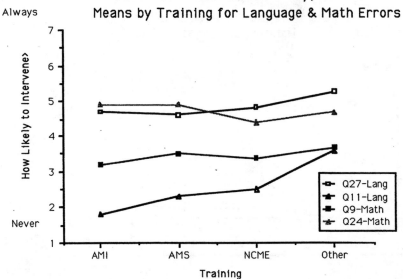

Individual teachers have widely different thresholds for their tolerance of disruption and fantasy play in their classrooms, but, in general, Montessori teachers say that they do not intervene when the child is making "mistakes" with materials that involve seriation, and classification activities, and intervene only some of the time in errors in reading and math areas. See Figures 5-4 and 5-5.

In Figure 5-6, you can see that there is more variation (by training) in teachers' response to math and language errors made by children. Teachers are most consistent about danger and quite consistent about seriation and classification errors. There is wide variability in their response to fantasy, as we will see when we come back to this data in the chapter on fantasy. Responses to math and language errors are moderately consistent across teachers in different training traditions and across nations. The AMI and AMS teachers seem slightly less likely to intervene than the other groups, especially on Question 11, an example of a child with an invented spelling. So, at least in this area of reported intervention in invented spelling, Montessori teachers vary by the type of teacher education they have received.

Of course, how a teacher intervenes is very important as well. After a teacher, through careful observation, has decided to intervene, the goal of the intervention is not to punish, but to redirect the child into work that will absorb him. The goal of the teacher is the "normalization" of the class. Montessori's term means that the children will have thrown off their abnormal behaviors and discovered the enjoyment and concentration that comes from work that challenges them at just the right level of difficulty. Normalization comes from work that meets the child's needs, and in Montessori's thought, this has a positive effect on all levels of the child.

To expand this idea of Montessori's concept of normalization, consider this from her 1921 course:

"*Thus we note this capacity in men of genius and in profound students, a capacity for concentration, analogous to that which we see in the children. We consider this phenomenon from our external point of view and say that men like this are distracted from their environment. But we may also say that they are concentrated within themselves, and these are the people that produce the great original works. This accounts for those incidents which we read in the biographies of eminent men who forget to eat, etc.*

I would like to define clearly the characteristics of this phenomenon and distinguish it from other phenomena already spoken about. I would like to distinguish this phenomenon of the concentrated attention from that other which we have described as the elementary psychic movement. This consists in accomplishing a series of actions which modify the external environment. Such series of actions are performed in carrying out the exercises of Practical Life; they are movements having as their scope an intelligent purpose. The purpose involves a whole, logical succession of actions, bound together for the fulfillment of that purpose.

For instance, when the purpose is to set the table, this work necessitates many small logical actions bound together; the unfolding of the tablecloth, the precise placement on the table of the silver, the plates, etc. The child is led to do work which has an intelligent purpose, where all the necessary actions are logically connected. When the child has accomplished the purpose, this group of logical actions is complete.

In this exercise, the child's whole attention is held by these external objects. We may say that the attention is taking a logical walk in the environment. The continuously varying muscular exercise is the prevailing experience of the child. The muscles in this case are really serving the environment. But in the other form of the exercise of concentration, there is a very small muscular exercise which is constantly repeated; and this muscular exercise represents the necessary external expression of the inner activity.

We may say that in this case the movement is serving the inner life. We may compare these two forms of concentration: the first to a pleasing discourse, the purpose of which is to give information, the second to the few words, always the same, which two people who are in love are always repeating. Those who are in love do not speak for the sake of giving information; the words come out simply because of the love which is within. These words, to other people, do not seem either interesting or useful, but merely a repetition of the same thing. And so, in the school, we find it easy to be interested in watching those actions which have a purpose, and we find it difficult to interest ourselves in the more intimate work which has its expression in simple movements repeated over and over again.

To conclude, the Montessori teacher has as her goal the normalization of the class through work. Her job is an indirect one in the sense that she spends a great deal of effort on the environment and the materials, as well as her interactions in the classroom. Although she intervenes to keep order, occasionally teaches the class in one group, and gives individual and small group lessons with materials, these are not the focus of the classroom. The focus is the child working with the materials, concentrated on what she is doing, interested in choosing a challenge from the shelves.

The Montessori teacher has a great deal of faith in the child, and in what he will learn through interacting with the Montessori materials that he chooses himself. The goal of the teacher's work is to provide an environment where this concentration can exist. Respect for the child should guide the teacher in doing this.

Summary: In this chapter, the Montessori model was examined in more detail. The layout of the Montessori classroom was discussed, and several comparisons between the Montessori classroom environment and that of the traditional preschool were made, such as between the Practical Life area and the Role Play area. In relation to the Montessori materials, several key concepts were introduced. Characteristics of materials were discussed, and the role of the materials in the classroom presented. The misconception that children are not allowed to use the materials in more than one way was discussed, and the freedom of the children (and the role of the teacher's short introductory lesson) are covered in a quote from Montessori's lectures.

The way that a Montessori teacher spends her time in the classroom is also discussed. One of her primary goals is the maintaining of order, with the goal that children's work with the materials of their own choosing shall not be disturbed by others. The teacher's expectations, and how these affect children, are also presented. The Montessori method is seen to be a whole system, in which all of the elements are necessary for the program to work well. If the materials are too few or unattractive, if the teacher does not present them in a way to attract and challenge the children, if a child is not free to choose and concentrate on work, if the teacher does not expect and maintain a degree of order to allow concentration, then the individualization that is so central to Montessori is not possible, and the teacher must return to whole group instruction.

A sample Montessori lesson plan is shown, to give the reader an idea of the detail needed to be known by the teacher. Also, data from the author's international study when Montessori teachers say they intervene is presented. Finally, the concept of normalization through work is presented.

Preprimary Montessori Teachers (3-6) Questionnaire:
        When to Intervene?

Instructions

Please enter the information requested about your Montessori training and the number of years you have taught in a Montessori 3-6 class **after** your training. Then, write in a percentage, from 1 to 100%, that represents the amount of time that children have free choice of any material in your morning classroom time.

Next, for each of the situations described below, please circle a number from 1 to 7 that indicates **how likely you would be to intervene.** Assume for the questionnaire that the work described is appropriate for the child in terms of his or her age and ability. Many Montessori teachers will want to answer that intervention depends on each individual child. While this is true, for this questionnaire, please imagine the "typical" child, with average self-confidence, initiative, and so on. Just try to imagine the situation as occurring in your own classroom, then give your immediate response on the scale below the question.

With your cooperation, we can respond to critics of the Montessori method and find out more about how and why the Montessori method works. Thank you for your cooperation.

Part I: **You**

1. Your training. (Please give the name of the organizational affiliation of your training program, such as AMI, AMS, St. Nicholas, NCME, etc.)................_____

2. How many school years since your training have you taught in a Montessori 3-6 classroom?.._____

3. What percent of the usual morning period in your classroom is free choice time for the children ?(1% to 100%)..._____

Part II: **Intervention** (Circle the number from 1-7 underneath each question to show how likely you would be to intervene.)

1. The child has taken two of the sound cylinders (one in each of his hands) and is shaking them next to the ears of another child working at a mat.

1	2	3	4	5	6	7
Never Intervene	Almost Never	Would not Usually	Intervene Sometimes	Would Usually	Almost Always	Always Intervene

2. The child has taken out the second box of colour tablets and is pointing to an orange tablet, saying,"Red."

1	2	3	4	5	6	7
Never Intervene	Almost Never	Would not Usually	Intervene Sometimes	Would Usually	Almost Always	Always Intervene

3. The child has sorted 12 baric (weight) tablets into 3 piles of heavy, medium, and light weights while blindfolded. There are several mistakes.

1	2	3	4	5	6	7
Never Intervene	Almost Never	Would not Usually	Intervene Sometimes	Would Usually	Almost Always	Always Intervene

4. The child has created an enclosure ("a corral") with the pieces of the long red rods. Some of the smaller rods ("the cattle") are enclosed within.

1	2	3	4	5	6	7
Never Intervene	Almost Never	Would not Usually	Intervene Sometimes	Would Usually	Almost Always	Always Intervene

5. A child has taken the flag of Brazil and placed it on the corner of her table. "I am the President," she proclaims, pointing to the flag.

1	2	3	4	5	6	7
Never Intervene	Almost Never	Would not Usually	Intervene Sometimes	Would Usually	Almost Always	Always Intervene

6. A child swings one of the number rods at another child, using it as a sword.

1	2	3	4	5	6	7
Never Intervene	Almost Never	Would not Usually	Intervene Sometimes	Would Usually	Almost Always	Always Intervene

7. A child using the rough and smooth tablets decides to use them like sandpaper rhythm blocks, moving them together to make a sound and marching through the classroom.

1	2	3	4	5	6	7
Never Intervene	Almost Never	Would not Usually	Intervene Sometimes	Would Usually	Almost Always	Always Intervene

8. A child working with the knobbed cylinders places a cylinder in an incorrect hole.

1	2	3	4	5	6	7
Never Intervene	Almost Never	Would not Usually	Intervene Sometimes	Would Usually	Almost Always	Always Intervene

9. A child doing addition with the bead stair writes down: 2+3=6.

1	2	3	4	5	6	7
Never Intervene	Almost Never	Would not Usually	Intervene Sometimes	Would Usually	Almost Always	Always Intervene

10. The child is sorting the tasting bottles into three groups (sour, sweet, and salty). He tastes a drop and says," Mmmm! What good wine! "

1	2	3	4	5	6	7
Never Intervene	Almost Never	Would not Usually	Intervene Sometimes	Would Usually	Almost Always	Always Intervene

11. A child using the movable alphabet has labeled an object, spelling the word "butterfly": buttrfli.

1	2	3	4	5	6	7
Never Intervene	Almost Never	Would not Usually	Intervene Sometimes	Would Usually	Almost Always	Always Intervene

12. The child has put several of the bells in ascending order. She then runs past them, holding out the striker and striking them, singing loudly.

1	2	3	4	5	6	7
Never Intervene	Almost Never	Would not Usually	Intervene Sometimes	Would Usually	Almost Always	Always Intervene

13. A child has sorted fabrics into three groups, but has placed nylon and silk together by mistake.

1	2	3	4	5	6	7
Never Intervene	Almost Never	Would not Usually	Intervene Sometimes	Would Usually	Almost Always	Always Intervene

14. A child has constructed an elaborate "castle" with the broad stair and pink tower together. "This is the fortress of solitude," she tells you.

1	2	3	4	5	6	7
Never Intervene	Almost Never	Would not Usually	Intervene Sometimes	Would Usually	Almost Always	Always Intervene

15. A child playing the banker in the Bank Game with the golden beads begins to call out softly, "Money! Get your golden money here! I'm the banker! See me now for changing money!"

1	2	3	4	5	6	7
Never Intervene	Almost Never	Would not Usually	Intervene Sometimes	Would Usually	Almost Always	Always Intervene

16. A child has laid out one color-set of the third color boxes, from darkest to lightest. She has made two mistakes.

1	2	3	4	5	6	7
Never Intervene	Almost Never	Would not Usually	Intervene Sometimes	Would Usually	Almost Always	Always Intervene

17. A child has taken a triangle from the constructive triangles and is poking other children.

1	2	3	4	5	6	7
Never Intervene	Almost Never	Would not Usually	Intervene Sometimes	Would Usually	Almost Always	Always Intervene

18. A child has placed the counters from the cards and counters exercise into two groups of "men" and is preparing to have one group attack the other.

1	2	3	4	5	6	7
Never Intervene	Almost Never	Would not Usually	Intervene Sometimes	Would Usually	Almost Always	Always Intervene

19. The child is explaining to another, pointing to Australia on the world map, "This is Greenland."

1	2	3	4	5	6	7
Never	Almost	Would not	Intervene	Would	Almost	Always
Intervene	Never	Usually	Sometimes	Usually	Always	Intervene

20. The child is using the farm, but rather than applying the labels, she is making each animal move and make its characteristic sound, such as, "Moo!"

1	2	3	4	5	6	7
Never	Almost	Would not	Intervene	Would	Almost	Always
Intervene	Never	Usually	Sometimes	Usually	Always	Intervene

21. A child has made a snake from plasticene. "This is a real snake," he informs you. "He is poisonous."

1	2	3	4	5	6	7
Never	Almost	Would not	Intervene	Would	Almost	Always
Intervene	Never	Usually	Sometimes	Usually	Always	Intervene

22. A child crawls along the floor to where some children are reading and gently bumps them with his head.

1	2	3	4	5	6	7
Never	Almost	Would not	Intervene	Would	Almost	Always
Intervene	Never	Usually	Sometimes	Usually	Always	Intervene

23. A child has laid out several of the color sequences from the third box of color tablets. "This is my beauty parlor," she says. "Show me what color you would like your nails done."

1	2	3	4	5	6	7
Never	Almost	Would not	Intervene	Would	Almost	Always
Intervene	Never	Usually	Sometimes	Usually	Always	Intervene

24. A child attempts to bring the number card for 300 and brings the 30 instead.

1	2	3	4	5	6	7
Never	Almost	Would not	Intervene	Would	Almost	Always
Intervene	Never	Usually	Sometimes	Usually	Always	Intervene

25. A child makes several constructions with the geometric solids, calling them a silo, a church, and so on.

1	2	3	4	5	6	7
Never	Almost	Would not	Intervene	Would	Almost	Always
Intervene	Never	Usually	Sometimes	Usually	Always	Intervene

26. A child is asked to say the sound his name begins with; he gives another sound.

1	2	3	4	5	6	7
Never Intervene	Almost Never	Would not Usually	Intervene Sometimes	Would Usually	Almost Always	Always Intervene

27. A child in the middle of the room begins singing loudly the theme music from a popular cartoon show, using gestures.

1	2	3	4	5	6	7
Never Intervene	Almost Never	Would not Usually	Intervene Sometimes	Would Usually	Almost Always	Always Intervene

28. A child has painted a castle with his paints. "I'm going to move to this castle and really live here," he informs you.

1	2	3	4	5	6	7
Never Intervene	Almost Never	Would not Usually	Intervene Sometimes	Would Usually	Almost Always	Always Intervene

29. A child pouring rice in the Practical Life area asks another child,"How much rice shall we use for our rice cakes? Let's be bakers, OK?"

1	2	3	4	5	6	7
Never Intervene	Almost Never	Would not Usually	Intervene Sometimes	Would Usually	Almost Always	Always Intervene

---

Thank you for your cooperation. Please return the questionnaire to Dr. Chattin-McNichols.

CHAPTER 6
The Practical Life Curriculum Area

Chapter Goals: In this chapter, you will learn:
- What is the Montessori curriculum area of Practical Life?
- What are the categories of activities that are grouped together as Practical Life?
- What are the issues in the Practical Life area, such as the use of breakable objects, sharp knives and scissors, etc.?
- What are appropriate activities for older children in the Practical Life area?
- Are computers ever appropriate for the Montessori classroom?

INTRODUCTION

The Practical Life curriculum area is paradoxical; it's filled with simple activities that have complex aims. It is the area that experienced Montessori teachers count on most often to draw children into purposeful activity, especially young or easily distracted children. It is of great importance in the Montessori classroom, yet it is the least standardized area, since almost all of the materials are teacher-made or teacher-assembled. This means that the teacher's aesthetic sense, her creativity, her financial resources, and her cultural background will all influence the quality and diversity of the Practical Life exercises. This area also spawns criticism from traditional early childhood programs since some of the materials are like the role play materials in traditional programs, but their intended uses are different.

The Practical Life exercises, also referred to as the exercises of Daily Living, are usually divided into categories, more for the adult's organization than for the child's.

Care of the Environment

Pouring activities are common in almost all classrooms. These activities can range from very simple pouring activities such as pouring of beans, to pouring of smaller things like corn or rice, to water pouring, to complex pouring into more than one container. The pouring activities that might be out on the shelves at any particular time during the school year should represent the range of the abilities of the children in the class. Almost never would the entire sequence be out at the same time, both because some of the exercises would be either too easy or too difficult for the class and because the Practical Life shelves must also hold all of the other sequences. Also, boredom would set in if one area was over-represented.

Transferring includes a sequence of spooning activities, first of dry materials and then of liquids, with increasing levels of difficulty. Exercises with tweezers or tongs (again, graded in difficulty and size), basters, sponges, eyedroppers, and even chopsticks would all be a part of a teacher's sequence of transferring activities.

Cleaning and polishing activities make use of many of the subskills developed in these two earlier sequences. Cleaning can range from polishing exercises, in which small objects of wood or metal are polished, to work with large objects such as desks, tables, windows, and even floors. More complex, multi-step processes, such as dish- or clothes-washing, would come toward the end of the sequence.

Care of the Self

This is another major category in Practical Life; it includes exercises that teach the child some of the skills needed for his own independence. This category includes one of the few manufactured Practical Life materials, the dressing frames. These are wooden frames with cloth pieces attached to the sides. The pieces are joined in the middle by a variety of fasteners, such as zippers, buttons, bows and so on. The concept of isolation of difficulty is apparent here: it's easier for a child to learn to tie a shoelace when the additional difficulty of the shoelace's location is removed. Other activities in this category are related to grooming and cleanliness, such as hand- and face- washing, brushing of teeth and hair (with the child's own brushes, which must be cleaned after each use), blowing the nose, and others. A mirror in the classroom can be considered an element in this area of the Practical Life curriculum. Montessori's idea was that the time spent by the typical nursery school teacher in wiping noses and tying errant shoelaces was not merely wasted but actually spent in making the child feel less in control, more dependent on the adult world.

Life Skills

A number of the other works in Practical Life are fasteners, with exercises such as fitting jars and lids together, lock and key exercises, nuts and bolts, and so on. The pouring activities can be extended quite naturally into measuring and then into cooking. Exercises such as peeling, cutting, and serving carrots are very popular. It's unclear if the fascination is the real knife, the eating of the carrots, or the serving of them to others. Other cutting exercises, nut shelling or even making peanut butter, and other simple food preparation exercises are available, as well as those connected with snack and lunch.

As with all Montessori exercises, each Practical Life activity includes cleaning up after oneself, and return of the materials to the shelf ready for the next worker.

Many of the craft projects that are shelved in Practical Life could also be considered as art works. Typically, sorting exercises of many types, bead stringing, and a sewing sequence are all important sources of the materials on the shelf on any given day.

Grace and Courtesy

The last category of Practical Life exercises is Grace and Courtesy. In this area, exercises might include laying a tablecloth and setting a table, how to offer someone a cup of juice or a carrot from the carrot cutting work, walking on the line, and so on. Also, lessons on what to say when you bump into someone, how to ask someone to move, even opening and closing a door quietly, are taught.

Issues in the Practical Life Area

As you can imagine, one of the major concerns in this area is the sequencing of activities, and how often to change the materials on the shelf. In general, there is consensus on the best sequences for most Practical Life materials: the earlier exercises involve work with larger materials and have fewer steps.

As far as how often the materials on the shelf should be changed, there is wide variation among schools and even among the models as taught in Montessori teacher education programs. Practical Life exercises, as has been mentioned before, are almost all assembled by the teacher. She selects a tray, the pouring pitchers, the rice, and so on. She must find the tops and bottoms and prepare the lesson to introduce them to the classroom. Because of this, more experienced teachers, in schools with more resources (and storage space!) are more likely to have a large store of prepared Practical Life exercises that they can draw from. Other teachers may find themselves too busy with their many other concerns to develop new activities as rapidly as they feel they should. This means that the Practical Life area is a very good one to take a close look at in evaluating a classroom.

To evaluate a Practical Life area, ask these questions:

- Are there enough exercises out? There should be approximately 12-20 activities out, although there may be fewer at the beginning of the year.
- Are the materials attractive? Do they show that the teacher has put some thought and effort into the choice of materials, and the arrangement? This is a difficult question to answer objectively, since personal taste, resources, and even the cultural background of the teacher and the class will influence the choice of materials and arrangement. In general, however, Practical Life should not look like a "poor relation" to the Sensorial and Math areas with their gleaming painted materials. A haphazard assortment of plastic trays of various sizes and colors is one sign of a neglected Practical Life area, except in schools in very low income areas. The pitchers, cups, etc., should be <u>glass</u>, not plastic, and of decent quality (more about this later). The trays and materials should be clean and filled with water, grains, etc.
- The arrangement of the exercises on the shelves and of the materials on the trays must be orderly.
- Most importantly, the materials should be in use! This is easy to observe, and is the single most important assessment of the quality of the Practical Life area. Although there will certainly be variations in the number of children in the Practical Life area throughout the year, in general it should be a busy area, with perhaps one-quarter of the total class engaged in this area.

In addition to providing some general guidelines in the above areas, a good Montessori teacher education program should also discuss how the Practical Life area should reflect the diversity of the cultures represented by the children in the class. For example, the cooking and food preparation projects should reflect the cultures of the children. The transfer activities can do this (chopsticks, shish-kebab skewers, etc.), as can the exercises that require the child to match tops and bottoms of containers by using small items from different countries. The availability of materials to reflect the cultural diversity of children may vary depending on where the school is located.

This child in a 3-6 classroom is concentrating on his paper cutting activity in the Practical Life Area.

As was mentioned earlier, one of the things that most frequently strikes the observer is the use of "real" things in the Montessori Practical Life area. Real glass glasses, pitchers, and so on are used for pouring. Real knives and graters are used in food preparation, and some classrooms even involve the children with baking. Mirror and glass polishing involve real, breakable glass and glass polish that many parents are concerned may get into mouths; other parents may worry about beans being put up noses. Part of the job of the Montessori teacher is to be aware of who is using what how. But that does not mean swooping down to intervene if a child is going to spill or even if a glass is going to break, as long (of course) as no one will be hurt.

Part of one shelf of Practical Life activities. The layout of all of the things needed to complete the activity in a clearly organized way is an important part of the design of new activities.

Montessori's basic position on the necessity for these real things in the school is based on the need for the child to get feedback from his interactions with the environment. For example, if the plastic glasses never break, then there is no inherent reason for the child to learn to be careful with them. His only reason is because of adult demands. So, again, the role of feedback from the environment forms a part of Montessori's thinking.

Another important reason for the use of real objects is the motivation for use that comes from real things. With a real, child-sized carpet sweeper, the child can actually do it; he can actually sweep the carpet, and, when the sweepings are emptied out into the trash can, he can see that he has cleaned the classroom. The same sort of thing is true in pouring, food preparation, and care of self. In food preparation, in particular, the old Boy Scout idea holds true: a dull knife is more dangerous than a sharp one. The type of knife is carefully chosen, and a Montessori teacher watches to see which children choose that work.

Montessori was quite clear on this need for reality as a characteristic of the child. She described being taken by an enthusiastic educator to an orphanage, where she was told, "See, we too, have your exercises of Practical Life." What she saw were children who had been given a doll's tea set and were pouring imaginary tea. Montessori wanted the children to have real tea in real, child-sized (not doll-sized) cups. But this does bring up the important point of the use of Practical Life activities in fantasy or role play. Montessori's position on fantasy is clarified in that chapter. Whatever Montessori's original position, children in Montessori classes do use the Practical Life activities for fantasy play: washing dishes in their "house", making carrot slices for "the family," and so on. They are more or less open about this aspect of their work dependent on the attitude of the teaching staff: children are no fools.

Most Montessori teachers would ask themselves whether the child is getting the benefit of work with the materials during these situations, but still allow the child these non-disruptive role play activities. It is unfortunately true that some Montessori teachers have either misunderstood Montessori's position on fantasy, or have blown this part of Montessori's philosophy all out of proportion and forgotten the more central precept: follow the child.

The Practical Life materials do allow the children to imitate adult activities, which is after all one of the central goals of the role play area in a traditional nursery school environment. The key difference is the reality of the tools and the reality of the results when the children imitate. Don't imagine that children don't understand the difference between imaginary doll tea and real tea. Since we're speaking of tea, I'll mention the story told by a long-time Montessorian in the Minneapolis-St. Paul area, who told of E. M. Standing's visit to her school during the early days of the second wave of American Montessori. Standing was by that time an elderly British gentleman who had been with Madame Montessori for a long time before her death. He had followed Montessori in her early days, translating her work and writing on Montessori. He had inherited Montessori's decidedly cool attitude toward American Montessori schools, especially those associated with the upstart rebels of the American Montessori Society. When Standing came to her school, he sat down in the visitor's chair, was approached by a very small child and asked if he would like some tea. Standing said that he would and the child left. Almost an hour later, when he had forgotten all about this offer, the child came struggling up with the tea tray, arranged with silver creamer and sugar bowl, napkin, etc. It had taken the child that long to arrange the tray, pour the milk, brew the tea, and so on. The report is that Mr. Standing's attitude toward American Montessori was quite changed by the arrival of his tea.

The last issue I wish to bring up is the under-use and under-valuing of the Practical Life area in some Montessori schools. I've described some schools as "clipboard" Montessori, from the way teachers are hanging over children, checking on their academic work. A common characteristic of these schools is a negative attitude toward Practical Life. First, these teachers see Practical Life as something important only for the youngest children. They have the notion of the three year Montessori program as being primarily Practical Life and Sensorial for the three-year-olds, Math and Language for the four-year-olds, and Science and Social Studies (and more Math and Reading) for the fives. This is completely inappropriate. Practical Life must attract and challenge children at age five as well as at age three. These same teachers complain to me of all the trouble they have motivating the children to do their homework! Questions like this can leave even me speechless. If children were choosing their own work from a variety of attractive choices, there wouldn't be a problem. The overall problem I see here is the over valuing of academic skills, of skills that will help the child stay ahead in first grade. These are probably the most transitory of the gains that Montessori experience can give children. What possible good will it do a nine-year-old, or an adult, that he could do multiplication tables at age four? Education is not a race, certainly not in Montessori's thought.

It is quite informative to talk to "older" Montessori children, say 4- or 5-year-olds, about what they choose and what they like in their classroom. Those who have moved to a traditional classroom may talk about what they miss from Practical Life, or even say that they "can't do anything" in their new class.

PRACTICAL LIFE FOR OLDER CHILDREN

One of my particular interests is Practical Life exercises for older children, both the five- and six-year-olds in the preprimary classroom, and the six- to nine-year-old children in elementary Montessori classrooms. One reason for this interest is that I feel that it's a neglected area. This is partly because of the mistaken perception mentioned above, that Practical Life is primarily for three- and four-year-olds. When a child starts to turn five or six, it's time to get serious--yes, with serious Practical Life!

This is also an important area because appropriate Practical Life activities are the best way I have found for dealing with the child in an elementary Montessori classroom who has not had the benefit of previous Montessori experience. This is common in many classrooms, because of the economics of running an elementary Montessori program, but often under discussed in Montessori elementary teacher preparation programs. It was just assumed in my elementary Montessori training program, for example, that all my children would have come from three years of Montessori preschool and would all be reading and writing. My first class full of real children was, therefore, quite a shock!

Practical Life seems to me to be the best way to reach a child new to Montessori, especially the child who has had academic problems in his previous school setting. These children can be over-represented in elementary Montessori classrooms, since that is why some parents have sought out the school and are paying the tuition. Because Practical Life exercises require concentration and periods of sustained work, but in areas far removed from traditional school work, Practical Life can be the key area in helping these children make the transition to the freedom and complexity of the Montessori classroom.

One of the areas that can be expanded from the preprimary level is Care of Self. In this area, a good deal of the content taught in traditional schools as health, safety, and nutrition can be taught, based on concrete activities. Presentations may be formally organized in a sequence, or may spring from incidents in the ongoing life of the class. A blister on a child's foot after a nature walk might lead (after first aid, of course) to a discussion on the care of the feet, preparations for hiking, and so on. Thus, the standard material covered in Health in traditional schools will also be covered in Montessori schools. An emphasis on care of the teeth is important for most American children. The goal here is to have hands-on activities replace dittos. For example, the models of various parts of the body such as the ear, the eye, and so on can be used. If these are painted but not glued together, they can be assembled and disassembled numerous times. Labels can be made to add to the value of the activity. I feel that all children can be taught some of the basics of First Aid. Again, this can be done with models or volunteers for bandaging, care for a nosebleed, and so on.

Some of the best source books for this area are the various Boy Scout handbooks. I find that the older ones are often better than the new; these can often be found in used book stores, Salvation Army or Goodwill stores. (These are frequently haunted by Montessori teachers in search of old National Geographic magazines and other treasures.) An example of an activity for use with older children is called "First Aid": Several descriptions of accident victims are available, and the child chooses one. The child reads the description and then must take various "response cards" and put them in order. Should you , for example, "Check breathing" first or "stop bleeding"?

Another key area in which Practical Life exercises can be developed is in <u>Nutrition.</u> This makes sense from a number of viewpoints. First, it is a natural outgrowth of the food preparation and simple cooking activities the children should have experienced in the prepri- mary classroom. Secondly, there is little developed in this area in the "standard" Montessori elementary curriculum. Some of the areas that have been explored by some Montessori teachers are given below; this is by no means an exhaustive list.

• Food preparation activities. These can now be more elaborate, requiring more ingredients, more preparation, and more complex cooking. These activities should be prepared so that children with a range of reading and measuring skills can do them. One solution is to pair reading and non-reading chefs. There are possibili- ties of writing extensions here: writing up descriptions of how things looked and tasted, and so on.

• Sensory experiences. This group represents the extension of the basic activ- ities of the tasting and smelling bottles. Begin with an expanded set of smelling cylinders, filled with changing herbs and spices (in pairs for matching). There are a number of opportunities here to develop extensions from the "cultural" area, such as finding the sources of the spices on a map, talking about how different peoples season their food, and so on. Why is it that the cuisine changes toward increased hotness (picante, non caliente) the closer the peoples are to the equator? A good ex- ample of a project that can require reading, writing, and math is to ask a team of 6- year-olds to design a new soft drink. How should their product differ from existing ones? Could it be made more healthy than existing products? How?

• Foods, food sources. This is typically given some coverage in the Montessori early elementary curriculum through a discussion of the Fundamental Needs of People, one of which is certainly food. The foods that the children de- scribe are also usually related to their work in science, such as looking for foods from each of the basic parts of the plant (leaves, branches, stems, roots, flowers) and from each of the groups of animals (invertebrates, fish, amphibians, reptiles, birds, and mammals). Cards of various types can be used and sorted in a variety of ways. Magazine pictures can be cut out by children to make displays of the various food groups. Certainly, food can be grown from seed (indoors if the climate dictates), and field trips organized to dairies, farms, supermarkets, restaurants, and so on. [1]

---

[1] With older children, it is certainly possible to begin to introduce some of the basic concepts in the politics of food production and distribution. Many Montessori schools have implicit or explicit goals of teaching a "peace curriculum," and hard facts on this area should be included. Two of the most important concepts to include would be the amount of wasted

• Nutrition. Some of the content in this area may be blended with the area above, but the focus here is on the use of foods by the body. The standard content covered in the traditional school curriculum can be covered, such as the body's needs for proteins, fats, carbohydrates, and so on. The role and abuses of vitamins should be discussed. Especially important for American children is a unit on junk foods and on advertising telling us to eat them. The Hygiene area should be covered as well, as an extension of the grooming activities offered at the 3-6 level.

In the area of Care of the Environment, the children's role should also be expanded. In the Children's House, the small children swept, dusted, and so on. Now, the burden of the majority of the cleaning tasks should come to the children. They should take all the materials from the shelves and clean them, dusting each shelf in the process. We did this weekly, but it should be done at least monthly. Tasks such as window washing and even painting and simple carpentry repairs are within the ability range of the elementary children if a clear and organized presentation is given and high quality tools are provided. The children seem to like especially any project done for a room of smaller children.

In Grace and Courtesy, the children can learn the correct way to set a formal table, introductions, bread and butter letters, apologies, and correct behavior at weddings, funerals of various types, and religious occasions drawn from the population of the school. Can you see that these are the same type of things that nose blowing was for the preschool child? We look at a 7-year-old who is misbehaving in a certain situation and say things such as "Behave!" or "Mind your manners!" Clear information on our complex culture will give the children a greater chance to behave appropriately.

What should be the appropriate extensions for the older child of early Practical Life exercises in pouring, or in jar and lids? Some of the more complex measuring skills that can be practiced can be done in connection with cooking. Another very important area is the physical sciences. The children can begin here as many college chemistry students do, with elementary lessons on the names of various items of glassware, with the use of scales and other tools, and with very simple "experiments" in measuring. Here is an example of a command card:

Pour 30 ml of water into the large Erlenmeyer flask. Add 20 ml of water to this. Pour off half and measure the amount.

I have found that the interest of the children is related to the quality and "reality" of the materials. Good test tubes, graduated cylinders, etc., generate much more interest and much more precision than old mayonnaise jars. This is certainly true in other areas in the Montessori classroom, at all age levels. I have also found that a brief explanation on how to use the materials and an explanation that the materials we have must last the entire year results in breakage rates somewhat better than those of college students. I usually lost only one or two test tubes a year.

---

food (including the current U.S. expenditures paid to farmers not to produce food) and the relative efficiency of eating plants vs. chicken vs. beef.

Other important science[2] things can be going on as well under the general format of the Practical Life exercise. Magnifying glasses and microscopes, ant farms, and electricity project sets (such as those from Radio Shack) can be used to create good Practical Life exercises for the older child. The key is to create an exercise that is clear but really involves that child at the limits of his competence.

I feel, for example, that if the role of Practical Life is to prepare the child for his life in the world, then our Practical Life area must include the machines that she will have to deal with. For example, telephone manners should be taught in Grace and Courtesy. The child can learn the basics of bicycle repair, at least how to make sure that all the parts are working properly, and how to lubricate and clean a bike. I taught my class how to change a car tire, with all the correct steps. The children who didn't pay attention and didn't loosen the lug nuts before they jacked up the car learned why I had presented this way. The control of error was there. Many children were very interested, and one boy with a number of problems changed the tire eight times one day.

A careful eye is needed to supervise this, and the teacher needs to watch to be sure that these activities do not grow to exclude reading, writing, and math. It is often the case, though, that reading, writing, or math activities can be structured around the Practical Life activity that has grasped the child's interest.

Another sequence of activities can be built around electronic machines. Old and new radios can be brought in, to be taken apart and reassembled by the children. Also, the children should be familiar with tape recorders, cameras, phonographs, and typewriters. More affluent schools may want to let older children explore with video cameras.

A CONTROVERSIAL SUGGESTION: COMPUTERS IN THE MONTESSORI CLASSROOM

Many people, certainly some Montessori teachers, would object to computers in Montessori classes at all, and certainly with their classification as a Practical Life activity. But it is certainly true that the children in our Montessori schools today will be using com-

---

[2]There is certainly the possibility of links between these kinds of experiments, the grammar command cards, and the imagination-striking experiments connected with the story of creation as told to the children in early elementary school. The grammar command cards are used to expand the children's knowledge of grammar from simple parts of speech to the subdivisions within these: abstract and concrete nouns, descriptive, numerical, and demonstrative adjective, and so on. As you might expect in Montessori, these distinctions are made to the children through concrete actions that they undertake. The set of grammar command cards is one way of organizing this work. The story of the formation and cooling of the earth and the origins of life, as well as content about the weather, seasons, the rotation and revolution of the Earth are given to the children in a unique way, incorporating story telling, posters, and experiments. The children's art during these lessons often reflects the deep interest and satisfaction that they get from this cosmogony, an area of knowledge which only Western culture restricts to college students.

puters in their future lives. The vast majority of them will be using them in later schooling, and certainly in their jobs or in college. If one of the roles of the Practical Life area is giving the child the skills and experiences she will need for daily living in our particular culture, how can the computer be excluded?

This is how one Montessori elementary school has set up the computer as a choice for children to work with.

The most common objection raised is that the computer is too complex, too abstract for children. If we are interested in computers for the 3-6 classroom, I agree that the focus must be on the older children in this age group. Many five-year-olds, however, and even some fours are ready to use the computer. We as adults sometimes make the computer out to be more complex than it really is, since we know all of the mathematical and electronic complexity that must exist inside. But the children are not fazed by this--to them it is an accepted part of their world, a "box that does things." To use it really requires no more skill than the use of a phonograph or a tape recorder, if the software is selected carefully.

The computer actually has the potential to be less abstract than, for example, a picture book. The computer can animate the picture, it can have music, sounds, and even speech. Most importantly, the computer can respond to the child. These are things that books can never do.

The key is the right software. Unfortunately, most of the software labeled as appropriate for young children is not. It is here that the criticism of "too abstract" needs to be directed. A best-selling program, for example, shows four shapes on the screen, one of which is different from the other three. These differ in obvious ways, such as three triangles and a square. Under each is a numeral. The child is to respond to the program by pressing the numeral key on the keyboard that is under the shape that is different. The problem with this best-selling piece of software is that if solving the shape puzzle is a challenging task for the child, how in the world will she find the correct key among the 88 on the keyboard? For the child who can find the keys, the task is trivial and worthless.

Few of the programs have any control of error. In another acclaimed and top-selling program, a key struck by a child produces a clever animated picture in which some element has an initial sound of that letter. The child's response, though, is to keep on pushing keys to make the pretty pictures come, and soon the novelty wears off. If only the program designers had thought about challenging the child and reversing the flow of the program: a child would see a picture and have to find the initial sound letter.

The list of errors also includes very poor use of the graphics capabilities of the computer, poorly formed letters and numerals, spurious "rewards," interesting explosions when wrong answers are given, indiscriminate use of all-upper case text, and so on.

Despite this, there are still a few worthwhile programs. For example, I am very fond of graphics drawing programs, especially those that don't make use of the keyboard. Graphics pads such as the Koala Pad^{TM}, light pens, or touch screen devices that let children draw directly on the screen are much less abstract and more direct for children to use. The artwork that children produce is different from their work in any other medium. There is a strong focus on process rather than product when the children are drawing on the computer. For example, most children do not choose to save their work on a disk when this is offered. This focus on process rather than product is very consistent with the children's orientation at this time in their development.

There is a final reason to consider the computer for children in the Montessori 3-6 environment. The children in today's schools will certainly be exposed to computers in their elementary or secondary school years. Wouldn't it be better to introduce children to the computer in an orderly way, and to allow them to have some positive experiences with computers before they are forced to type in the answers to multiplication problems or the capital of South Dakota? Don't you think that drawing--an open-ended activity that appeals to both boys and girls--might be a better way to have a first experience with computers?

CONCLUSION

The latter part of this chapter may all seem very far afield from pouring grains of rice or learning to buff one's shoes to a high gloss. But the intrigue and the power of the Practical Life curriculum area is that it is truly and incontrovertibly an open ended, expandable part of the Montessori curriculum. It can, it should, and it must respond to the particular children of each class. It must provide the motives for activity, and so bring the child along to other work. The work of the child, the success, and the satisfaction must come first before this power of work can be turned to the other important areas for growth.

Summary: In this chapter, the Montessori Practical Life curriculum area is presented. The sub-parts of this area include Care of the Environment (cleaning, transferring skills, etc.), Care of the Self, Life Skills, and Grace and Courtesy. Evaluation of Practical Life areas is discussed, including the attractiveness of the materials, and Montessori's somewhat controversial use of real, breakable glass and china objects, sharp knives and scissors, and so on. Montessori's insistence on real objects (child-sized, functional, rather than toy-sized) is explained, and is seen as a central aspect of the model.

Practical Life activities for older children including the use of the computer, are presented.

CHAPTER 7
The Sensorial Curriculum Area

Chapter Goals: In this chapter, you will learn:
- What is the Montessori Sensorial curriculum area?
- What are the standard Sensorial materials?
- What are the issues in the Sensorial area, such as the relationship of the children's work with these materials to Piaget's concepts of seriation, classification, and conservation?
- Montessori's ideas about internal, rather than external, motivation for learning.
- Montessori's ideas for Sensorial activities for older children.

The Sensorial curriculum area in the Montessori 3-6 classroom is easy to spot. A majority of the materials displayed there are standardized. Despite the fact that there are now many more manufacturers of Montessori materials than in the past, these materials are very consistent in appearance. Here are some of the sensorial materials you would expect to find in a Montessori classroom:

- The cube tower: 10 cubes, from 1 cm to 10 cm on a side. This is usually painted pink. (Freudians may draw their own conclusions.)
- The broad stair: 10 prisms, which look as if each of the cubes described above had been lengthened to 20 cm. Usually brown.
- The long rods: ten 2 x 2 cm rods, ranging in length from 10 to 100 cm.
- 4 sets of knobbed cylinders, inset in blocks of wood. One set varies in diameter and height, one in diameter only, one in height only, and the fourth varies in both dimensions, but inversely--the cylinders go from wide and flat to tall and narrow.
- 4 sets of these same cylinders without knobs or blocks. Color coded. Stored in boxes.
- Color tablets: painted wooden rectangles with plastic handles. Three sets of increasing complexity, stored in boxes.
- The binomial and trinomial cubes: two cube "puzzles," in wooden boxes with patterns of red, blue, and black rectangles and squares on them.
- The constructive triangles: six[1] sets of flat colored triangles, stored in distinctive wooden boxes shaped like a triangle, hexagons, and so on.

---

[1] Most classrooms have only five, leaving out the "pinwheels," which are considered elementary work (wrongly, in my opinion).

• The geometric cabinet, with 6 drawers of plane geometric figures: circles, quadrilaterals (rectangles and a square), triangles, polygons, etc. Cardboard cards with the same shapes for matching (three sets) and name labels for each shape.

• Sound cylinders: six red and six blue paired cylinders for shaking and listening.

• The bells: mushroom shaped bells give a very clear tone with a pleasing resonance, unlike the musical instruments more often given to children. The size of the bells does not vary with the pitch. Classrooms may have only a few bells, a set of 8 white based bells, or more elaborate sets with black based bells (the colors match piano keys) and a set of natural wood based bells for matching. The set may also include staff boards and small black disks for notes. Tone bars, rhythm instruments, and so on may also be present. The lovely materials used in Orff music are very popular in Montessori schools because of the high quality and beautiful tone.

• A variety of other materials used for feeling, such as mystery bags (reach inside and identify objects by feel), smelling and tasting exercises, exercises for the baric (weight) sense, for thermic (temperature), etc., are also found in the Sensorial area.

USE OF THE SENSORIAL MATERIALS

Near the Sensorial shelves should be ample room for children to work with the materials. With few exceptions, Sensorial work is typically done on a mat on the floor. This means that the storage of mats should also be nearby. The child lays out a mat before choosing her work. When she is done, she is responsible for returning all of the parts to the storage shelf in the same way that she found them, and rolling or folding her mat to return it as well.

Some of the Sensorial materials encourage children to work in pairs or small groups. Variations (more complex exercises) with the tower and broad stairs, the red rods, the geometric solids or geometric cabinet, tasting bottles, and baric tablets are among the Sensorial exercises that are commonly worked on by more than one child.

There is only one copy of each material in a Montessori class. This means that at some point the material a child wants will be already in use. Not just a way to save money on materials, this set-up offers children a chance to learn important lessons about themselves and others. They are developmentally able to learn to wait in the later preschool years, but will not do so if given neither the opportunities nor the expectation that they will do so. The role of the teacher here is to reinforce the ground rule of non-interference with children's work. She might do this indirectly, through suggesting alternatives, or more directly, by stating the rule and reminding the child of the consequences.

Montessori's Rationale for the Sensorial Area--and Her Critics

Now let's consider what the Sensorial curriculum is about, and why Montessori's writings about this area have caused misunderstandings. In writing about this area, Montessori uses the phrase "sense education" or even "sense training" to describe what she felt the child gained through his interaction with the materials: She writes about systems of objects that share a definite quality, such as color, shape, dimension, and so on. By this, she refers to the idea of materials that have one dimension that varies, while all others are kept constant.

For the educators and psychologists in the early part of this century, the phrase ("sense training") meant that the children needed to have specific associations made for them between the perception of red and the word "red." This associationist model of human learning was assumed to be the primary model on which Montessori was based--at least, that is what Kilpatrick and other early American critics assumed.

One of Montessori's biggest and most effective critics was William H. Kilpatrick. His book, The Montessori System Examined (1914), had a profound impact on the first wave of American Montessori. One of the flaws Professor Kilpatrick felt was most damning was that Montessori seemed ignorant of the controversy surrounding general transfer; that is, Montessori did not seem to be aware of the debate that was going on in educational circles at that time about whether or not this kind of association learning would transfer to other situations and other concepts.

At a more basic level, was this kind of teaching necessary at all for children to master these links between sensory impressions and verbal labels? Dewey's answer, and Kilpatrick's, was that it was not necessary. These two professors, and the rest of the faculty at Teacher's College, Columbia University, were to have an enormous influence as Dewey launched the Progressive Education Movement. The Progressive Education point of view was that the child would acquire the basic links through ordinary human interactions and especially through play.

This position, reinforced by other theoretical perspectives, has come to represent the mainstream of the early childhood education movement in the United States. Montessori represents a stream toward a more carefully structured environment, with a view to allowing the child more specific interactions with materials designed to foster development. On the opposite end of the continuum, another stream is growing in popularity. The behaviorist theories predict maximum effectiveness from preschool programs with direct instruction and little or no free play.

It may well have been the case that Montessori had an association model in mind in her writing about the Sensorial area. Montessori was a very eclectic borrower. [1] But Montessori's method--the materials and teacher behaviors-- were to a large extent developed empirically. She made up materials, drawing on her own work with children and on that of Itard and Seguin. These materials went into the laboratory of the classroom. What "worked"--what attracted children and facilitated concentration--was kept, and the failures were scrapped. Montessori's theories for the method were developed either at the same time

---

[1]An excellent paper by Mary Boehnline at Cleveland State University outlines Montessori's theory of personality and the role of then-contemporary theorists in Montessori's development of her theory.

or afterwards; it's not the case that Montessori developed a full-blown theory and then set out to implement it. See what she says about this in *The Discovery of the Child:, p. 143.*:"Color, size, shape, all their qualities in brief were experimentally established."

Because she did experiment and observe the children, her materials were not limited to those that would be the best from an associationist viewpoint. In particular, the Sensorial curriculum, as it exists in Montessori classrooms today, seems tailor-made to allow the child to experiment with Piagetian cognitive skills, especially one-to-one correspondence, classification, and seriation.

PIAGETIAN DEVELOPMENT AND THE SENSORIAL AREA

Piaget's theory and the relationship between Piaget's and Montessori's ideas are discussed in a later chapter. In this section, the relationship between Piaget's theories and the work of the child in the Sensorial area is discussed. Consider, for example, one-to-one correspondence activities. One example of this type of activity is the child's work with the the the four sets of the knobbed cylinders--each cylinder fits in only one hole, if you want to be able to put each cylinder away. The same sort of work can be done with more complex shapes, such as the drawers of the geometry or leaf shape cabinets. The stream of matching activities gets more and more complex. Some of these activities lead to complex matching in other curriculum areas, such as the puzzle maps of the continents and countries. More abstract matching can also involve reading, such as the standard exercise for older preschool children of matching shape names to shapes.

To complete your picture of the matching activities, and to see why the Sensorial curriculum is so much richer than what is offered in other preschool curricula, remember that these activities are going on at the same time in <u>other sense dimensions</u>. The child is also working on one-to-one correspondence in sounds, with the sound cylinders and the bells. The sound cylinders and the bells look (and feel and weigh, etc.) identical; only one sense dimension (pitch) varies among them. And that sense dimension varies evenly from one to the next. The child also matches color tablets, and wooden tablets varying in weight. He handles the tablets with a blindfold on, to sharpen his perception of weight. Tasting and smelling cylinders, graded pairs of sandpaper tablets, and pairs of fabrics to be felt, and so on, are all offered to the child. So the sharpening of the child's matching skills is proceeding from simple to complex in all sense dimensions at once, guided largely by the child's interest.

Montessori Concepts: *Isolation of Difficulty* and *Control of Error*

One of the reasons that these activities differ from similar ones found in traditional or developmental-interaction preschool programs is the materials themselves. As described above, the materials are constant in all sense dimensions except the one on which the child must concentrate. Thus, the child is not distracted from putting the bells in order from lowest to highest pitch by differences in color, size, shape, etc. The ability of the child to tolerate distractors is not great at this time, and this Montessori concept of <u>isolation of difficulty</u> allows the child to do a great deal of successful work with the materials.

It is also clear that the Montessori Sensorial curriculum area affords children a wide variety of opportunities for matching exercises, not merely the more typical color, shape, and size matching activities available in other programs with materials such as attribute blocks. If Piaget's theory is correct, matching activities across a variety of materials and sense dimensions will allow the child to understand the concept in a medium she likes best and practice it in other media, at her own pace. The child can find her own balance between assimilation and accommodation--between practicing and new learning--and thus learn at an optimum rate.

Since we have introduced the idea of work with the Sensorial materials allowing the child to move forward through Piaget's stages, let's examine this idea in more detail. First, it is not clear that Montessori understood the importance of skills like one-to-one correspondence in the same way that Piaget did. Nor is it clear that she understood how these materials would allow the child to master these skills. Quotes from Dr. Montessori that seem to support a Piagetian conception of learning can be balanced with quotes that seem to suggest sense training for its own sake, associationism, behaviorism, or an entirely mystical rationale for the child's work with the materials. But whether or not Montessori was able to articulate a theory that agrees with Piaget's, her genius for design and winnowing out only the best materials has resulted in an almost ideal set of materials. The Sensorial materials are ideal in that they interest the child, provide him with a clear task, and give him feedback about his work.

This notion of feedback is also central in Montessori's thought. The child working to put the knobbed cylinders into their holes will find that each pairing he makes either works or it does not. If he puts a too-small cylinder into a hole, his last cylinder will not fit. Montessori placed great emphasis on this control of error. Especially important is the idea that the control of error comes directly from the child's manipulation of the materials, not from an adult correcting a child. Montessori felt that it was essential that children learn to see error as information, not as something to be avoided at all costs. This is in line with her overall ideas on motivation, and certainly consistent with Piagetian ideas of development.

Motivation in Montessori's Thought

Montessori felt that the child should be motivated by his own interests and his unconscious drive to develop himself. The materials should challenge the child; that is where the teacher wishing to motivate a child should turn, not to praise. This may seem cold when contrasted with our usual picture of an early childhood educator moving through the classroom, patting children on the head and warmly praising their work, regardless of the child's effort. I can only urge you to observe in several good Montessori classrooms, so that you can discover that it is possible to be warm and supportive without excessive praise.

In this area, as in many others, Montessori anticipated current early childhood education theories and practices. The relationship between Montessori's ideas on motivation and the "competence motivation" theory of White [1] is well-covered in an article by Seattle Montessori teacher Laurie Ross in an article in the AMS *Constructive Triangle* (1982).

The Montessori teacher can and does use praise and other social reinforcers, such as her attention and even physical contact. But she uses them perhaps somewhat less than a traditional nursery school teacher, and typically much less effusively. She is especially careful about praising or reprimanding a child in relation to his work. The goal is that the child will develop a sense of satisfaction from the work itself, not be dependent on the approval of the teacher or others. The Montessori teacher, then, should be warm, open, friendly, but not bubbling over with "What a good boy!" and "What a lovely painting!" and dispensing pats on the head to each child she passes. In response to a child showing her a completed piece of work, she might smile and say,"Good." or "I see you've gotten every piece back in." To say to a child, "You're so smart, you matched them all up!" gives the child the message that he's not smart when he doesn't get them all matched up.

MATERIALS BESIDES MATCHING: SERIATION AND CLASSIFICATION

The examples we have used so far have focussed on one strand of the Sensorial area: one to one correspondence, or matching. As we have seen, the Sensorial materials provide the child with a rich array of opportunities for working on matching activities. The activities vary not only in difficulty but also in the sense dimension on which the child must concentrate in order to match: size, loudness, pitch, weight, shape (both plane and solid), color (both hue and intensity), smell, temperature, taste, roughness, and so on.

But there are also seriation and classification activities available in the Sensorial area. For example, the cube tower, broad stair, and red rods are all early seriation materials. Again, the Montessori concept of isolation of difficulty is seen in the design of these materials. The first one in the series, the cube tower, consists of ten cubes (an indirect preparation for our base ten number system) which vary in all three dimensions, from a one cm to a ten cm cube. They are identical in color, finish, and so on, in contrast to the almost universal tendency of toymakers to paint a series like this in rainbow colors. The second set of materials, the broad stair, has removed one dimension; the prisms now vary in cross section only (height and breadth) and all have the same length. Thus, only two dimensions are salient in seriating, and the third is constant. Finally, the long rods have the two dimensions of their cross section constant, and only the length varies.

In later seriating work, the child can put the knobless cylinders in order. There are four sets of these, corresponding to the four sets of knobbed cylinders. The matching work the child has done by placing the knobbed cylinders back in their holes prepares her to seriate the knobless cylinders without the additional cue of the permanently ordered block of holes. The four sets also increase in difficulty. The first set of ten varies from thin/short to thick/tall: two dimensions moving in the same direction. The next two sets vary in one di-

---

[1] Robert White's article, Motivation Reconsidered: the Concept of Competence, in *Psychological Review*, 66,#5, 1959, is considered the classic statement. See also the excellent review article, Praise or Encouragement, by Hitz and Driscoll, *Young Children*, July, 1988.

mension each, keeping the other one constant: the one from thin/tall to thick/tall, the other from short to tall, all being the same diameter.

Figure 7-1

Extension for the Knobless Cylinders: Floor Chart

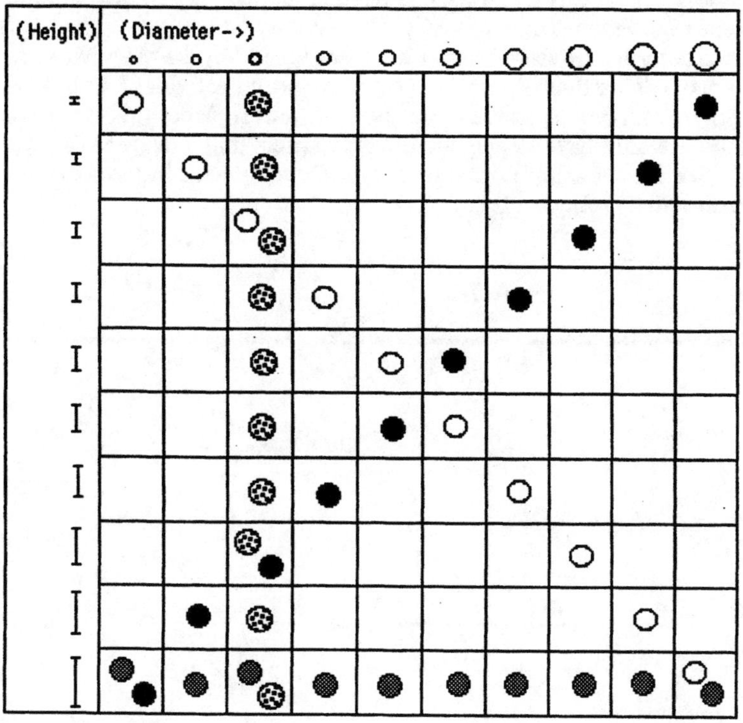

(Height)	(Diameter→)									
I	O		Blue							●
I		O	Blue						●	
I			O / Blue					●		
I			Blue	O			●			
I			Blue		O	●				
I			Blue		●	O				
I			Blue	●			O			
I			Blue / ●					O		
I		●	Blue						O	
I	● ●	●	● Blue	●	●	●	●	●	●	O ●

The Yellow Cylinders: O   The Red Cylinders: ●

The Blue Cylinders: ⊕   The Green Cylinders: ●

The final set varies inversely from thin/tall to thick/short, the most difficult type of two-variable seriation, according to Piaget. The arrangement of these four sets of ten cylinders can be seen on the graph shown above. This graph (Figure 7-1) is used as an advanced exercise (as a floor chart) in many Montessori classrooms.

Again, seriation goes on in other sense dimensions, too. The sound cylinders, the bells, the rough and smooth (sandpaper) tablets, the thermic bottles, the color tables, and so on, can all be put in order.

Some classification work is done in the Sensorial area; for example, the bells are sorted into high and low pitches. In working with the shapes of the geometric cabinet, a common work is to sort the shapes into those that have straight and curved sides. More complex types of classification skills, such as sorting objects into groups based on two characteristics, such as red and yellow cars and trucks, is beyond the majority of the children at the three to six age group (See Figure 7-2).

I would like to describe the classification work engaged in by the older Montessori children; their science work is particularly rich in complex sorting activities. I could then comment on when these sorting activities are out of order, according to Piaget. Unfortunately, to do this I would have to plagiarize a fine article that already exists which covers this in detail. See Pam Lanaro's "Classification Development in the Montessori Classroom" in the *Constructive Triangle* (1986).

Figure 7-2

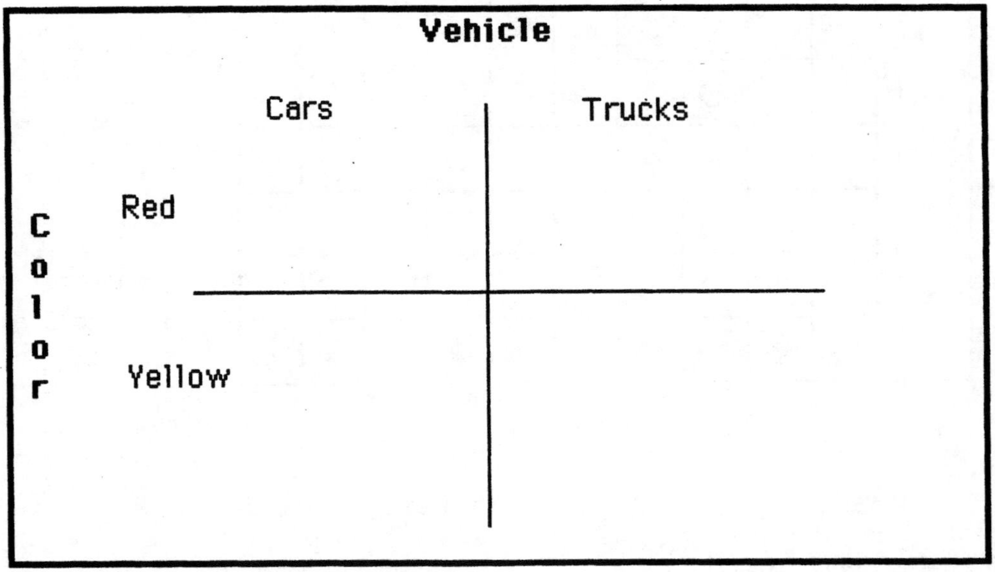

Although sorting red and yellow cars and trucks onto a grid like this is easy for adults and older children, most children below eight or nine years cannot do it successfully.

SENSORIAL PRESENTATIONS AND THE CHILD'S WORK

How are these materials actually used in the classroom? Sometimes, the careful arrangement of the Montessori materials and the detailed presentations learned by Montessori teachers are seen by non-Montessorians as evidence of a too-structured approach, as was discussed in Chapter 2. If the child's life in the Montessori classroom consisted only of children sitting still for group or even individual lessons on these materials, then their concern would be justified. It is certainly inappropriate for young children to spend long periods of time sitting still to listen to adult lessons--but that's not Montessori, as can be easily seen in a classroom observation! Children in a Montessori classroom may sit still for a short group time, and for one or two individual lessons from a teacher. The group time is typically the least distinctively Montessori part of the entire day's schedule. It consists of songs, stories, fingerplays, sharing, and possibly the discussion of rules or upcoming events. The individual lessons seldom last more than a few minutes. The children's work with the materials is the theoretical and actual focus of the classroom, not the 1-3 minute introduction by the teacher. This is especially true of the Sensorial materials.

Children work on Sensorial materials at the Bengali Education Society and School. Courtesy Seattle University and Estate of E.M. Standing.

A final point in this area concerns the many indirect aims of the Sensorial materials. You may have already noticed the fact that a large number of the Sensorial materials consist of ten pieces, as a preparation for the decimal system. The majority of the Sensorial presentations are given in a left-to-right, top-to-bottom order, preparing the child for the directionality of reading in English. (In Hebrew or Japanese schools, the directionality of the presentation is appropriately adjusted.) Another very common indirect aim is the preparation of the child's fingers for careful gripping of a pencil. Both the pencil-sized materials (such as the knobs on the knobbed cylinders) and the teacher's introductory presentation serve to help the child develop control of objects held in a pencil grip. Finally, the materials are frequently sized according to metric lengths--the one to ten cm size of the cube tower, and the final one meter length of the long rods, are examples of this.

A variety of more specific indirect aims is associated with individual materials. For example, the red rods prepare the child for the number rods in the math curriculum, which are in fact the same-sized rods, painted to show the division of the rods into ten centimeter lengths. The bells are primarily a sound matching and seriating exercise, but lead directly into actual music work with older children, including associating notes with written music notation, playing songs, and composition. The exercises of taste and smell lead to cooking activities, which can become quite complex with older children. The broad stair's largest prism is the same one used in 9-12 classes for the study of volume. These children, for example, derive their own formulae for volumes of prisms (including hexagonal and other unusual prisms) and pyramids! The old cube tower is met again by the child in the cube root material. Without belaboring the point, the Sensorial curriculum is full of indirect preparations for later work in math, language, science, and so on.

THE MONTESSORI TEACHER:
TO INTERVENE OR NOT TO INTERVENE?

The focus on Montessori teachers' precision in their lessons has led some people to assume that they are swift to intervene or even punish children who make mistakes. This has been discussed in Chapter 2 in relation to the idea of structure in the Montessori classroom. A clear understanding of the difference between a child's errors and actions requiring discipline is essential. Actions requiring discipline would include actions that could harm another or the child himself, actions that could damage property, or other violations of the classroom ground rules such as running, disturbing another child, and so on. Error, on the other hand, occurs when the child incorrectly sorts, matches, or seriates a material.

The control of error in the exercise replaces the need for teacher correction with a source of information for the child: "It won't fit." Not only is error unavoidable: it is, according to Montessori and Piaget, the source of the child's learning. It is the moment when the child gets the message that his model of the world doesn't quite match the real world--he'll have to look closer, to think again. This reexamination is much more likely to occur, claims Montessori, when the error is just information, not the emotionally charged correction that a teacher, even a well-meaning one, can give.

The teacher must not intervene in this feedback process. She should also refrain from intervening when the child begins to explore new ways to use the material, as long as these are consistent with the aims of the material. Different ways of building up the cube tower or the broad stairs, or even combining the two in a new extension, are indications that the child is furthering his knowledge of the concepts in the material. The key to the teacher is the concentration and intensity of the child or children. If they are only half-focussed on a task, some new difficulty or combination may be needed to involve them.

Montessori teachers have been criticized for intervention in the child's use of a material when the child uses the material for fantasy play. For example, many Montessori teachers would intervene when the broad stair becomes a space fortress; all would intervene when the red rods become light sabers! While this is discussed in Chapter 2 and elsewhere, the most important points are these: Montessori teachers should probably not intervene if the fantasy play is not damaging the materials, deeply involves the child or children, has some aspect of the original intent of the materials, or if there are no appropriate alternative materials for similar play.

> *From E. M. Standing's notes on Dr. Montessori's course in 1923. May 3rd, lecture 38. Copyright © 1989, E. M. Standing and Seattle University.*
> *(Emphasis by the author)*

Where I recommend exactness in certain movements, I do not intend that this exactness should be stereotyped and become mechanical. When I speak of exactness, I refer principally to the purpose of the exercise.

Take, for example, some of the Sensorial exercises. Those objects intended for the education of the sense have a purpose to accomplish, such as developing a finer discrimination of sensations, more refinement of muscular coordination, and so on.

In order to attain these ends, it is necessary to use these objects in a certain way within certain limits. The one who is directing these exercises should have a very clear idea upon this point, in order to be able to distinguish between those movements which are useful to attain that purpose and those movements which are not.

For instance, if the rough and smooth surfaces were to be touched roughly by the hand, there would be no point in the exercise. If the objects which are graded in dimension were all replaced without first being mixed, the purpose of the exercise would be lost, and so on.

When, however, the child himself makes variations in the use of the material and the variations lead to the same definite purpose, they should not be stopped. *In this case we could speak of individual variations in the use of the material. One can see the originality and differences between individuals by the way they use the external objects.*

*We should, however, always bear in mind the principle that these variations must lead to perfection. **In this lies the teacher's art, to be able to initiate the child into the use of the object or material without inducing a stereotyped mode of use.** She must present the*

*material with exactness, giving as it were a fundamental
type, upon which individual variations are possible.*

*To use a somewhat exaggerated parallel which
may make this idea clear, we could say that it somewhat
resembles Nature, which has a fundamental type and
then individual variations. Thus, if something fundamental is not first established, variations cannot exist. In this
case, there would be a lack of form, there would be that
which the individual could produce if we did not have the
fundamental basis. If we did not have this definite something established beforehand, these objects would be
used for purposeless and useless exercises. Perhaps the
child would himself eventually discover their real use. **In
this case his energies would either be dissipated in useless movements or they would be consumed in bringing
him to the starting point. But as we indicate the starting point with exactness, all his energies are then devoted to perfecting his powers--his motor powers, his
sensorial powers, and all those inner powers which are
developed by the exercises.***

Summary: This chapter presents the Sensorial curriculum area, beginning with a list
of the standard Sensorial materials. This curriculum area is often misunderstood, due at least
in part to the way Montessori has written about the exercises. In fact, the area contains a
large number of sets of materials allowing seriation, classification, and to a lesser extent,
conservation activities in a variety of media. The materials are designed to be of varying
difficulty. In addition to examining these materials from this Piagetian perspective, the
chapter returns to the Montessori concepts of control of error and isolation of difficulty.
Control of error refers to the aspect of a material that gives a child feedback, such as a final
puzzle piece that will not fit in if other pieces have not been put in correctly. Isolation of
difficulty refers to the design of the materials to focus the child's attention on one concept at
a time. The red rods vary only in length, the bells have different tones, but are of identical
size, weight, and color, for example.

Montessori's ideas on the internal motivation for learning, and the consequent
deemphasis on teacher praise, are discussed. Extensions of the Sensorial area for older children are discussed.

CHAPTER 8
The Mathematics Curriculum Area

Chapter Goals: In this chapter, you will learn:
- What is the Montessori math curriculum area ?
- What are some of the Montessori math manipulatives?
- How do the Montessori concepts of indirect preparation and isolation of difficulty apply in the math area?
- What is the Montessori concept of abstraction-- how does this concept explain how Montessori math materials are used in a way different from other math manipulatives?

INTRODUCTION

When someone thinks about Montessori, her wonderful math materials are often the first things that come to mind. The Montessori method is much more than materials, certainly, but even the materials are different from other manipulatives, such as Cuisinaire rods. Important goals of the Montessori method are that each student be taught at exactly the level he or she is on, and that students will be both willing and able to work on their own. The goals of individualized instruction and self-motivated, independent work by students are difficult to achieve, however. In this chapter on the math curriculum, I will focus on the use of the math materials to get to these two goals.

There are two characteristics of the math area and the math materials that will be our main focus for the chapter. These two areas are perhaps the most important differences between the Montessori math curriculum and other manipulative approaches. These two differences are the depth and complexity of the materials, and Montessori's concept of abstraction vs. memorization. These two differences are part of why Montessori schools have been able for 80 years to achieve individualization and student independence. The subject area I have chosen is algebra because it represents an area difficult to make concrete to children and therefore more usually taught only to older children, using traditional "chalk and talk" methods.

The concept of **abstraction** begins with the idea of a sequence of materials and activities with those materials that the child engages in. An important fact in this sequence is that the sensorial cues to the child are gradually removed; that is, the work she is required to do becomes more and more abstract over time. But what Montessori meant by abstraction was not this process, nor even the carefully prepared presentations made by the teacher. The real abstraction is a creative process undertaken by the child to construct her own knowledge. The indirect preparation and the presentations lead the child to discover important facts, derive formulae, and so on. This process Montessori contrasted very strongly with the child memorizing the same formulae given out by the teacher.

One of the key concepts in Montessori's thinking is her idea of the role of the subconscious mind in learning. As has been discussed previously, Montessori believed that any experiences undergone resulted in an <u>engram</u>, or memory trace. This memory trace of the experience is stored in the subconscious. (See, for example, Dr. Montessori's *To Educate the Human Potential*, Chapter 3.) Although not always or immediately accessible to the conscious mind, these engrams are permanent. Thus, a sensory experience in early childhood, according to Montessori, can be counted on to help a child both feel more comfortable with certain materials and activities, and provide a sensorial basis for more abstract concepts.

Central to Montessori's thought is the idea that these engrams are not merely passively stored in the subconscious, but are actively processed, and that new combinations and reorganizations of them may and do occur. The indirect aims of the Montessori materials are thus based on the idea that different aspects of the child's experience can be called upon at a later time to make the learning of new, more abstract concepts easier. The previous work with the materials that have algebra as an indirect aim serve to increase the child's attention span, give her success experiences, but also provide specific sensory experiences that can later be elaborated into new concepts.

An early topic in algebra is often graphs and graphing. Typically, after some work with number lines, the child is supposed to learn to plot a point on an X-Y graph that corresponds to a particular order pair of numbers. Children learn, eventually, to count over on the X axis, then slide their fingers up from that point on the X axis to the Y number to find the point. This skill has already been learned, practiced literally hundreds of times by Montessori children using the memorization charts for addition and multiplication. The children check their math work by looking up the correct answers with these charts. The addends (or factors) are ordered along the edge of the charts. To find 6 x 7, the child counts over to the six, then across to the intersection of the line of the seven, finding 42 there. Later, a more advanced material, the long multiplication checkerboard, gives him additional practice with a different material on the same concept.

AN EXAMPLE FOR ABSTRACTION: SQUARE ROOT

When I give presentations on Montessori math to teachers and parents, I often ask how many of the group ever learned to take square roots, using a process like long division. Most of the people have learned this way. Then I ask how many would be able to take a square root today, using that same process. Typically, one hand in 30 will go up.

To refresh your own memory, let's go through this square root algorithm from the days of adolescent disinterest in algebra. (An algorithm here means simply a process or series of steps used to get the answer. There is a set algorithm for square root just as there is for long multiplication or division by a fraction.)

1. Take the square root of:

$$\sqrt{1\ 5\ 1\ 2\ 9}$$

2. First, mark off the numbers in groups of two, beginning from the right. The number of groups will determine the number of digits in the answer. In our case, the answer will have three digits.

$$\sqrt{1\wedge5\ \ 1\wedge2\ \ 9}$$

3. Next, find the largest square of a single number that will be less than the value of the leftmost group.

In school language, you might have been told to find the largest square that "fits under" the first group.

In our case this is one. This number is then squared, and written underneath, and subtracted from the first group:

$$
\begin{array}{l}
\quad\ 1 \\
\sqrt{1\wedge5\ \ 1\wedge2\ \ 9} \\
\quad\underline{1} \\
\quad 0
\end{array}
$$

4. The next group is brought down.

$$
\begin{array}{l}
\quad\ 1 \\
\sqrt{1\wedge5\ \ 1\wedge2\ \ 9} \\
\quad\underline{1} \\
\quad 0\ \ 5\ \ 1
\end{array}
$$

5. (This next step is one that many teachers and parents report drove them to ask, "Why?" Few reported getting satisfactory answers from their teachers.)

In this step, we **double** the digit from the first answer and write this out to the side, as shown:

$$\begin{array}{r} 1 \\ \sqrt{1_\wedge 5\ 1_\wedge 2\ 9} \\ \underline{1} \\ 0\ 5\ 1 \end{array}$$

2

6. Now we must find a digit such that when it is placed to the right of the two <u>and</u> in the second place of the answer, the product must be just less than the brought down number, 51 in our case.

One would give 1 x 21=21; two would give 2 x 22 = 44; three would be too large at 3 x 23 = 69. Our digit is two:

$$\begin{array}{r} 1 2 \\ \sqrt{1_\wedge 5\ 1_\wedge 2\ 9} \\ \underline{1} \\ 0\ 5\ 1 \\ \underline{4\ 4} \end{array}$$

22

7. Subtracting and bringing down the next group gives:

$$\begin{array}{r} 1 2 \\ \sqrt{1_\wedge 5\ 1_\wedge 2\ 9} \\ \underline{1} \\ 0\ 5\ 1 \\ \underline{4\ 4} \\ 7\ 2\ 9 \end{array}$$

22

8. Now we must repeat the mysterious doubling trick. We need to find a third digit for the answer, such that that number times 24 X ("two-hundred-forty-something") will "fit under" 729. (This step is a little like a division problem; we need the largest possible digit, but it can't give us a product greater than 729. This can be determined by trial and error.) Three works:

$$
\begin{array}{ccc}
1 & 2 & 3
\end{array}
$$

```
        1   2   3
     _____
   √ 1∧5 1∧2 9
     1
       0  5  1
22         4  4
              7  2  9
24
```

9. Our final answer, then, looks like this:

```
        1   2   3
     _____
   √ 1∧5 1∧2 9
     1
       0  5  1
22         4  4
              7  2  9
243           7  2  9
```

In most groups, going over this algorithm brought it back to the minds of most of the adults in the audience. Why, then, were so few of them able to remember it? One reason is obviously disuse; we are not often required to compute a square root. Those of us who have to, buy a ten dollar calculator to do the work for us quickly and accurately. Why then has this part of the math curriculum been left in?

Many educators feel that it is important that children learn what square roots are, even though they may be pushing buttons later in life to do the actual calculating. I agree with this; my problem is with the teaching of this algorithm as a tool for helping children to understand square roots. I don't think it works. One step forgotten and the algorithm is useless. It's particularly easy to forget that one step, too, since the whole sequence is an arbitrary sequence of steps undertaken for no reason. This is the sequence; memorize it and it will tell you the answer.

In contrast, the Montessori way of teaching this concept begins with materials. In this case, the materials are some color coded pegs and a pegboard. The pegs are green for units, blue for tens, and red for hundreds. In the newer sets of these materials, the colors are shaded so that thousands are a darker green and millions the darkest of all. Along with these pegs are some rules for their arrangement. Let's take a simple example; find the square root of 121.

First, make the number 121 by taking one red hundred, two blue tens, and one green unit peg:

Then, arrange these on the pegboard according to the following rules:

1) Start with the highest value peg, and place it on the pegboard. If there are more than one, make a square out of them. Change in any left over pegs for the next hierarchy down. For example, three red hundreds pegs would be made into a "square "of one, and the two remaining pegs traded in for twenty blue tens.

2) Using the next hierarchy down, make two lines of pegs leading away from the square at right angles. These two lines must be as wide as the square, and must be even in length. (See illustration below.)

3) Fill in the space between these two lines of pegs with the pegs from the next hierarchy down, making a complete square:

Figure 8-1

a)   b)   c)

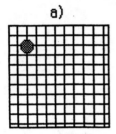   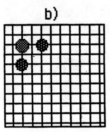   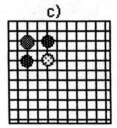

Look at the arrangement of the pegs which total 121 in c) of Figure 8-1. Can you see that the bottom line of the square is one 10 and one unit, a total of eleven? Eleven is one side of the square of 121; that is, the square root of 121. Thus, this simple process of laying out beads according to some rules has not only given the child the correct answer, but has shown him the meaning of square root. The square root is one side of the square.

Now let's follow through the example already given by finding the square root of 15,129. For these larger problems, the child makes use of a square root guide, which shows which colors to begin with. First, the student counts out the pegs needed:

Figure 8-2

●	●●●●●	●	●●	●●●● ●●●● ●
1	5	1	2	9
dark blue	dark green	red	blue	green
10,000	1,000	100	10	1

Next, the pegs are placed on the pegboard, following the rules described above:

Figure 8-3

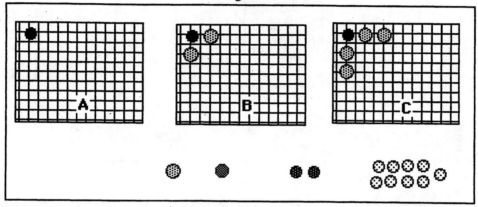

In the Figure 8-3 A, the student has laid out the one dark blue 10,000 peg. In the B and C, two "wings" of dark green 1,000 pegs are laid out. The remaining pegs are: one 1,000, one 100, two 10's, and nine 1's. The remaining 1,000 peg can't be put into a "wing" on the pegboard since this would make one wing larger than the other.

In Figure 8-4, the 1,000 has been exchanged for ten hundreds.

Figure 8-4

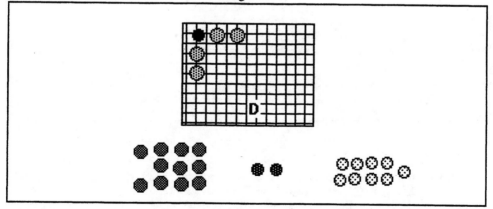

Figure 8-5

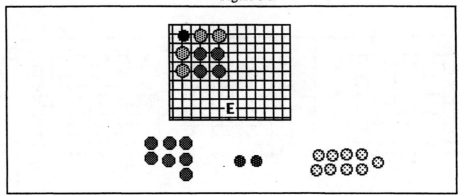

In Figure 8-5, four of the 100's have been used to fill in the square made by the wings of 1000's.

Figure 8-6

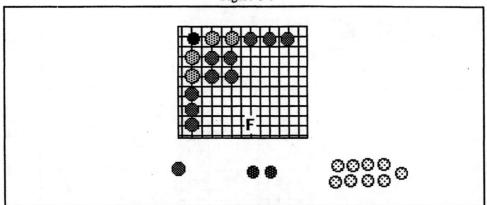

In Figure 8-6, new wings are made of the remaining 100's, extending the lines made by the thousands. One 100 remains; there are also two tens and nine units. In Figure 8-7, no new pegs have been added, but the left over 100 has been traded in for 10 blue ten pegs. In Figure 8-8, the squares formed by the 100's will be filled in with the 10's.

Figure 8-7

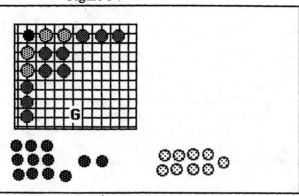

Figure 8-8

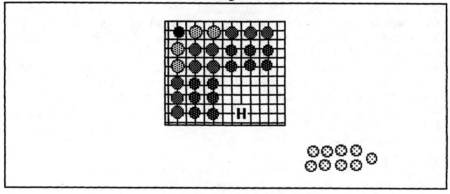

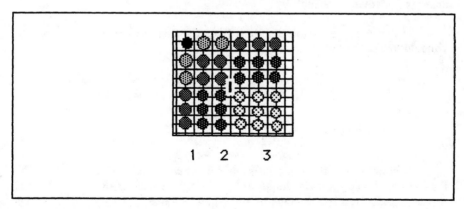

In the lower half (marked I) of Figure 8-8, the 1's fill the square. A completed square has been made out of pegs whose value is 15,129. The edge of the square is made of one 100, two 10's and three 1's--one hundred twenty three. This is the square root of our number.

To really understand what is happening with this material, to understand why this way of doing things is different from just the use of some materials to illustrate a concept, you must see the several parts of the process of abstraction in this example of teaching square roots. First, the child can be shown how to manipulate the materials quite easily, so that she can get the right answer to square root problems while practicing concepts of place value, multiplication, etc. But more importantly, **the child <u>discovers</u>** the paper and pencil algorithm herself, as a shortcut to the pegboard. This could not happen if the materials and the sequence of their use did not exactly parallel the algorithm. It also cannot happen unless the teacher is firmly committed to this discovery learning approach. In my experience as a teacher and a teacher educator, I have found that it is very hard for us to keep our mouths shut when we have the right way to do it and we feel a student is so close...

To see how this way of manipulating materials is a guide to the paper method, look back at the first step of the paper and pencil algorithm. This was to determine the number of digits in the answer. This step is done through the use of the square roots guides: if a child is working with a number less than 100, she just uses that many green pegs, makes a square and counts the bottom edge. For numbers greater than 100 and less than 10,000, the same pattern as with 121 is followed: red hundreds in one corner, blue "wings" of tens, and complete the square with units. The next largest size is shown in the example of 15,129.

The next step in the algorithm is to find the largest square that "fits under" the first group. Can you see that this is what is done physically on pegboard "A" when a square is made with the largest-valued pegs?

The most mysterious step is next--remember it?

5. (This next step is one that many teachers and parents report drove them to ask, "Why?" Few reported getting satisfactory answers from their teachers.)

In this step, we **double** the digit from the first answer and write this out to the side, as shown:

$$
\begin{array}{r}
1 \\
\hline
\sqrt{1{\wedge}5\ 1{\wedge}2\ 9} \\
\underline{1} \\
0\ \ 5\ \ 1
\end{array}
$$

$$\underline{2}$$

6. Now we must find a digit such that when it is placed to the right of the two <u>and</u> in the second place of the answer, the product must be just less than the brought down number, 51 in our case.

One would give 1 x 21=21; two would give 2 x 22 = 44; three would be too large at 3 x 23 = 69. Our digit is two:

$$\begin{array}{c} 1 \quad\quad 2 \\ \hline \sqrt{1_\wedge 5\ 1_\wedge 2\ 9} \\ \underline{1} \\ 0\ 5\ 1 \\ 22 \quad\quad \underline{4\ 4} \end{array}$$

Now, look at this step with the pegs:

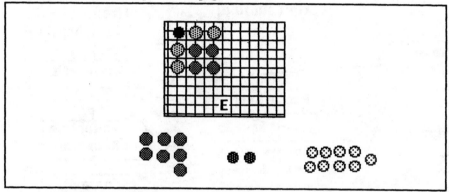

Do you see that the wings added to the single dark blue 10,000 peg are green thousand pegs--a value of two of these, or 2,000 per pair of pegs? What we're doing is really like a division, determining how many of these wing-pairs of two green beads, with a value of 2,000, we can take from our remaining number of 5,129. The first digit in our answer is a one--this was determined by the size of our first square, 1. The length or extension of these green pegs, a length of two in our case, determines the second digit of the answer.

Although it can't be gone into in detail here, the point of the square root materials is that the materials and the manipulation that the student goes through to reach the answer is not an arbitrary one. Each step of the entire paper process is modeled in the manipulative process. In fact, the goal of the whole situation--materials, teacher education, and so on--is to have the child discover the paper process, the algorithm, as a shortcut to what she has learned. The big hidden aim is the deeper understanding of what a complex concept like long division, division by a fraction, square or cube root, and so on, really means.

EXAMPLES OF INDIRECT PREPARATION

Next, let's examine a second example, in which I'll focus on the variety of preparatory materials for a complex operation. The extraction of the cube root of numbers is one of the most advanced mathematical operations for which a separate set of Montessori didactic apparatus exists. It is also a material that has received some criticism, since the extraction of cube roots is not usually taught to children under ages 11 or 12.

Figure 8-9

Indirect Preparation for Square and Cube Roots

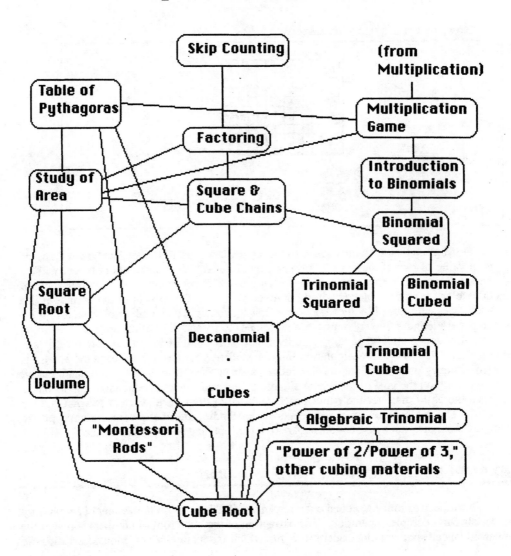

I've shown the approximate sequence and direction of the materials that prepare a child for cube roots in Figure 8-9. Bear in mind that almost all of the pieces of apparatus or presentations indicated with a single box in the chart have a <u>series</u> of exercises associated with them, each with different direct and indirect aims.

The "bead cabinet," containing squares and cubes of each of the numbers 1-10, and chains that have the same values, is the most obvious material with an indirect aim of preparation for cube root. The early activity of skip counting, useful in itself, is easily taught and readily practiced by the children. In skip counting, the child chooses a chain, such as the sevens chain. A container of arrows of the same color (white, in this case) is selected. The child lays out the chain on her mat, then orders the arrows: 7,14,21, etc.. The chain is counted and the arrows arranged to point to the correct beads on the chain of seven-bars.

The "Table of Pythagoras" material is sometimes referred to as the plastic decanomial material, to contrast it with the decanomial that is constructed by the children out of bead bars. A decanomial is a number with ten terms. A binomial has two terms, such as (2+3), a trinomial three (3+4+5), and a decanomial ten. The decanomial used for the Montessori material is made up of the first ten integers: (1+2+3+4+5+6+7+8+9+10). These polynomials are like ordinary numbers; they can be added or multiplied and so on. The Montessori materials usually concretize the multiplication of two integers by showing an area: thus 2 times four is shown as two four beads, or an area of two by four squares. The plastic decanomial is a representation of the decanomial $(1+2+3...10)^2$, as shown in Figure 8-10.

The numerical facts of which the plastic decanomial is the concrete representation are:

	(Squares)	(Pairs of rectangles)

(Red) 1^2

(Green) 2^2 + $2(2 \times 1)$

(Pink) 3^2 + $2(3 \times 1)$ + $2(3 \times 2)$

(Yellow) 4^2 + $2(4 \times 1)$ + $2(4 \times 2)$ + $2(4 \times 3)$

(Lt. Blue) 5^2 + $2(5 \times 1)$ + $2(5 \times 2)$ + $2(5 \times 3)$ + $2(5 \times 4)$

(Purple) 6^2 + $2(6 \times 1)$ + $2(6 \times 2)$ + $2(6 \times 3)$ + $2(6 \times 4)$ + $2(6 \times 5)$

.
.
.

(Golden) 10^2 + $2(10 \times 1)$ + $2(10 \times 2)$ + $2(10 \times 3)$ + $2(10 \times 4)$ +
$2(10 \times 5)$ + $2(10 \times 6)$ + $2(10 \times 7)$ + $2(10 \times 8)$ + $2(10 \times 9)$

The values of the squares and rectangles are not given to the child when the Table is first presented as a Sensorial material. Variations of the basic exercise of building the square include asking the child to cover a given square or rectangle with other pieces. She is limited in the way this can be done by the fact that the pieces include only one 1^2 piece. This work can be made more challenging by asking the child to use no pieces of the same color to cover the chosen piece. That is, if the white 7 x 6 piece is chosen for the child to cover, the simplest method of doing this is to choose some of the other white seven pieces to cover it, such as the 7 x 2 and the 7 x 4 or two of the 7 x 3's. When this is ruled out, the child must try more complex solutions, such as 6 x 4, 3 x 3 and 4 x 3, or even 3 x 1, 4 x 1, 5 x 2, 2 x 2, 3 x

3, and 3 x 2. When the child has had the work on multiplication and factoring to be described next, she can return to this pleasant Sensorial puzzle with the new knowledge of the **values** of these shapes. Combinations can be copied onto graph paper with colored pencils or markers, and the values and sums written down. This work is also a preparation for the bead bar decanomial, square root, and area.

Figure 8-10

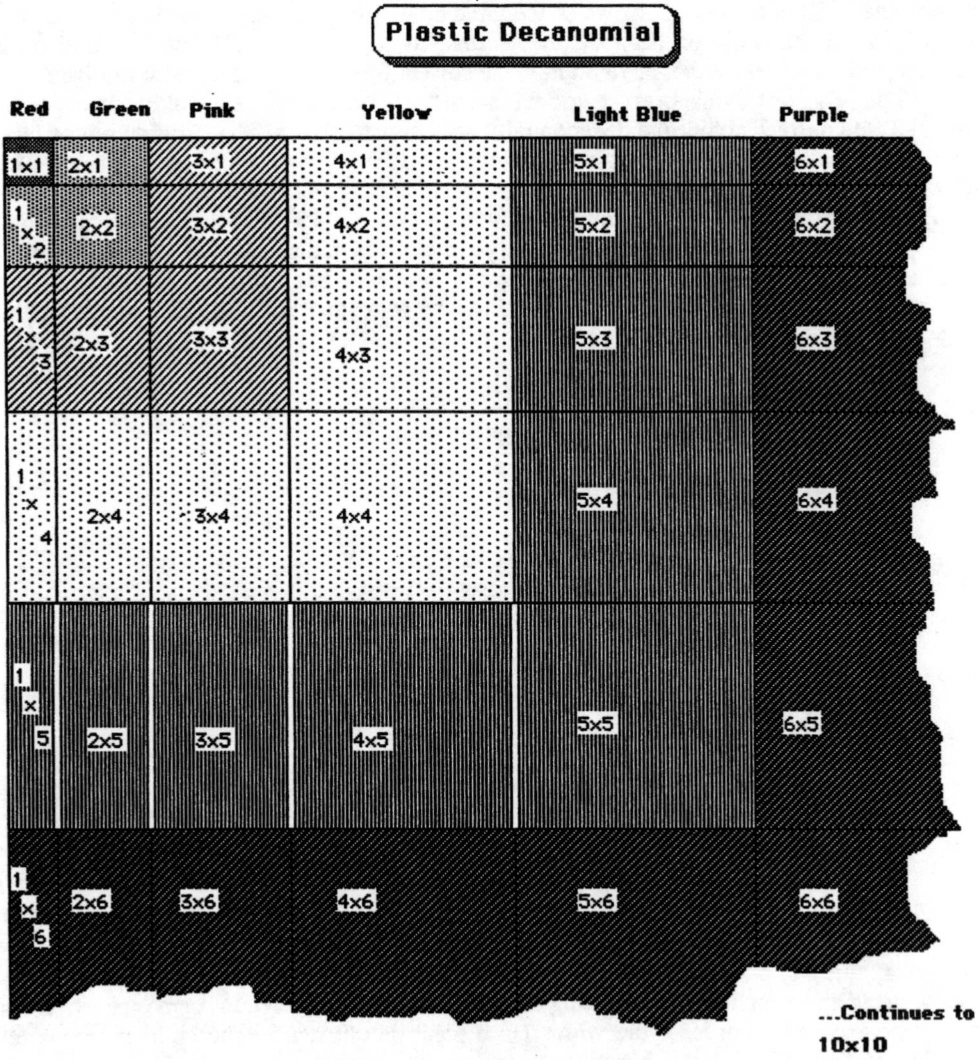

Plastic Decanomial

Red	Green	Pink	Yellow	Light Blue	Purple
1x1	2x1	3x1	4x1	5x1	6x1
1 x 2	2x2	3x2	4x2	5x2	6x2
1 x 3	2x3	3x3	4x3	5x3	6x3
1 x 4	2x4	3x4	4x4	5x4	6x4
1 x 5	2x5	3x5	4x5	5x5	6x5
1 x 6	2x6	3x6	4x6	5x6	6x6

...Continues to 10x10

MULTIPLICATION & FACTORS

The concept of multiplication and the memorization of the multiplication facts (the "times tables") are taught separately, with separate sets of materials, in keeping with the Montessori principle of isolation of difficulty. A multiplication exercise with the bead bars is an important preliminary to the introduction of factoring and the concept of a binomial.

Figure 8-11

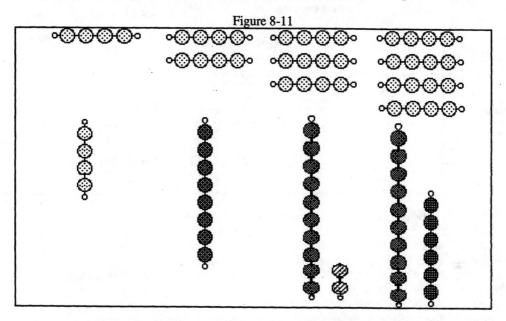

In this multiplication exercise, the child lays down beads (Figure 8-11) representing the particular times table she is practicing, so that the upper beads are all the specified kind of bead bar, e.g. fours, and the lower half represents the "answers." Points of interest include the repetition of patterns in the answer digits, which appears as a repeating pattern of colors, and the rectangles and single square formed by the upper half of the bead layout.

This concept, the geometrical representation of numbers, is as obvious indirect preparation for the study of area. The child's experience with this idea grows when he begins to study factors and factoring. Factoring can be presented by using the square root board and pegs. The square root materials manufactured in Sri Lanka (Kaybee) formerly included pegs of colors other than the red/blue/green pegs used for square root. These were specifically designed for work with factors.

The child is taught the concept of factors through an exercise of making as many different filled rectangles as possible with a given number of pegs (Figure 8-12). Twenty-four pegs, for example, can be arranged in a 1 x 24, 2 x 12, 3 x 8, or a 4 x 6 rectangle. There are also the opposites of each of these, 24 x 1, etc., which would be shown with the pegs vertically if the first layout was horizontal. There are thus 8 possible rectangles for 24.

Figure 8-12

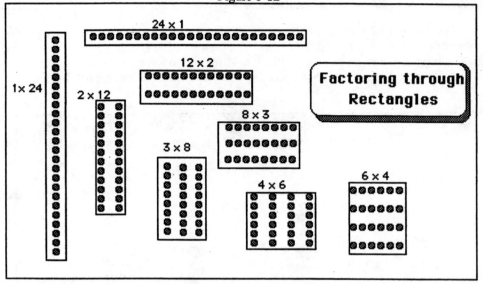

This idea of a geometric representation of multiplication is a central theme in the Montessori math materials. The child sees it in the factoring exercise above, in the values or names of the pieces of the plastic decanomial, and in the calculation of area. When the child is introduced to the idea of a binomial, shown by pairs of bead bars, the step to binomial multiplication is an easy one. The binomial 2 + 3 squared is just 2 + 3 taken two times and then three times. Each of these multiplications produces a square and a rectangle. These shapes are first made by the child with beads, then with a fixed square (a five-square in this case) with the portions of the binomial squared shown by two rubber bands, and finally by the pieces of the plastic decanomial. These are more abstract, of course, since they don't contain the actual beads, but are the same color as the beads they replace and the same area.

CRITICISMS OF THE MONTESSORI MATH AREA

Some would certainly criticize the Montessori math curriculum for going too far in the elementary years--cube and square roots, volumes of odd shaped solids, a good ways into geometry, and so on, but I'm afraid I can't take this very seriously. First, American children are consistently ranked far too low in their math skills in comparison with European and Japanese agemates. It is quite clear that other children can master these concepts. Secondly, I have taught children with these materials. I have many questions about Montessori, but virtually none about the strength of her math materials for older children--the children, in general, take to them easily, learn well, and frequently choose math or geometry in free choice time.

A more serious concern has arisen, however, about the math curriculum for the 3-6-year-old child. Piagetians, especially Kamii[1], have suggested that very little formal work in math is appropriate for children who are non-conservers of number. Non-conservers would typically choose a long, spread out row of pennies or candies (containing fewer) over a shorter, more dense row containing more items. That is, they concentrate on the length and ignore the density. These children can often say the names of the numerals in order, and even count, that is, enumerate objects, counting each one just once. But because they don't relate their counting to more, it's hard to know what their understanding of number is.

Kamii has also made use of a simple test. She has the child draw seventeen circles. The child and she count these together, and write the numeral 17. The child agrees that this numeral stands for the number of circles drawn. The tester then asks the child to draw a circle around all of the circles that are represented by this numeral (pointing to the seven). Almost all children are able to count off and circle seven of the dots. But when asked to do the same for the 1 in the ten's place, children as old as eight circle one dot. When asked about the remaining uncircled nine dots, children shrug, call them "left-overs," and so on. Yet, Kamii says, we expect these same first and second graders to understand carrying and borrowing!

Two friends at an elementary Montessori classroom work together on the long multiplication checkerboard, which helps reinforce concepts of place value notation.

Along the same lines, criticisms have arisen about the Montessori math curriculum, in which 4- and 5-year-olds (with materials) perform addition and subtraction, sometimes

[1]Kamii, C. *Young Children Reinvent Arithmetic*. New York: Teachers College Press, 1985.

with four digit numbers, and sometimes multiplication and division as well. Montessori adherents counter with the fact that these operations are all performed concretely, with material--and that children are demonstrably able to do these things, since they do them every morning in thousands of classrooms around the country. Piagetians counter that it is not clear what the children have actually learned from these manipulations of the materials-- could they not be just pushing around materials, according to rote, with no real understanding of what they are doing?

This is certainly an area for more research. The fact is that we don't really know how deeply Montessori preschoolers understand the concepts embodied in the math work they do. [1] We have data on their performance on math tests, summarized in a later chapter. They do very well on math, in general. In fact, one long-term study (Miller and Dyer, 1975, and follow-ups) found that Montessori children, particularly males, showed statistically significant differences in math achievement test scores as late as tenth grade, in comparison to both other preschool programs and no-preschool control groups. Something is clearly happening to these children's understanding of math that is unrelated to the content of the math they did in preschool eleven years previously.

In some unpublished research conducted by members of the Teachers' Research Network, Kamii's test was replicated with children from Montessori and traditional preschool backgrounds, both in preschool, and afterwards, through second grade. Results were statistically significant, favoring the Montessori children. [2]

It is certainly not the case that these small studies, or the long term success of Montessori children in math in the Miller and Dyer study should cause us to ignore the validity of Kamii's questions. Clearly, we need more research on what Montessori children understand from what they do with the math materials. We may also need to make sure that the children in Montessori classrooms have enough unstructured work with quantities and comparisons, and so on, before they move on to the more abstract Montessori materials such as the number rods, spindle boxes, and so on, traditionally the earliest math materials. Montessorians must always see the curriculum as a series of opportunities for each child to choose from, not a pipe, with children put in one end and pumped along, willy-nilly.

Summary: In this chapter on the mathematics curriculum, a number of examples of the Montessori math materials have been discussed. Several points about the Montessori math curriculum have been made:
   • The curriculum makes extensive use of <u>manipulatives</u>, not materials for the teacher to demonstrate concepts with.
   • The principle of <u>isolation of difficulty</u> is shown by materials that are designed to be used to teach one concept only; for example, different sets of materials

---

[1] See "The Interpretation of Subtraction held by Children in the Association Montessori Internationale Curriculum,"an unpublished masters' thesis at the University of Maryland, Kay Baker, 1988.

[2] This research by Pape and a partial replication by Basu can be obtained through contacting the Teachers' Research Network, c/o the author at Seattle University, Seattle, WA 98122.

are used to introduce the concept of multiplication than to teach the multiplication facts.

• A "web" of <u>indirect preparations</u>-- experiences with materials that help the learner at critical points with new materials and new concepts-- is found throughout the math curriculum. This is perhaps one of the strongest (and least well-known) aspects of the Montessori math curriculum.

• The Montessori concept of <u>abstraction</u> means two distinct things. The materials the child uses change as the child matures, becoming more abstract and less concrete. In the bead frames, a red bead stands for a hundred, whereas in the earlier golden bead material, a hundred is actually one hundred golden unit beads wired together.

But also, Montessori describes the process of abstraction in mathematics as an important goal of her math curriculum. By this, she meant that concepts, such as area, and formulae, such as the one for the area of a rectangle, could be either memorized by the child, at the teacher's urging, or abstracted by the child herself, from experiences with materials, guided by the teacher. This process of abstraction is an "Ah-ha!" experience for the child. The concept, formula, or an algorithm, such as a pencil and paper process for long division or square root, is individually discovered by the child. The learning is truly the child's own. Montessori describes this as a creative act, even though these abstractions are not the first: a child is creative who discovers the formulae, even though it is already known to mathematics.

CHAPTER 9
The Language Curriculum Area

Chapter Goals: In this chapter, you will learn:
- What did Montessori write about how children acquire language--is this correct in the light of current theories?
- What does Montessori say about the teaching of reading?
- Are the Montessori practices similar to phonics, whole language, or unlike any current reading theory?
- What are four levels of Montessori language materials/activities and the materials that make up each level?

INTRODUCTION: MONTESSORI'S THEORIES ON LANGUAGE[1]

Everyone, it seems, has an opinion on how and when young children should learn to read, and on whether that learning should be left up to the child, or to the parents and the child, or to a formal program of instruction. In this time of great concern over America's millions of illiterates, parents are understandably concerned about their children's reading. There are few areas in the Montessori model less well-understood than her language curriculum. To try to separate what Montessori really said (and what Montessori schools really do) from the fog of common misconceptions, let's begin with Montessori's theoretical work in this area.

Language Acquisition

This section examines the theories of language acquisition put forth by Maria Montessori in the light of current theoretical and empirical knowledge in developmental psycholinguistics and related areas. Montessori's writing style is a clear lecturing style[2] (in

---

[1] Thanks for some of this information to fellow Bergamo graduate Dr. Larry Schaeffer of the St. Paul area, and to a paper prepared for the Toronto public Montessori schools.

[2] See, for example, *Secret of Childhood*, pp. 178 and following; *Education for a New World*, Chapter 7, pp. 39-41; *Discovery of the Child*, pp. 268-277, 303-310, 318-325; and *Absorbent*

Italian), a fact not readily apparent in some of the currently available translations of her work. One difficulty for modern readers is that her writing is full of allusions to then-current theories and practices, as well as responses to criticisms that are unknown to the modern reader.

Montessori speaks of the development of language, rather than the teaching of language, and states that this development follows fixed laws that are the same in all children. She feels that each child absorbs the language of his group, whether it is simple or complex, learning all the rules of syntax and grammar. Since most adults are unable to state the rules of grammar, we must assume that Montessori meant children speak as if they know the rules. She also noted the fact that our early language development affects the ability to distinguish sounds in language. If the distinction between S and Z, for example, is important in the rules of the language, as in English, then the child will learn to distinguish, and later to produce these two sounds distinguishably. But an adult raised in a Spanish speaking environment would confuse these two sounds. Montessori believed that the acquisition of language was not a conscious act of the child, but that the mind of the child was set to absorb the language of its environment unconsciously.

In *The Absorbent Mind*, Montessori talks at length about the process of language acquisition. She writes about how the child may seem to be making no progress at all, but then will suddenly display a new skill. She also used her concept of sensitive periods extensively in describing language acquisition: she writes about how a child who has the power to pronounce syllables will work at that stage with great enthusiasm until a higher level of performance can be seen.

Montessori also used her idea of an innate push or drive for development (horme) in her description of language acquisition. To Montessori, the idea of needing to motivate young children to learn language would be absurd. Finally, she comments on the fact that humans come with a capacity to learn any language--the language of their environment-- rather than with a pre-programmed or instinctual language. See pages 113, 117 and following in the *Absorbent Mind*.

She then reasons that the child must be specially sensitive to the sounds of speech, attending to and retaining these above all others. She gives the example of the wild boy of Aveyron as a child deprived of exposure to speech during his crucial period for the acquisition of language.

As we have discussed earlier, Montessori referred to the potential of language learning as a "nebula"; she felt that each experience undergone by the child results in an engram or memory trace stored permanently in the child's subconscious. These engrams interact and produce new learning which on occasion rises to the conscious mind.

In the earliest stage, before 8 to 10 months in most children, language has been primarily for the child himself. Now, at one year, he wants very much to make his needs and feelings known to others. At eighteen months, the child discovers that everything has a name. Soon after this he begins to use "one word sentences" or "fusive" words. "Seeing his

---

Mind, p. 124, 138, 140, 166, 172, 174, 181, 186. (These are the paperback edition page numbers.)

supper prepared, the child says, 'Mupper,' meaning 'Mummie, I want some supper.' A marked feature of this condensed speech is that the words themselves have become altered. Often the shortened form is united with some mimetic sound, as in bow-wow for dog, or the word is invented." Montessori, *Absorbent Mind*, p. 125.

Just before age two occurs what Montessori called the explosion into words, a sudden radical increase in vocabulary. After two comes the explosion into sentences or the pulling together of the new words into ordered strings--the discovery of syntax. Montessori felt that if two languages were used during this crucial period, one by each parent for example, the creative system of the child's mind would allow him to absorb both, speaking the correct language to each.

She also concluded that frustration, through incapacities in the auditory, vocal, or cerebral parts of the language acquisition system or through an impoverished environment would have grave consequences not only on language, but on the behavior of the child and the adult.

Montessori's Ideas and Contemporary Psycholinguistic Theories

Now let us examine Montessori's ideas in the light of current theories. A highly recommended summary is Slobin's (1970). He states, "Until recently, behavioristic psychology looked upon language, and the task of first language learning, as just another form of human behavior which could be reduced to the laws of conditioning. The picture we are now beginning to form, however, is that of a child who is creatively constructing his language on his own, in accordance with innate and intrinsic capacities - a child who is developing new theories of the structure of language, modifying and discarding old theories as he goes." (1970, p. 40)

Slobin and his associates conducted an interdisciplinary project, studying the acquisition of grammar in children from black and white, lower and middle class American, German, Russian, Finnish, Kenyan and Samoan backgrounds. Grammar he defines as "a device for relating sounds to meanings." His report of all the cultures examined shows a general sequence of developmental stages very similar to that proposed by Montessori:

> . . . *Typically, in all of the cultures we have examined, there is a period of babbling ending somewhere around 18 months of age. Overlapping this period is a stage of single-word utterances, followed by a stage of two-word utterances at around 18-24 months. The two-word stage is often quite brief, but its structural and semantic characteristics appear to be universal. There is no prior reason why child speech, at a certain stage, should be limited to utterances of two words in length, for children can babble much longer strings of sounds. The universality of this phase suggests the maturation of a "language acquisition device" with a fairly fixed programming span for utterances at the start.*

Slobin, like Montessori, recognized the enormous and unique task of the construction of language, and its importance for the continuation of civilization. Slobin: ". . .human language could not be so defined if it were not so defined by children, because, in a profound sense, language is created anew by children in each generation." Montessori (1967, p. 115): ". . .if (the child) lacked this power (special mechanism for language) and could not spontaneously master his language, no effective work would ever have been done by the world of men. There would be no such thing as civilization. This is the true perspective in which we must see the child. This is his importance. He makes everything possible. On his work stands civilization."

Montessori gave the child credit for being able to use his senses at a much earlier age than then-current child psychologists did. She describes the child as displaying a sensitive period for language by both producing sounds and showing a predisposition to watch the source of sounds--the mouth of the speaker. Both the ability and the preference have now been firmly established in infants (McCandless and Trotter, 1977; Bower, 1979). Montessori's ideas on the early stages of speech, however, have received less investigation and support.

As far as Montessori's rejection of the infant's feat in learning a language as being the result of adult-like learning, this issue has not been entirely laid to rest. Although fewer in number, proponents of a modified stimulus-response theory of language acquisition still exist.

Noam Chomsky would agree with Montessori that language is not learned at all, in the behaviorist sense:

> . . . *Knowledge of grammatical structure cannot arise by application of step-by-step inductive operations (segmentation, classification, substitution procedures, filling of slots in frames, association, etc.) of any sort that have yet been developed within linguistics, psychology, or philosophy. . . . It seems plain that language acquisition is based on the child's discovery of what from a formal point of view is a deep and abstract theory - a generative grammar of his language - many of the concepts and principles of which are only remotely related to experience by long and intricate chains of unconscious quasi-inferential steps. A consideration of the character of the grammar that is acquired, the degenerate quality and narrowly limited extent of the available data, the striking uniformity of the resulting grammars, and their independence of intelligence, motivation, and emotional state, over wide ranges of variation, leave little hope that much of the structure of the language can be learned by an organism initially uninformed as to its general character. . . (1965, p. 58)*
> . . .*On the basis of the best information now available, it seems reasonable to suppose that a child cannot*

help constructing a particular kind of transformational grammar to account for the data presented to him, any more than he can control his perception of solid objects or his attention to line and angle. Thus, it may well be that the general features of language structure reflect, not so much the course of one's experience, but rather the general character of one's capacity to acquire knowledge - in the traditional sense, one's innate ideas and innate principles. (1965, p. 59)

Other researchers comment, "It seems then, to be truth value rather than syntactic well-formedness that chiefly governs explicit verbal reinforcement by parents. Which renders mildly paradoxical the fact that that the usual product of such a training schedule is an adult whose speech is highly grammatical but not notably truthful." (Brown, Layden, and Bellugi, 1967, pp. 57-58)

One of the areas of Montessori's theory that was (and is) attacked is her idea of sensitive periods, of which language is a prime example. Once again, it appears, contemporary science has caught up with Montessori. "The complexity of (the task of language acquisition) has made it plausible (to some) to postulate that the child's mind is somehow 'set' in a predetermined way to process the sorts of structures which characterize human language. . .the child has innate means of processing information and forming internal structures, and that, when these capacities are applied to the speech he hears, he succeeds in constructing a grammar of his native language. Indirect evidence for this approach also comes from the fact that there seems to be a biologically determined 'critical state' for language acquisition in humans (during childhood), and that there are probably special structures in the human brain, lacking in all other animal brains, which perform language functions." Slobin, 1970, page 56.

Research evidence also supports Montessori's description of the stages in language acquisition and the idea of language "explosions"; stages, or non-continuous development, appears to be the best description of child language development, especially in vocabulary. (Mussen, Conger, & Kagan, 1969; McCandless and Trotter, 1977) Also, Montessori summarized the whole idea of transformational grammar when she stated, "We must come to understand that the child reaches his knowledge of grammar by himself; but this is no reason for our not speaking to him grammatically or for not helping him to construct his sentences." (1967, p. 123) In general, then, Montessori's ideas on early language acquisition have been borne out--if not in detail, then certainly in her general approach.

Reading and Writing

In her approach of considering writing and reading as integrated, and as closely related to the child's oral language, Montessori has placed herself in the mainstream of most current thought on early literacy curricula. (See, for example, Jenson and Hanson, 1980;Teale and Sulzby, 1989; Schickedanz, 1989.)

The debate on the best method of reading instruction continues to rage on, as it has for decades. To the old debate of phonics vs. sight words, new terms have been added: skill tactics vs. ideational tactics, whole language, language experience, and emergent literacy.

(Strickland and Morrow, 1989) The fact is that most programs incorporate at least two strategies: direct teaching and indirect teaching or discovery learning. Most programs also use two content areas: decoding or letter/sound combinations, and the uses of language. Debates about which of these four possible combinations (such as discovery learning in the uses of language or direct teaching in letter/sound recognition) is the most effective are not useful because almost every program really makes use of all four possibilities.

Chalkboard writing, date unknown. Courtesy Seattle University & Estate of E.M. Standing.

A more useful question to ask is about the type of direct teaching that goes on: when a lesson is taught on sound/letter matching, is it done with a manipulative or with a dittoed worksheet? The worksheet-oriented approach, instructionally similar to primary grade work, rather than preschool, is in fact the most common type of reading instruction in American kindergartens today. (Durkin, 1987) These approaches focus on letter naming and letter/sound matching. Montessori avoids letter naming altogether, but does present (with the sandpaper letters[1]) letter/sound matching. As discussed later in this chapter, it is important to keep in mind that these lessons are short demonstrations to the child and that she or he

---

[1] The sandpaper letters are letters on hardboard cards, approximately 3 by 5 inches; the background of the card is colored and the letter is a fine grain sandpaper. Two colors are used for backgrounds to distinguish vowels and consonants.

should then be offered the option to choose to work with the letters or not. Unfortunately, the wide linking of the sandpaper letters with the Montessori language curriculum has led many people to forget about all the other parts of the curriculum that exist.The movable alphabet[1] is an important part of the language area. These sets of letters allow the young child to write--to use the letter shapes to communicate--at a time when the physical act of drawing the letters may be so difficult and tedious that he would not undertake it otherwise. This is another example of the Montessori principle of isolation of difficulty. This idea is in keeping with the suggestions of current theorists, who suggest that the child be given a wide variety of ways to be able to write. (Teale and Sulzby, 1989)

Other important components for an ideal early childhood curriculum for reading and writing include the following (Schickedanz, 1989):

• Learning that speech can be segmented into phonemes. Although the usual Montessori oral language activities would help children here, the most useful teaching techniques involve allowing the child to see the juxtaposition of oral and written language. (Cossu, et al., 1988; Ehri and Wilce, 1980; Mann, 1986) The composition of words with the movable alphabets, phonetic reading materials, and labeling of objects in the environment are important examples of Montessori work relating to this category of learning.

• Children must develop a rich vocabulary and a good understanding of concepts. The use of detailed vocabulary in Sensorial, Practical Life, geography, geometry, and other areas is clearly an asset to the child.

• Children must learn about print conventions, such as left to right, etc.

Montessori presentations in almost every area have a left to right, top to bottom orientation. The child has practiced with materials with this indirect aim of left to right orientation hundreds of times. Let's examine the curriculum in more detail.

MONTESSORI'S LANGUAGE CURRICULUM

This section presents the major kinds of activities that are grouped together as a language curriculum in a Montessori preschool (3 - 6-year-old) class, including some general Montessori principles important for the language area. Much of what Montessori wrote about the language area is similar to sources describing the open classroom method. In an article in Ascheim's *Materials for the Open Classroom* (1975), Rosemary Williams considers the invaluable first step toward language competency to be the building of *attitudes*, not skills. If the child sees the uses of labels, the utility of written instructions and directions, the joy of reading, then the teaching of the skills necessary for reading and writing will be a matter of feeding the child's interest, not a battle of wills. Williams produces a very

---

[1] The movable alphabets are several series of letters, ranging in size from a large set which matches the sandpaper letters exactly, to smaller sets printed on cards.

Montessori-like simile: a child's reading progress is like a tree; without the strong roots of attitude preparation the tree will not support the heavy trunk and branches of skill development.

Before beginning the presentation of basic Montessori ideas in the language area, it is important to remember the basic principle of allowing the child to move at his or her own pace. A parent or teacher who would not think of "moving a child through" the sensorial or Practical Life curriculum to achieve a certain level by a certain age may in fact have just such expectations for reading level. Pressure exerted on the child can have extremely undesirable effects, such as lowering his positive self-concept or turning him off to a whole area of learning. Undoing this damage can take years of patience. When a learning disability or a bad experience prevents a child from moving as expected and pressures mount for him to "catch up," secondary problems can arise. Aversions to reading, teachers, or school in general require far more effort to remediate than the original problem. Have faith in the child. Neglect the area of attitudes toward reading and you will increase the risk of turning a child away from reading permanently.

Word building work, Good Shepard Montessori House of Children, Columbo, Sri Lanka. Courtesy Seattle University & Estate of E.M. Standing.

Another concept basic to Montessori's language curriculum is sensitive periods. The child from 3 - 6 is riding the crest of a wave of development in spoken language. His absorbent mind is adding new words to his recognition and speaking vocabularies at a rate he will never again equal. All areas of the Montessori language curriculum seek to take advantage of the child's interest in language and communication, and his incredible capacity for learning from his surroundings.

This answers a common criticism of the Montessori preschool: that such programs somehow "force" early language work on children. Many children of average intelligence who have had the advantage of Montessori experience are in fact able to read in their "kindergarten" year; some read before this, some not until later. It is important to point out to such critics that nothing is forced on the Montessori children. A good Montessori classroom does not include long hours of language lessons, patterned language drill, fixed assignments in pre-reading workbooks, or similar activities. Much is shown and told to the child, in both group and individual presentations of short duration, but the child **always has the option to choose not to do the work shown.**

A good teacher will choose the correct activity or material at the correct level of difficulty, and present it in a way to attract the child's interest. This, the materials themselves, and the awareness of the sensitive period for language achieve the results you may observe in any good Montessori class, and this has been documented by research.

This sensitive period for language has weakened and transmuted itself by age six. At this point, the child has an interest in the structure of things--in classifying and organizing. Having already acquired some proficiency in reading, the average Montessori child at this time shows an interest in grammar. Critics see their own childhood experiences with grammar and cannot imagine 6- to 9-year-olds doing such study willingly. If they observed a classroom, they would find children in happy concentration pasting colored shapes representing the parts of speech over words, cutting up sentences to analyze them, and other activities, quite unlike the dry work they recall. Thus, the sensitive period of the child is met with developmentally appropriate materials and activities.

This discussion of the 6- 9-year-old child brings me to another common misconception about the Montessori language curriculum. Montessori's sandpaper letters are so well-known that they are taken by many to be the sum of her curriculum, which is then criticized for being entirely a phonetic system. Phonics is seen by these observers as suitable for Montessori's phonetic Italian but inadequate for English.

First, the sandpaper letters form the bases for several language activities out of hundreds that should occur in a well-run Montessori classroom. Secondly, and more importantly, it is not correct to categorize the Montessori curriculum as a phonics approach. All of the other curriculum areas, particularly Practical Life and Sensorial, prepare the child for language learning, giving what some early educators define too narrowly as "pre-reading skills," such as concentration, left-right sequencing, pencil control, and visual and auditory discrimination. Many alphabetic materials, including the sandpaper letters, are made available to the child; she usually learns the shapes that "make" most of our speech sounds very easily. But unlike other approaches, these early awarenesses are not used to enable her to complete workbook pages or mimeographed sheets. Montessori anticipated the focus on the child's use of language that characterizes the emergent literacy approach (see Strickland and Morrow, 1989). The child's phonics skills are used by him to communicate, such as by writing telegraph-style messages to his friends. Later, descriptions, labels of objects that interest him in the rich environment, and so on, are "written," using the sandpaper letters or the smaller movable alphabet. Thus, these materials should be seen as tools that the child uses to communicate things important to him, at a stage when the "drawing" of each letter is simply too tedious.

At the same time, the oral language of the classroom is rich and exact. How many times have parents and educators been surprised at Montessori teachers' use of words like "peninsula" and "corolla" with preschoolers? Slowly, more and more of this extensive oral vocabulary is made reading vocabulary, while the child works on more advanced phonics skills. The balance point usually comes at about age six; here, more than half of his reading work is actually in content areas: botany, geography, science, geometry. Even persons who carefully study the Montessori preschool language curriculum often miss the fact that the early emphasis on phonics is gradually replaced by an emphasis on sight vocabulary.

With children at age six, many traditional reading teachers are attempting to develop the children's attention span and spark their interest in an area for which the children no longer are sensitive. Montessori teachers, on the other hand, can continue the necessary work on the more irregular phonics rules, continuing to increase the number and complexity of the child's sight reading vocabulary words through the materials and experiences available in the other Montessori curriculum areas, and feeding the child's interest in grammar.

Listening to a child read in an elementary classroom.

Let's examine the teacher's role in more detail. The teacher's task is to offer choices to the child from a wide array of possibilities. An experienced Montessori teacher has a wealth of materials and activities to offer, only a small part of which can be used by any one child. The child's interests and learning style, as well as his general level of development and language ability, shape the curriculum the child experiences. Allowance for individual differences must be given more than lip service, if the Montessori methods are to be successful.

The teacher must be careful to include the full range of language experiences in the Montessori language curriculum. My observations have shown me that many Montessori classrooms are weak in the area of oral language, in building good attitudes toward use of language, and in allowing children to express themselves. Although Montessori felt that oral reading to a group was a difficult skill and should be postponed until later years, other forms of self-expression are suggested, such as interpretive reading games similar to charades. Unfortunately, during group time some Montessorians neglect finger-plays, songs, discussion of the calendar, days of the week, etc. and chances for the children to tell of their own experiences. All are essential for the child's preparation for language learning, reading, and writing. The attractive, impressive-to-parents Montessori materials are <u>not</u> the curriculum!

The language curriculum of the traditional or developmental preschool is often centered around the teacher's insertion of language or other curriculum content into an activity of the child's own choosing. A good Montessori teacher, while being careful not to interrupt or distract the child, also makes use of this technique, in addition to the standard Montessori curriculum.

Montessori's position on fantasy and fairy tales and her ideas on creative dramatics are a source of much confusion and histrionics. Montessori's original position, discussed in the light of current early education and child development research and practice, is given in a later chapter. In brief, as far as fantasy is concerned, most modern Montessorians try to avoid this with the youngest preschoolers, and try to make very clear the distinction between reality and "made up stories" with the older ones. Science experiments and observations in the classroom help a child acquire some rules to distinguish fantasy from reality, dragons from dinosaurs, Venus from Krypton. Creative dramatics should be allowed for older preschoolers, and encouraged for early elementary children. This is an area where Montessori teacher education programs need to examine their positions and intent very carefully in the light of existing research.

One more basic idea is central to the Montessori language curriculum. Reading and writing are taught "together," that is in parallel, with writing usually assumed to be slightly ahead of reading with most children. This linkage, as has been discussed earlier, is receiving wide support outside of the Montessori community. But these two parts of the language area make use of different materials, following the Montessori concept of isolation of difficulty. Contrast this with the sequence still used by many teachers: the alphabet song and a book with a first sentence such as, "Look, look, see Dick and Jane." The sentence quoted has capital letters and punctuation and 9 of its 22 letters are non-phonetic. None of them, except the letter <u>e</u> in see and the <u>a</u> in Jane, have the sound value they are assigned in the alphabet song -- the names, rather than the sounds of the letters.

Since reading and writing are taught in parallel, which does a child learn to do first? Again, the individual child will decide. Most of the children I have seen learn to decode, to read, before they write (with pencil), but <u>after</u> they have learned to "write" by composing words with the movable alphabet. Often the first words they read are ones they themselves have just created with the letters.

NUTS AND BOLTS: FOUR STAGES OF MONTESSORI LANGUAGE WORK IN THE PRESCHOOL

1. Oral/Auditory

This stage rests on the work the child has already accomplished: his concentration, his sharpened perceptions, his love of order, etc. and on the previous work of the teacher in giving the child a love of language and an appreciation of its importance. From wherever the teacher assembles her oral and auditory language activities and materials, at least the following should be included:

Stories, both read and told

Finger plays

Songs

Poems

Naming activities from the clapping game type--*Who stole the cookie from the cookie jar / John stole the cookie from the cookie jar / Who, me?/ Yes, you / couldn't be / Then who?/ Jane...etc.*--to naming the objects in the room, including the correct names of the Montessori didactic apparatus. Another example is the Question Game: "What did you have for breakfast?" "Toast." "You had toast for breakfast?" "I had toast for breakfast." "Where did you have toast for breakfast?" "In the dining room." "With whom did you have toast for breakfast?", and so on.

As with any work with children, your expectations determine to a large extent the level of performance -- I have found this to be especially true in group activities such as singing. Crucial to this period are a variety of games that focus on developing the child's ability to hear the initial, terminal, and finally the medial sounds of words. Classic Montessorians play "I spy with my little eye something that begins with /b/." Let the children pick objects and have others try to guess the object. Insufficient work at this level, particularly with terminal and medial sounds, is probably the single greatest cause of children remaining at the "doorway" to reading for a year or more.

2. Mechanical Level

Here the child masters the skills she will need to begin both reading and writing. The metal insets[1], when correctly presented to the child, prepare her hand for writing (as have a large number of materials in the Sensorial and Practical Life areas). The sandpaper letters[2] give the child the link between the sounds she has been working with and a particular

---

[1] These are a set of shapes, from a circle to more complex shapes, each made of an inner piece and a matching template. They are like a simple one-piece puzzle. They allow for a large number of different tracing and drawing activities, appropriate to a wide range of pencil skills.

[2] Some time needs to be spent by neophyte Montessori teachers in learning to correctly pronounce single sounds --/l/, not "el" or "luh" --as strange an occupation as this seems, it is necessary.

shape, thus preparing her for both reading and writing. The double sandpaper letters do the same for the most common phonetic difficulties: *ai* (<u>ai</u>m), *ar* (c<u>ar</u>), *au* (P<u>au</u>l), *ch* (mu<u>ch</u>), *ee* (s<u>ee</u>), *er* (h<u>er</u>), *oa* (<u>oa</u>t), *oo* (b<u>oo</u>k), *or* (<u>or</u>), *ou* (<u>ou</u>t), *oy* (t<u>oy</u>), *qu* (<u>qu</u>it), *sh* (pu<u>sh</u>), *th* (mo<u>th</u>), and *ue* (bl<u>ue</u>).

The movable alphabets (at least the first, largest one) must also be considered here, under the mechanical stage. The child can assemble words with the letters to create messages for a friend, to describe pictures or objects, etc., and still be able to read these words. The Montessori teacher must encourage the child, but must be patient and not push. Care is needed at this time not to flood the child with pictures and objects that are supposed to "encourage" him to create words with the movable alphabet; let him make up most of the words out of his own head. This encourages creativity, enhances relevance, and will prevent the child from coming to depend on you or any outside source for inspiration.

Another important way in which Montessori anticipated modern work in early writing is in training teachers (sometimes with difficulty) not to correct children's invented spellings, although the results from my intervention study show that more work is needed here.

3. Word Reading Level

In this stage falls the majority of the prepared reading activities in the Montessori classroom. Only classes of activities are listed, with the understanding that a well-equipped classroom would have many examples of each, although not necessarily all out at one time.

Object Boxes -- Boxes of objects, grouped by a phonic commonalty --all have a short <u>a</u>, for example: rat, cat, bat, hat, mat. Later, two sounds can be used, in a sorting exercise.

Picture Boxes-- as above.

Command Cards-- run, sit, etc.

Simple Nomenclatures-- name and picture matching cards, such as names of the parts of a flower or of a hamster, etc.

Classified Nomenclatures-- from a particular content area such as botany or geography, which usually has a hierarchical organization.

Dictation Games-- the child spells words with the movable alphabet or words are written on small chalkboards or on paper.

Word Cards-- includes the Phonograms (folded slips of paper for more difficult phonetic difficulties-- <u>dge</u>, for example) and Puzzle Words.

Sorting Games with Cards-- an important sub-group teaches the child the many ways the sounds he has learned from the double sandpaper letters can be formed. The <u>er</u> sound can be produced by er, ur, and ir; the <u>au</u> sound by au, aw, and ough, and so on.

Early Grammar Exercises-- nouns ("Bring me a _____.")and verbs ("Can you <u>jump</u>?")

4. Sentence Reading Level

Montessori saw a distinctly different stage appear when the child is able to read words quickly and easily enough to be able to comprehend a sentence. Some of the more important activities include:

> Definitions--for each of the words in the classified Nomenclatures. Four levels of difficulty are available for the work with these definitions.
>
> Small Books-- preferably nonfiction. These can be as simple as descriptions of the Montessori apparatus in the room.
>
> Longer Commands, Experiment Cards
> Interpretive Reading (Like charades)
> Early Grammar
> Dictionary Work

Let me stress in closing that it is an <u>attitude</u> -- a respect for the child and his power, and a love of language--in the teacher, rather than an abundance of material, that is primary in the Montessori language curriculum.

Summary: In this chapter, Montessori's thoughts on language and the Montessori language curriculum area are presented. First, Montessori's writings, mainly from her book *Absorbent Mind,* are discussed in light of contemporary theories of language acquisition. Then, Montessori's ideas and theories and actual classroom practices in the area of language, especially in reading, are considered. Contrary to a common belief, Montessori's ideas on reading are more similar to what is currently called a Whole Language approach than a phonics approach. Perhaps this misconception comes from the material, especially the sandpaper letters. In any case, many contemporary ideas, such as the linking of reading with (prior) writing, the focus on use of writing to communicate, and the labeling of objects in the environment, have been a part of the Montessori language curriculum since its inception. The chapter concludes with a list of Montessori language exercises.

CHAPTER 10
The Montessori Elementary Classroom

Chapter Goals: In this chapter, you will learn:
- What is the Montessori model for the elementary years, and how does this model reflect Montessori's understanding of the developmental needs of the 6-12-year-old child?
- What are some of the sensitive periods of this age range?
- What is the Montessori curriculum area of the "Cultural Subjects,"and why are these content areas so central to the elementary-age child?
- Why does Montessori advocate a social studies curriculum that is the exact opposite of the "expanding horizons" notion of beginning with the child's own city and moving outward towardthe country, continent , and world?
- What are the issues in the Montessori elementary classroom?

This chapter presents an introduction to the Montessori elementary, which is typically defined as classrooms serving children from 6 to 12 years, or from first through fifth grades. In the chapter, I'll lay out some of the basics of all three of the levels that were discussed in relation to the 3-6 level of Montessori: the **theory/philosophy** behind this level of Montessori, the **model**, and **actual classroom practice**. I'll try to describe both the strengths and the weaknesses that I've seen in American elementary Montessori classrooms.

I can still remember vividly many things about my year of Montessori elementary training in Bergamo, a beautiful Northern Italian city. It was an international group of students the year I was there (1970-71!), although the largest group was from the USA. Our classes were held in an old building in the older part of the town. Our lectures were given in Italian, with a sentence-by-sentence translation into English--when a translator was available. My three strongest memories from that year are: the Montessori information itself, the shock of being in a foreign country (I had had only one quarter of Italian before I had left), and close friendships I developed with the other students.

When I returned, I experienced something that has come to be almost a cliche among Montessori elementary teachers--I was the only Montessori elementary "expert." Everyone assumed that I had all the answers, even some of the experienced 3-6 level teachers, who knew more about Montessori teaching than I did. When I returned, there were so few Montessori teachers in California that I felt I knew them all after a year.

MONTESSORI PHILOSOPHY FOR THE ELEMENTARY YEARS

One of the central ideas in Montessori is that the school must adapt to the developmental level--the readiness, the mode of learning, the interests--of the child, not the child to the school. That is, curriculum must be placed in sequence according to the abilities and interests of the child; teaching methods,too, must be governed by child needs and abilities, not by considerations of efficiency. For elementary Montessori teachers, many of whom are former 3-6 teachers, most training programs spend a good deal of time on the difference between the two levels. Here are some of the most important differences: new sensitive periods, and a different conception of motivation.

Sensitive periods

Many of the important sensitive periods described by Montessori for the 3-6 period have faded by age 6. Certainly the young preschooler's interest in small objects and her fascination with movement and order have almost disappeared. One major sensitive period, that of sensitivity to language, has begun to change, but has not yet completely faded out. Montessori's ideas about this period are discussed in detail in the chapter on language curriculum, but her basic idea was that the child has a series of successive interests in different parts of language. Infants attune themselves to their mother's voices; later, they focus their vision on the mouths of the speaker. At two or so, productive language begins, and the child soon moves into an age of nouns, asking the name of every object.

Montessori built upon this interest with her language curriculum. She felt that children should be given the free choice of language materials such as the sandpaper letters and the movable alphabet, in a language-rich environment that was structured enough to allow the child to work on these and other materials without being interrupted. Montessori felt that a child with these opportunities would make the transition to both reading and writing during the late part of the 3-6 period; that is, he would understand the idea of a symbol-sound correspondence, and use this system, typically writing before he reads.

The sensitive period for language for the elementary years is also described as important by Montessori.[1] (See, for example, *Spontaneous Activity in Education,* and *The*

---

[1] From her viewpoint as a sensitive periods theorist, Montessori would feel that children who had not had the experiences of a language-rich environment, materials for working with letters (before the child's hands are capable of writing easily), and the ordered environment to work, would be at a disadvantage in learning to read or write at age six or older. The placement of reading and writing at ages four through six comes not from a desire to speed up children's growth or get them reading early, but from Montessori's conviction that this is the easiest and most appropriate time for this learning.

Montessori Elementary Material.) The child now is much less interested in the simple relationship of sound to symbol; consequently, it is now slightly harder to teach him to read. One part of the sensitive period from early preschool years is an impressive rate of acquisition of new words. This continues strongly into the elementary years. Montessori responds to this through extensive use of both oral and written words in many curriculum areas, but especially in social studies and science. One of the more controversial aspects of the way Montessori classrooms feed this hunger is through use of long words to precisely define parts of plants, animals, etc. Many people think it's the desire to impress on the part of the child or the teacher (or perhaps the pushy parent) that is behind word cards with words like *reticulate* and *echinoderm*, but these are the correct words, which the child learns with ease. Doubters should recall the ability that young children have with the names of dinosaurs or anything else they are interested in.

This sensitivity to language in the elementary years is different from that of the 3-6 child in two other ways. First, there is an interest in the origins of words. Typically, a Montessori elementary teacher giving a presentation involving a new word would give the etymology of the word. Secondly, Montessori theory predicts an interest in the structure of words and language in general. So the work of children in the early elementary includes work on the parts of speech, and on the parts of sentences, much like diagramming sentences.

Montessori theory predicts (and my own teaching experience confirms) that this is a short-term surge of interest. Many six- and seven-year-olds are excited about drawing or pasting the colored shapes (the symbols of the various parts of speech--see Figure 10-1) above words, but very few children age eight or older are interested. The same is true for the work with materials for finding the predicate, subject, etc. Many two-and three-person groups of sixes and sevens will happily cut up sentences written on slips of paper into parts and "diagram" a sentence in this way, a job that bores most eight- and nine-year-olds.

There are several other changes in the sensitive periods of the child in the elementary years. For example, the child in the 3-6 environment has finished with her work on herself--the work of building up her mind and senses through the hormé-driven repetition of exercises. The elementary child is more interested with things outside her classroom, and is no longer content to stay within the classroom walls. In addition to leaving the classroom with field trips, the good Montessori elementary teacher must do his best to bring the world into the classroom. The personality of the teacher becomes more important. The materials on the shelves, speaking to the child's interests, and the personal interaction with the teacher are important in motivating the child to choose and complete her work.

But perhaps the most important sensitive period in the elementary years is the sudden awakening of the imagination. This is linked to the cognitive development of the child, but it is a true sensitive period, a window of opportunity for development. In an environment rich with vivid sources for imagination, the child will grow and learn to use this capacity. Without these opportunities, the facility can atrophy. In addition, the use of imagination-striking lessons can be both a motivating tool, and a way for concepts to become lasting memories of the child. Some of the most important lessons, especially in the early elementary years, take advantage of what Montessori called the "impressionistic" approach to lessons; that is, a lesson or science demonstration designed (through the use of the child's imagination) to make a lasting impression on him.

Figure 10-1

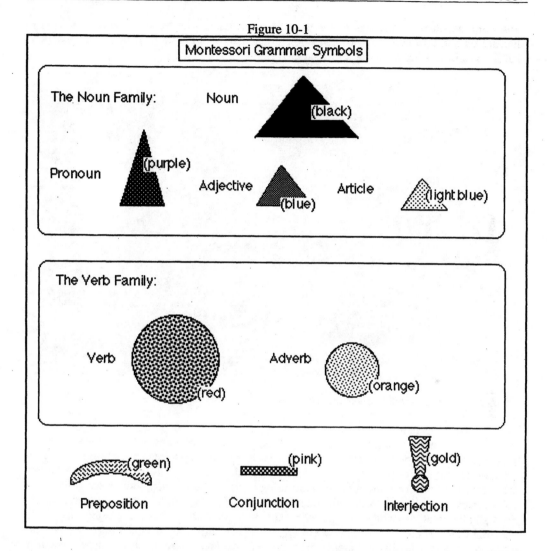

Motivation and Child Choice Vs. Teacher Direction
==

As discussed above, the child in the early elementary years is not as pulled by horme to work. Her motivations are more complex. Certainly, the attractiveness of the materials is a strong motivator. Another is the sensitivity to imagination: this helps account for the popularity of dinosaur and solar system work. The personality of the teacher, however, emerges as a much stronger factor in the elementary classroom. Despite the ideal that some Montessori teachers have--that the work itself will be so attractive that they themselves will fade into unimportance-- the elementary-aged child does notice the teacher, and is conscious of her approval and disapproval.

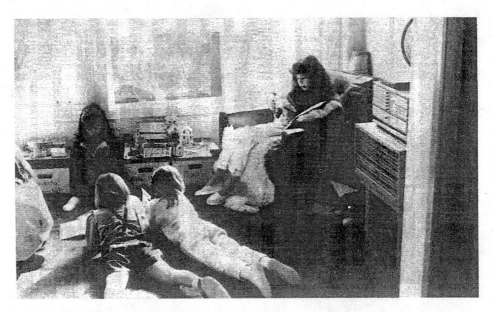

Elementary children in this classroom have chosen quiet reading in the reading corner.

       Another source of motivation is the parents. It is an unfortunate truth that the majority of Montessori schools in the U.S.A. today are private, which means that the majority of children in them are middle-class children whose parents have chosen to pay for Montessori rather than place their child in a free public school. While many of these parents have chosen Montessori out of an understanding of the method, many others see Montessori as a means to accelerate their child's development, or at least their academic learning. To them, "moving at the child's own pace" means, with their child at least, moving faster than the traditional school. In other words, many of the children in elementary Montessori schools come to school with parental expectations that above average learning will occur in every subject area. Sometimes these expectations are quite detailed, including how many minutes or hours of homework per night is appropriate. Sometimes the expectations are inappropriate. I still remember the anger of a father (who had just given his son a calculator for his fifth birthday) when he decided to pull the child from the school after my third refusal to move his son beyond operations with fractions, on into decimals. So it goes.

       The reality in most Montessori elementary schools is that students are usually given a good deal of free choice, with some work (often in math and reading) required on a daily or weekly basis. The way in which the required work is assigned, corrected, and monitored varies a good deal from school to school. Many classrooms move through a variety of strategies in the course of the year. In the beginning, work is primarily teacher-chosen for a good part of the day, with a variety of materials available for the students to choose from during a free choice period. As the class normalizes[1] and each child begins to develop an interest in working on his own projects, the amount of free choice time is increased. Individuals may be monitored with some form of contract, with assignments chosen by student and teacher together, and completion checked on a regular basis. Still later in the year, the teacher may decide that some or all of the students are ready to discontinue the contracts and move into free choice for the entire time. Sometimes teacher-made or commercial achievement tests are used to check overall academic competence.[2]

A final source of motivation for work is normalization. Simply put, if the norm in the classroom, the "thing to do," includes a good bit of self-directed work, then everyone in the classroom will feel motivated to do it. This can be seen most easily in students coming into the classroom later in the year, when normalization of the class has been fairly well established. Sometimes it is subtle, in influencing children to choose a popular work, and thus leading them to learn more about something they had had no previous interest in. It can also lead to raising expectations for the amount or quality of work done. Other times, it can have a more dramatic effect. I still remember teaching a class of early elementary students one winter morning. The class was well normalized, and this particular morning (not due to any particular excellence on my part) everyone seemed to have selected their work and settled in. The classroom was actually unusually quiet, with only a few children talking quietly, the soft click of materials being used, and the scratch of pencils. That morning, a school bus was late, and about 9:30 or so, its arrival could be heard as the children ran noisily down the hall, my three late ones talking quite loudly as they ran to class. Rather than meet them at the doorway with my best stern look, I decided to see what impact the effect of a normalized class at work would have on them, to see how long it would take them to notice that they were the only ones talking and not at work. So I continued where I was, giving an individual presentation to a child, down out of sight on the floor. The three noisy ones came barreling in, still talking in loud voices, glanced around once and stopped as if electroshocked. They looked once again at each other, and then separated to find their work. They had gotten perhaps three steps into the classroom and the whole process had taken less than fifteen seconds. Best of all, I did not have to intervene in any way!

---

[1]Normalization is Montessori's term for the process by which a class and its members become normal--that is, learn to work productively and cooperatively.

[2] Many schools monitor overall academic competence through yearly achievement tests, despite the fairly poor mismatch of the Montessori curriculum to the subject matter of these tests. For example, the elementary Montessori curriculum covers quite a bit of geometry, well beyond the "names of shapes" material, into similarity, congruence, and equivalence work typically covered in late junior high school or second year high school geometry-- remember "angle-side-angle"? Large amounts of other materials-- from physical geography, to plant and animal taxonomy-- are not covered on achievement tests. In addition, some Montessori students are unfamiliar with the whole concept of testing, especially timed tests, so that their performance may not reflect their real abilities. (As can be seen from the research reported in Chapter 14, however, Montessori children generally do quite well on achievement tests.)

THE MONTESSORI MODEL AND PROGRAM FOR ELEMENTARY

There are a number of topics that could be covered to try to give you a sense of what the Montessori model is like and what actually goes on in Montessori elementary classrooms. Other sections of the book give some hints; for example the chapters on math and Practical Life give some hints of curriculum for the older child in these areas. In the chapter on process research, Dr. Pat Felton's research gives us a good snapshot of the daily lives of elementary Montessori students. In this section, I've decided to give the reader a glimpse of the cultural subjects area--the sciences and social studies. This is because these content areas haven't been touched on before in this book, and also because of the uniqueness of these curriculum areas. The social studies areas. in particular play a central role in the Montessori elementary.

Why are the social studies (the "cultural subjects" in Montessori jargon) so central to the elementary curriculum? First of all, they are designed to work with the sensitive period of imagination. From the early science experiments to a story told of humanity's discovery of fire, the content is designed to make an impression on the children's imagination, an impression they are encouraged to communicate in artwork and writing. Secondly, Montessori had ulterior motives in mind, as she often did, in the design of the social studies curriculum. As we will discover, she used this area to bring home to children the fundamental similarities of people all over the earth, rather than bogging the young learners down in a mass of details about how people in other cultures are different from us. More about her ideas in this area can be read in her books, especially *To Educate the Human Potential*, *Formation of Man*, and *Education and Peace*. Let's examine the content of the cultural subjects in more detail. [1]

The best way to conceive of the cultural subjects curriculum is as parallel streams, running from ages 5 or 6 through age 12, each stream representing a curriculum strand. Before we move into the social studies area, consider one other strand from the cultural subjects. A good example is biology, which separates into botany and zoology. From early presentations in the 3-6 classroom on Living-Not Living, the children work on a number of materials designed to sharpen their perceptions of the plants and animals around them. Bird walks, plant walks, trips to the zoo, etc., sharpen and expand their perceptions. At the end of the 3-6 period and during the beginning of the 6-9, children work with cards that isolate one aspect of the plant or animal under study. For example, there are sets of zoology cards for fish, amphibians, reptiles, birds, and mammals. For each of these sets, a representative animal is shown with a simple line drawing. In each line drawing, one aspect of the animal is shown in red, to highlight it and isolate it from the rest. One sets of cards shows the external parts--the child can see the fins of the fish, the wings of the bird, and so on. In later work, the child can learn about the different fins--the caudal, pectoral, and dorsal fins, and more detailed parts of a horse--the fetlocks, withers, and so on. At the same time in zoology, children are sorting colored pictures of the animals into groups-- they learn to sort by those

---

[1] For more information on this (other than taking an elementary Montessori training course), see Tim Seldin and Donna Raymond's book, *The Word in the Palm of Her Hands*, Barrie Press.

that have backbones and those that don't, and then sort within the vertebrates into fish, amphibians, and so on.

One exercise in zoology could be replicated at home or in most traditional classrooms. Simply post a large piece of butcher paper on a wall, and mark off vertical spaces for as many of the kinds of animals as the children have learned. If they know simply invertebrates, and fish through mammals, then make six divisions and label them. A pile of old *National Geographics* and tape and scissors on a nearby table completes the materials. When the children choose this activity, they leaf through the magazines, find a picture of an animal, cut it out and post it in the appropriate place. Be prepared for some heated discussions when they come across the inevitable hard-to-classify cases--the pangolin, the platypus, the lungfish, and why are turtles not invertebrates, teacher?[1]

On the top of this shelf in a classroom for children ages 6-9 years are pictures and examples of the various phyla; on the shelves below are sets of cards and other materials for working with this content.

As the children move through these exercises, they can begin re-classifying the colored pictures on animals. In one exercise, they can sort the animals into groups under header cards that read "Eats Plants," "Eats Animals," or "Eats Plants and Animals." These cards can be turned over to reveal the words herbivore, carnivore, and omnivore. Eventually,

---

[1] I still remember one six-year-old that came out of the room that had this exercise on one of its walls (this school was in a converted house), with his fist in the air, yelling, "The invertebrates are winning!" Perhaps it was a betting pool.

in the 9-12 age group, the children will work their way up to the final classifying exercise, the tree of life. This is simply the basic taxonomy of zoology, shown as a tree with two main trunks. On the left are the chordates, and the non-chordates are on the right. The main trunks show the phyla: on the right, the worms, the echinoderms (starfish), the mollusks, the arthropods, flatworms, sponges, and so on. Important phyla sprout branches--the mollusks have a branch to show that the cephlapods (squids and octopi) are here, and the arthropods branch to show crustaceans, insects, and spiders. Insects is such a complex class, that it is further broken down into the most important orders.

On the chordate side, the vertebrate phylum is subdivided along the main trunk into the fish to mammal sequence of classes so familiar to the child. Each of these groups is broken down in orders--the five types of reptiles[1] , mammals broken down to include the whales and dolphins, and so on. I wish that I could take the space here to go into the wonderful detail and clear educational design that went into the tree of life materials and the reference box--the "Chinese boxes"--that went into it. Each picture shows exactly those features of this animal that make it different from the other groups at that level. For example sharks are different from other fish in four main ways--they have a very different type of scales, producing their rough skin; they have a special, primitive type of gills; they have teeth in rows, so that a broken one is quickly replaced; and their skeletons are cartilage, not true bone. The shark illustration is divided into four parts, with a schematic drawing showing each of these, red color highlighting the important parts. What a study aid-- where were materials like this when I was in school or college? Why are similar things not available for medical students trying to learn anatomy?

In botany, an elaborate set of cards does similar work with plant taxonomy. The flower, for example, is broken down into its parts: the calyx, the corolla, the pistil, and the stamens. Then a new series shows the many varieties of corolla; another series shows the parts of the stamen, and so on.[2]

Before leaving the life sciences and moving on to social studies, one thing needs to be considered. With all of these cards and other materials, new teachers sometimes make the mistake of equating the materials with the curriculum. This is wrong at two levels. First, the material is there for a child more like an encyclopedia than a workbook. That is, it is a reference tool, for use by some of the children in service of their seeking after particular bits of knowledge, not a programmed sequence of learning and tests that every child is expected to go through. Most children will get a presentation on the first few botany card sets, it's

---

[1] Snakes, lizards, turtles and tortoises, alligators and crocodiles, and--the tuatara, a very ancient lizard-type fellow. There will be a quiz for the reader, so don't forget these.

[2] An important article by Pam Lanaro in the *Constructive Triangle* in 1984 deals with a proposed reorganization of the cards with labels that are such a central reference tool in the Montessori elementary classroom, especially in the life science and geography. Following the work on the development of classification skills in children by U.C. Berkeley professor Larry Lowery, she proposes that many of the classic Montessori activities are too complex for the classification abilities of the children . Her article indicates that Montessori has created, as she intended, a scientific pedagogy. I hope that Montessori teachers everywhere will read Pam's article, especially teacher educators, and that they will try the new ideas with students and carefully observe the results.

true. But they always have the option of taking them from the shelf to work or not. And the majority of the cards are there for those children when they have an interest in the subject. The children's natural explorations with real plants or animals are the true focus of the curriculum. The children's observation of plants in or out of the classroom leads them to questions, to new and more precise observations. Having the materials on tap lets the child create his own curriculum without each Montessori elementary teacher having to be an expert in all areas, or without having to turn the child to dry, often poorly organized adult reference books for what she wants to learn. Even when the teacher is giving a short presentation (such as our first flower nomenclature cards described above) the lesson is given around a real flower (usually a hibiscus); the parts are shown and discussed and finally named. Then the cards are brought out as a way that the children can work further with the new names, checking their knowledge, perhaps tracing the pictures and copying the names to make their own books.

Social Studies in the Montessori Elementary

In the social studies, Figure 10-2 shows that there are actually several streams moving in parallel. One interesting Montessori innovation is splitting the geography strand into two: one strand deals with physical geography--the features of the earth, leading eventually to weather, the seasons, and into basic geology. Political geography deals with the location of countries, cities, and so on.

In each of these strands, you can see another Montessori principle that is central to the elementary model--the concept of moving from the whole to the part. In the study of the countries of the world, for example, Montessori starts with the globe. This is a very simple globe; there are no political divisions, no equators or lines of longitude and latitude, no undersea mountains. This globe (first presented in the 3-6 classroom) has blue paint for the oceans and sandpaper for the land. The presentation is equally simple: showing the globe, letting the child touch it, showing him how to turn it, letting him feel the smooth blue parts and the rough tan parts. The teacher talks briefly about how this globe is a model of the earth we live on, though smaller. It has the same shape as the earth. The earth has two kinds of things on it: land and water. The land and water are shown on the globe with, "This is the land; this is the water." The child can then be asked in the second and third periods discussed earlier to identify the land and water. A second globe removes the tactile clue of the sandpaper. A third globe has the continents colored in different colors. The child will be given presentations on the names of these and on the oceans.

The point here is the extreme simplicity, the isolation of difficulty. A second point is that the study of geography starts not with the child's own neighborhood, community, city, county, and state, but with the world. The many variations of this "expanding horizons" curriculum has dominated American social studies for several decades. Montessori, in contrast, shows the world first, and then narrows the focus. Her curriculum says to the child that you are a citizen of the world first, then of a country. No wonder Mussolini closed her schools, and Nazis burned her books.

The next steps in the sequence of political geography link the globe with the continents on it to a world map, with the same color coding of the continents. Nearby in the room are files of pictures for the children to look at (color coded to the continents) showing the many kinds of people, the ways they live, and flora, fauna, and geology of the continents. The puzzle maps are quite popular with the children; they learn to match the continents to paper maps (called control maps), how to assemble the pieces, both in and out of the frame, and eventually how to make their own map of the world. They trace each continent piece onto paper, and color it in with pencils, watercolor, or markers. These are usually objects of great pride.

      Next, the North American continent is singled out for the child's attention, and a new map of this continent is introduced, as always with a link to the known, in this case, the North American piece from the world map. The North American map is divided by country.

Figure 10-2

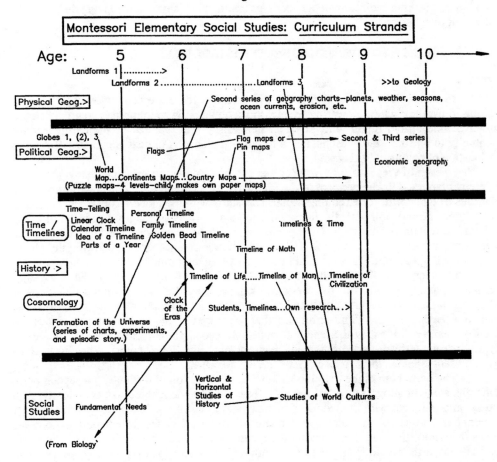

A good example of the Montessori concept of indirect preparation can be pointed out here. The puzzle piece for the USA is a large one in the North America map, perhaps ten inches long and four or five inches wide. The knob for picking up the piece is located at the far right or eastern side. This makes picking up the piece a more challenging task, and calls the child's attention to that particular spot. As is the case with all the countries on each of the continents' maps, the knobs in the puzzles are located not where they would balance the piece, but where the capital of the country is.

Display on Asia in a Montessori elementary classroom.

Still later in the sequence of political geography, the students work with maps with holes drilled in them, for the insertion of tiny flags. These may be small reproductions of the actual flags, or small banners with the names of capitals and countries. In a more advanced version, rivers, other cities, mountains, etc. are named with the small flags. Throughout, you can see that there is an emphasis on the child becoming actively involved with the content of geography through movements--whether making his own set of maps, or trying to label the rivers of the U.S. with small blue flags. Since available research done on Montessori elementary students is so limited, and since achievement tests typically neglect geographic knowledge, we can't be certain that this approach results in lasting greater knowledge of the world and its parts. But given the results of several recent surveys of the knowledge of geography of American school children, it's hard to imagine how this approach could lead to worse results than the systems now in place.

Physical geography can continue with an exercise that might look to a casual observer like making mud pies. Pairs of land forms that are mirror opposites, such as island and lake, bay and cape, and so on, are made by the child out of clay or plastecene. Water from a small pitcher (often tinted blue) is poured in. Many Montessori set-ups for this exercise include a small toy boat, to further emphasize the distinctness of the water and the land. This physical model building is level one of landforms work. A second level makes use of illustrations rather than a three dimensional model. By the time students are using these cards, usually in the early elementary years, they are able to read. The names of the landforms are printed on cards, and students match names to picture cards. The answers are either on the backs of the cards or in a separate book, which the student can get to check her work. At the third level, particular examples of these landforms in the real world are studied. The students work with maps in which the real bays and real islands are highlighted. Even with more advanced landforms--the parts of volcanos, the parts of glaciers, rias, colls, estuaries, and so on, the ideal curricular flow is from real models, to more abstract but general illustrations with matching word cards and matching definitions, to the location of real examples in the world.

As you might imagine, not every child makes his or her way through all of this work. But even the average child in a Montessori classroom has done much more with geography of both kinds than his age-mate in a traditional school.

Social studies proper includes both history and the study of people. Before we plunge into what goes on in the Montessori classroom, recall from your own or your children's schooling, the way that these subjects are approached. As was mentioned earlier, the expanding horizons approach dominates American social studies. Early primary graders learn about their community, its workers, and so on. Then, their city, county, and state are studied; and at this point some history begins, covering the Revolution and the Civil War.

After this, in my opinion, the model breaks down and children are exposed to a bewildering array of U.S. and other history--dinosaurs mingling with George Washington, Thomas Edison with knights in armor. Social studies is then a series of units on different cultures--the Japanese, South America, exports of the United Kingdom, and so on. Could anyone make sense of this much detail, presented in an apparently random order?

Despite its intentions to familiarize the students with other times and other places, it seems to me that the result of this curriculum is to leave a hodgepodge of random facts in the minds of the students who retain anything at all. Brazilian soccer players, side by side with koto drummers from Japan and the Aswan Dam, dance through the minds of children who, in high school, will be unable to locate the Pacific Ocean. The result, as far as trying to build positive attitudes toward the cultures of other peoples, seems likely to me to be a failure. What students seem to retain are just those aspects of culture which they find most outre´and unusual: the high price of beef in Japan, the oddity of traditional costumes, the supposed awful tastes of native dishes made with rotted fish, and so on.

As with the curricular decision to start with the world, Montessori wants to start with the general and move to the particular. So, in social studies, one strand is a series of discussions on what people need. There are commercially available Montessori materials for this activity, but I and many other Montessori teachers prefer to have the fundamental needs of people emerge new from each year's class discussion, so that each year comes up with their own short list. Almost always, food, clothing, shelter, and transportation make the list.

As this discussion moves forward, other things are often added. Although the discussion focuses on the group's own society, examples from other places and times are soon brought in by the students to prove or disprove the universality of needs. One of the most hotly debated needs is defense; many would argue that it is not a fundamental need of people, yet our culture, for one, spends large sums on this. Non-physical needs are also subject to a good deal of debate, yet religion and personal ornamentation seem to be cultural universals. Can you see how this curriculum segment makes good use of the sensitive period for imagination?

This concept of fundamental needs is used throughout the Montessori elementary social studies work as an organizing theme. As students study other ages, they can look to see how these peoples satisfied the same needs we satisfy in our society with the different means at their disposal.

A display of rocks and minerals might be put out in conjunction with stories of the earth's formation.

Another central part of the curriculum is the story of the formation of the universe. Montessori's background in anthropology led her to believe that the imparting of this knowledge was important for all cultures. All teachers must be able to satisfy the need that children have for a myth or story that tells where they and the earth came from. In the Montessori elementary, the story of the formation of the universe, the origins of life, and the evolution of man are told as if around a campfire, in segments.

Each part of the story is illustrated with one of a series of what Montessori called impressionistic charts and experiments. An example of an impressionistic chart would be a picture of the planets swirling out of the proto-sun. These are commercially available, but again, I and many other Montessori teachers prefer to draw our own on the spot to go with each lesson. You should not suppose from this decision that I have any artistic talent whatever. The mere fact that the teacher is making the picture as the talk is being given, and the ability to make the picture dramatic, are the important factors. The best already-made set of charts I have seen were made by an artist-parent (with no Montessori background) drawn in acrylics on black backgrounds.

The experiments that are done are described by Montessori as impressionistic because their aim is to make an impression in the minds of the children, not to be a model or an example of the scientific processes that are being described. In the section of the formation of the universe in which the particles are coming together, the teacher demonstrates this by tearing postage stamp sized pieces of paper and floating them in a large basin of still water. Gradually, by surface tension, these pieces will drift together, forming larger and larger islands of soggy paper. This illustrates the way the particles accreted, forming a clear image in the child's memory. These experiments are presented by the teacher along with the story, so as to strike the imagination of the child as much as possible. Afterwards, materials are made available for the children to replicate the experiment themselves, as often as they would like.

Thus, the story of the formation of the universe and the beginnings of life is conveyed to the child. Another strand has prepared the child, with a lot of preliminary work, to understand the concept of a timeline, the main idea being representing equal lengths of time with equal lengths on the timeline. A material that unites these two strands is the Clock of the Eras shown in Figure 10-3. This is a pair of circles, with clock numerals on each. They show the period of time from the formation of the Earth until the present day as a full 24 hour day.

Figure 10-3

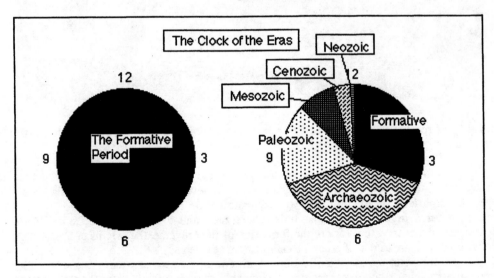

The formative period, including the cooling of the earth, (shown in black,) is the longest one, followed by a period in which life began. The Paleozoic (a blue wedge,) was the period of invertebrates, fish, and amphibians, as well as a great diversity of plant life. The Mesozoic (shown in brown) is the ever-popular age of the dinosaurs. The Cenozoic (shown in green) is the period of the mammals, from the sabre-toothed cats and mastodons to early man. The thinnest sliver at the end, the red Neozoic period, represents the last 1-3 million years in which man, or manlike primates have existed. The child works with a cut-up version of the clock that she can assemble and compare to the completed one.

After this, the seven-year-olds attack a massively detailed timeline of life. This makes use of the same color-coding as the Clock, and shows the eras across the top--the Paleozoic through the Neozoic. The scale is such that the Paleozoic gets several feet, while the Neozoic only a few inches. Under the top line of blue on the timeline in the Paleozoic is a line showing the periods--the Cambrian through the Permian. There is also a line with Montessori's "nickname" for each period, such as "Age of the Trilobites," and so on. The timeline itself is a pageant of animal and plant pictures. Red lines show when a species, such as the trilobites, dominated life. When a red line drops to the bottom of the timeline, such as the line of the armored fishes, it signals extinction.

The presentation of the timeline has several phases, and can take weeks or even months. The children often work with a blank version of the timeline and a container of the same pictures, arranging them in their correct spaces and checking their work against the master timeline. A great deal of tracing of pictures, fossil classifying, dinosaur card games, field trips, and other work springs from the central skeleton of this timeline, which can remain a focus of classroom work for a month or more.

In the same way that the timeline of life is an expansion and intensification of the study of a subset of the time on the clock of the eras, the timeline of man is an amplification of the last few inches of the timeline of life. The timeline of man expands those few inches to another large timeline, and lets the 8- and 9-year-old child study the various early hominids in great detail. As was mentioned earlier, this is a part of the curriculum in which the teacher can use the children's sensitivity to imagination very effectively, having the child try to imagine the evolution in the discovery of fire, from being able to keep a fire going to being able to start one. The work of fundamental needs of people can be brought in here as well.

Finally, the end of the timeline of man is expanded with the timeline of civilizations. This shorter timeline is a permanent reference tool in the 9-12 classroom. It shows nations as horizontal stripes. One can see clearly in this timeline the difference between the empire of Alexander the Great, whose stripe expands to cover many adjacent countries, but lasts in the horizontal direction only a little beyond his own life, and the Roman empire, which not only conquers more territories (vertically) but lasts for hundreds of years. Another example of the kind of thinking that can be engendered with this timeline is to examine what was going on in other countries, such as France and England, during the American Revolution.

The main benefit from the use of timelines is to make the relative lengths of time more concrete to the learner. The use of these, especially the child's active use in constructing her own timelines, is designed to give the child some idea of the relative distances involved in past events. The dinosaurs were a **long** time ago, they know, far back on the timeline of life, while George Washington and the founding of the U.S.A. is only a few inches backwards in time on the third timeline, of civilizations.

To conclude this whole example from social studies, think now of how social studies might be taught and learned in a classroom of 10- or 11-year-olds in Montessori. Rather than being subjected to a whirlwind of units--the Mid West, Japan, Brazil, Micronesia, ancient Greece, knights in armor--a child of 10 who wants to study or is invited to study Brazil in a Montessori classroom is able to do so. She begins with a review of the physical geography of Brazil--what is the country like? How big? What are the rivers, mountains, and bays? What will the climate be? Next, the materials available in the classroom, even if this child hasn't studied them, can provide a good deal of information on the political geography of the country. What are Brazil's neighboring countries? And lastly, the timeline of civilizations can provide information on the historical context. How is it that Brazil uses Portuguese, not Spanish, as its national language?

Taking all of this information as background, our young researcher then begins a study based on the fundamental needs of people. How do the Brazilian people satisfy their need for protein in their diet--given their resources, would beef be more or less expensive than in Japan? How about fish? Given what you know about Brazil's climate and geography, what would be a likely grain for them to grow--wheat or rice? What about clothing and housing? In this way, many of the same facts would be learned that a child in a traditional classroom would learn, but in a different context. What Montessori wants children to see in their study of world cultures is that everywhere in the world, people have the same needs, and that how they satisfy these needs is determined by historical and geographical forces. Culture is explainable; it is understandable; it makes sense in terms of the climate, the ancestry, and so on, of the people being studied. Montessori has as a very important secondary aim for social studies the promotion of a sense of unity in the children, a sense of brotherhood for all nations. This is of course something about which we have no research information, but her ideas make sense and many teachers and parents vouch for their effectiveness in this area.

ISSUES IN MONTESSORI ELEMENTARY

Training

One issue is clearly the provision of good Montessori training for enough teachers to meet the needs of schools at the elementary level. Many people have criticized Montessori elementary training courses. One of the most telling criticisms has been that the programs are not set up efficiently, that is, they do not make use of what is known about effective adult learning. Should these teachers be required to make their own albums, which are compilations of writeups, or should good albums be created and distributed to students for study? (A writeup is a detailed description of how to use a particular Montessori material; there is a sample one shown in Chapter 8.) Some programs have in the past been guilty of distributing science materials that were not correct--the age of the earth keeps being revised upwards, and several reorganizations have taken place in the taxonomy of both plants and animals. The principle of respect for the child requires that the information given out be correct, but the changing of these materials to keep them in line with the latest scientific findings is a big task. This task is made more difficult by the attitudes of competitiveness and even secrecy, rather than cooperation, that exists across training organizations. Another criticism of training programs has been their unwillingness or inability to put Montessori in context through the pointing out of similarities and differences between Montessori and other educational theorists, philosophers, and psychologists.

In addition to these issues, what is the best time structure for the delivery of the approximately 400 contact hours needed for Montessori training? Year-long programs contend with summer-intensive courses here. Another issue is the need for a practicum or internship year. Traditional teacher education programs consider student teaching to be the capstone of their programs and go to great lengths to set up a good experience, with an outstanding lead teacher and supervision from the program. This is not the case for several of the major training traditions. A few lessons given to normalized children, while the lead teacher maintains order in the rest of the room, especially given late in the year, is an experience that can lead to a fool's paradise. Teachers for whom this is the only teaching experience can find themselves in real trouble in the first weeks of school, when children new to Montessori, and those who have been gone all summer, need frequent reminders of ground rules.

These teacher-training issues are related to two other important concerns that affect teacher supply: low salaries and high turn-over. We have little hard research data on how long a trained Montessori teacher stays in the classroom, but 5 to 7 years is probably an optimistic estimate. It's difficult to ask them to do more than this, with salaries typically below that of traditional school teachers, and benefits virtually nonexistent in private Montessori schools.

Two final concerns are university credit for Montessori training, and state teaching credentials. It's an unfortunate fact that relatively few Montessori teacher education programs are located at universities, so that student-teachers are not very likely to receive credit for all their hard work. Some courses offer credit through nearby institutions, but this is not always the ideal solution it may seem. Students need to examine the kind of credit offered very carefully-- is it transferrable or "continuing education" credits? Some of the credit offered for Montessori courses is not only not transferrable, but will not be accepted by the university itself for its own degrees! The fact that some states require state teaching credentials for teachers in private Montessori schools, and some states do not, had led many courses for elementary Montessori training into accepting candidates without state teaching credentials. Especially if this is not clear in the advertising, it can lead students into a year's work in Montessori and then leave them unable to teach.

Public Schools

Perhaps 100 districts in the U.S. today have Montessori programs. Most of these are elementary level, while only a few offer 3-6 level programs. How can a good Montessori program fit into the constraints of a public program? For example, will the program offer a full three year age span, the traditional one year age span, or some compromise? Will there be money for an aide in the classroom, or a parent volunteer? Can class sizes be kept down below 30? Where does the money for materials come from? What about district required achievement tests and state standards? Will substitute teachers have Montessori elementary training? This last seems unlikely, since there are still many districts that have trouble hiring trained teachers, even with the enticement of superior compensation packages. This area will be discussed in more detail in the last chapter, but it is an important one, since it offers Montessori to those who would not be able to afford it in private schools.

Curriculum Development

This is another important issue, especially at the 9-12 level of the elementary. I've already mentioned the tedious task of updating materials when a reorganization of phyla occurs, or new findings change what should be on one of the timelines. But more than this is needed. Because of the way that most of the "standard" Montessori elementary curriculum came to the states, it is very strong in some areas and weak in others. For example, development in life sciences is very strong, although uneven between botany and zoology. But physical sciences is weaker, and earth sciences, especially the more advanced levels, is weak to nonexistent in many classrooms. Second language instruction, which is very much in line with Montessori's overall aims, is by and large made up by each individual course or school. The best programs should publish what they do, and other schools and training programs adopt them. Computers should almost certainly be a part of elementary classes, but other than one book advocating Logo, there is little guidance from the literature or from training centers. Composition and handwriting are typically weak as well.

The attitude of Montessorians toward their curriculum as perfect and complete, unalterable by mere mortals, must change.

Conclusions

I have tried to give some of the Montessori elementary philosophy and some of the actual model--what goes on, including sample pieces of curriculum. There are two points I would like to leave with the reader after this brief overview of the Montessori elementary. First, I would like readers to think about the developmental stages proposed by Jean Piaget, whose work is discussed in detail in the next chapter. In Piaget's theory, most normal Western children make an enormous transition and change in their thinking abilities at around age 11. They move from Piaget's stage of concrete operations to his stage of formal operations. Basically, Piaget thinks there are limits on the abilities of children in logical mathematical thinking before the stage of formal operations. In the stage of concrete operations, children's thinking is not abstract, not determined by premises and logic, but governed by the appearances of the materials before them. They can reason correctly, unlike the earlier preoperational thinkers (from 2 to 7 years approximately), but **only if they can do so concretely, with materials**. The Montessori elementary period, just as much as the 3-6 period, provides a developmentally appropriate environment for the child to grow and learn.

Secondly, I would like the reader to think about the goals not just of Montessori education, but of good education. What is it that you want, that all of us want, for our children in elementary classrooms? There is actually surprisingly good consistency for what we want. We all want students who can express themselves well, who are readers and are excited about reading. We want students who have learned some basics in geography, social studies, and the sciences, and who have a good feeling for the basics of math. Most of us realize how important attitude toward school is for children's future learning. With these common goals in mind, I invite you again to do some observations at a Montessori elementary school.

Summary: In this chapter, the elementary Montessori years, and the "cultural subjects" curriculum area (botany, zoology, social studies, history, geography, and earth sciences) are presented. First, the philosophy of the elementary years is presented: in Montessori the curriculum and teaching methods must "follow the child"; that is, they must fit the developmental nature of the child, rather than outside needs. One area discussed was sensitive periods in the 6- to 12-year-old child. For example, the sensitive period for language is beginning to wane, and the most interesting thing for the child in the period from 6-8 is grammar--parts of speech and sentence analysis, a form of sentence diagramming. A strong new sensitivity is imagination, and so this new ability is to be used a great deal in working with the 6-12 aged child.

The different motivation for work of the 6-12 child is discussed. This child is seldom motivated solely by the attractiveness of the activity, but rather by more social forces. The cultural subjects are then discussed. These content areas are important as a central area for study for the elementary age child--they represent his need to acquire the culture of his group and his need to escape from the classroom out into the real world. Montessori concepts--indirect preparation and isolation of difficulty -- are examined again in the light of such elementary materials as timelines and the puzzle maps. The Montessori idea of using the fundamental needs of humans everywhere, such as food, clothing, and shelter, is presented as a backbone to the Montessori social studies, the study of world culture. Another key is studying world cultures later, when a background of the physical geography, history, and biome of a country can provide details that give explanations for why cultures are different. Thus, the Japanese eat rice because of their ancestry and their climate and growing conditions; we eat bread for the same reasons--ancestry and type of land for agriculture. This unifying idea is designed to unify the study of world cultures, and to lead to the important indirect aim of respect for all peoples.

Issues in the Montessori elementary presented include: training, public Montessori program, and the development of new curriculum.

CHAPTER 11
Piaget And Montessori

Chapter Goals: In this chapter, you will learn:
- The basic components of Piaget's theory of the development of logical-mathematical thinking.
- How do the theories of Piaget and Montessori compare?
- In the view of Piagetian researcher Rheta De Vries, where do the practices differ in Montessori and constructivist (Piagetian) preschools?
- What does the research say about the differences between Montessori and other preschools in Piagetian terms?

PIAGET'S THEORY OF COGNITIVE DEVELOPMENT

Piaget's theories of cognitive development are considered to be among the most important theoretical advances made in child development this century. Despite criticisms about the details and especially the comprehensiveness of his theory (Flavell, 1982, 1985, for example), Piaget's ideas are very important as a theoretical support for much of what goes on in early childhood education classrooms today. Piaget's voluminous writings have covered numerous aspects of the child's development. Even the central, skeletal ideas of his theory cannot be discussed fully here. Ginsberg and Opper (1969) provide a good summary of central portions of his work. A slightly more detailed explanation is offered by Furth (1969) who has also written *Piaget for Teachers* (1970). Specialized sub-theories of Piaget are available in translation, such as *The Child's Conception of Number* (Piaget, 1952), *The Child's Conception of Space* (Piaget and Inhelder, 1956), *The Child's Conception of Geometry* (Piaget, Inhelder, and Szeminsia, 1960), *Play, Dreams and Imitation in Childhood* (Piaget, 1962), and *The Moral Judgement of the Child* (Piaget, 1965).

Piaget's theory is, first of all, a stage theory, in which each stage represents a qualitatively different kind of thinking than the previous stage. Next most important is Piaget's conceptualization of learning as an *active* process. The changes that come about when a child makes the transition from one stage to another are profound, affecting a wide variety of behavior, and these changes are the result of actions that the child has performed. This can be seen as a contrast to a behaviorist theory, in which development is achieved through a gradual accumulation of new bits of behavior. See Figure 11-1.

The first stage, from birth until sometime near the second year, is called the **sensori-motor stage**. Thought is not inferred in the child by his actions; here, the child's actions *are* his thought. The goal-directed activity of the child is the primary object of study. One simple activity, such as reaching toward a rattle, Piaget calls a *scheme*. The infant builds his repertoire of schemes by two methods. By applying the same scheme to a slightly different external object, the child *assimilates* doll-reaching, for example, into his repertoire of schemes as an extension of his rattle-reaching scheme. When the object to be grasped is different enough, the child must *accommodate* his scheme to take into account the difference. So a rattle-grasping scheme is modified to become a bottle-grasping scheme. Assimilation (of new objects into existing schemes) and accommodation (of schemes to fit new objects) are the way the infant expands his repertoire of schemes. This expansion of schemes is the way in which the child constructs his picture of the world. *Equilibration* is the state of balance the child seeks between these two processes. Later, schemes will include thinking about actions and their results, as well as performing them.

One important fact about the world that is learned in the sensori-motor period is that objects do not cease to exist when they are not perceived by the infant. Very young infants will stop reaching for an attractive object when it is hidden. For slightly older infants, there is a period where the child will search for partially hidden objects, but not for completely hidden objects. Next, the infant will be able to find a covered object, but unable to find an object that has been displaced twice. That is, if you hide the object under a cloth, then in full view of the infant, move the object out from under the first cloth and hide it again under a second cloth, the infant persistently looks for it under the first cloth! Finally, at almost the end of the sensori-motor stage, the child will be able to search for an object which has been displaced twice without having to follow the object's course by searching physically in each place successively.[1]

The transition between the sensori-motor and the **preoperational** period is reached by many children at around age two. Although there are many differences between the sensori-motor and preoperational child, one of the most important is that the preoperational child has begun to move along the long path that will lead to formal logical thinking. The preoperational child has the first key to this important achievement: the ability to symbolize things. The first, most important symbol system being mastered by the child at this time is language.

It is important to recognize that Piaget's ideas about the role of language in thinking and in development are one of the ways in which his theories differ most markedly from other theories. For Piaget, language comes after cognitive understanding, and it is possible, even probable, that a developing child might understand a concept and be unable to express her understanding in language. Those stressing the role of language in cognition, such as Vygotsky (1934), assign language a much more central role. For behaviorists, there is no cognitive development to worry about, only behavior, of which language is a very important category. The preoperational period, from two to about seven years of age, is often characterized by the things that children cannot do. The child has increased mobility, language, and a new sense of self. The beginnings of social relations with peers and a reputation of testing

---

[1]This object permanence has attracted quite a bit of research attention. T. G. R. Bower (1974) has claimed that the infants' failure in this task is due to the lack of the concept of insideness, not the permanence of objects, which he believes develops much earlier.

the limits set by parents are also characteristics of this age period. But let's return to the puzzling inabilities of the preoperational child.

Figure 11 - 1

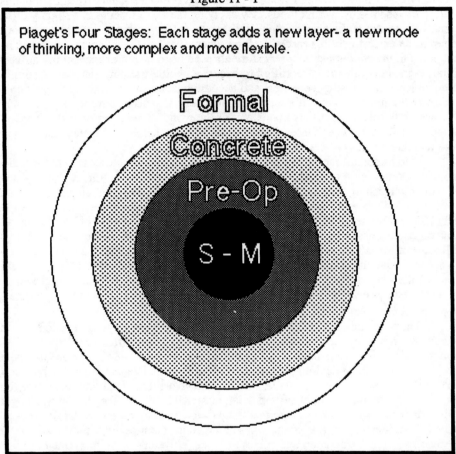

Piaget's Four Stages: Each stage adds a new layer- a new mode of thinking, more complex and more flexible.

Formal

Concrete

Pre-Op

S - M

One area in which the child surprises adults is in *seriation*--putting things in order. Although children can do this well in the preoperational period, further inspection of their ordering skills shows some limitations. For example, when a series of objects differs on two sense dimensions inversely, it is much harder for the child to put in order. (An example from the Montessori classroom is the green set of knobless cylinders, which vary from a tall, thin one to a thick, short one.) Also, children usually have trouble if an object from a seriated array is removed, and the array closed up. Adults and older children can quickly reinsert the removed object into its correct position in the array. Preoperational children can't--they often must re-order the entire set to find out where the one removed piece goes.

A second focus for observing development in the preoperational child is *classification*. Here, the child moves through a series of levels, becoming increasingly able to classify things. Lowery (1974) has given these substages, discussed in detail in relation to the Montessori curriculum in an excellent article by Pamela Lanaro (1984):

1) Inability to classify/Accidental representation (1-3 years)

The child at this substage generates groupings or arrangements, without real forethought.

2)Pre-classification abilities/Resemblance sorting (3-6 years)

The child at this substage can use one-to-one matching. One-to-one matching may be used to classify groups of objects. While the outcome of one-to-one matching is an array of objects correctly grouped by a particular criteria, the process used by the child is different from that used in later substages. The child's pre-classification development begins with color, then dimension, pattern, and size. (Goldman and Levine, 1963)

Figure 11-2
"Traditional" Montessori
Elementary Zoology Chart

Kingdom	Animal Kingdom													
Sub-Kingdom	Invertebrata								Vertebrata					
Phyla	Porifera	Coelentrate	Platyhelm.	Nemathelm.	Annelida	Arthropoda		Mollusca	Echinoderm.	Chordata				
Class					Insecta	Arachneda	Crustacea			Pisces	Amphib.	Reptilia	Aves	Mammalia

Lanaro's (1984) Proposed Reorganization

Kingdom	Animal Kingdom								
Phyla	Porifera	Coelentrate	Platyhelm.	Nemathelm.	Annelida	Arthropoda	Mollusca	Echinoderm.	Chordata

3)Pre-classification abilities/Consistent and exhaustive sorting (6-8 years)
The child can actually sort a group of objects using the same criteria all the way through (consistently) to the end of the group (exhaustively). Figure 11-2 shows an example (Lanaro, 1984) of a revised Montessori elementary zoology material that would require consistent and exhaustive sorting, rather than the traditional Montessori chart that requires the much more difficult horizontal reclassification.

4) True classifying ability/Multiple membership classifying (8-10 years)
At this, the first level of true classifying ability, the child must be able to think about objects as being members of more than one category at a time. For example, triangles in the triangle drawer of the geometry cabinet can be classified into three groups according to the angles they contain: acute, right, and obtuse. Alternatively, they can be classified according to the number of equal sides: scalene, isosceles, or equilateral. The combination of these two groupings gives all of the possible triangles, and gives each of the seven possible triangles its complete name: right scalene, acute isosceles, etc.

Three additional levels exist beyond the age span of interest to us here:
5) True classifying ability/Inclusive classifying (10-12 years)
6) Flexibility in classifying ability/Horizontal reclassifying (12-14 years)
7) Flexibility in classifying/ Hierarchical reclassification (14-16 years)

Figure 11-2 shows how the traditional Montessori elementary material of the zoology classification chart can be reorganized to be appropriate for the 7-9 year olds who typically use it.

A third focus for the preoperational child's development is *conservation*. If a preoperational child agrees that two glasses each contain the same amount of water, then one is poured out into a wide, shallow container, the child will often assert that the amount in the shallow container is less. In Piagetian terms, the child has failed to conserve the amount of liquid across a transformation. Children who are able to conserve know that the shape of the container does not matter. In a test of conservation of number, a conserving child knows that 7 pennies in a closely spaced array are more than 6 widely spread out pennies. Other kinds of conservation include conservation of weight, area, and volume.

The **concrete operational** child--from seven to eleven years old--is able to "conserve" weight, area, liquid and solid volume, and to classify objects by more than one characteristic. But concrete operational thinkers need their concrete objects to "think with".

Formal operational thinkers can work with logic--with premises and deductions. My favorite example of a "test" to distinguish formal from concrete thinkers is the following: Take a ring or a small piece of chalk and then tell the child or group to close their eyes so that they won't see whether or not you have concealed this in your hand. Then write down the statement, "There either is or is not a ring in my hand." Let the subject(s) think about this for a moment, then ask,"Now tell me is that statement true, false, or do you need me to open my hand before you can tell?" Formal thinkers know that the statement is always true, axiomatically true. Concrete thinkers must see what's in your hand to be able to answer.

In the formal operational stage, the child or adult can deal with the verbal logic problems described above. When faced with the task of determining whether the weight of the object, the length of the string, or the starting motion of a pendulum influences its motion, the person at a formal operational level will proceed "scientifically." By holding all other variables constant, he is able to verify the results of the variation in one factor.

These stages represent broad backgrounds for the other cognitive developmental achievements of the child. Moral development, development of concepts of time, space, and number, and so on, are all taking place simultaneously. Piaget's work has been primarily to describe this process and offer a theory of how pieces of this developmental panorama fit together. Others (Bower, 1974) have disputed parts of the theory, and offered new theories to account for the facts of development. Much of the American interest in Piaget has come from educators, who want to facilitate the child's movement through these stages.

ELKIND ON PIAGET AND MONTESSORI

David Elkind (1967) has noted several similarities between Piaget and Montessori. First, their common knowledge of biology, which is the base of both theories of development. Secondly, Elkind notes the common interest in normative development rather than individual differences, at least at the theoretical level. The third similarity he refers to as a genius for empathy with the child. Elkind feels both have such an ability to describe the feelings and mind of a child, that their work has the ring of truth, even without the support of confirmation by repeated empirical validation by controlled experiment.

Elkind sees Piaget and Montessori as agreeing on a key question, the roles of environment and heredity in development. The environment is seen as both providing nourishment for the development of structures and abilities (whose pattern of unfolding is laid down by the genes), and the environment also determines the particular content--language, values, etc., that will fill these completed structures of intellectual capacity. Piaget and Montessori are also seen as agreeing on the futility of attempts to accelerate the child's development beyond his capacity. The Montessori "prepared environment" is intended to allow each child to maximize her capacities, not to push the child beyond them to meet some normative schedule of development.

Lastly, Elkind notes that both Montessori and Piaget have observed in detail the repetitive actions of the young child's motor behavior. Rather than meaningless drudgery, both feel these actions to be crucial for intellectual growth, despite how such repetition would be perceived by older children. Elkind (1967) also cites research evidence for each of these concepts, mostly done under the aegis of confirmation of Piagetian principles, which supports these ideas.

OTHER SIMILARITIES AND CRITIQUES OF MONTESSORI

Montessori's "Four Planes of Education" are similar to Piaget's stages. The first half of the first plane--birth to 3 years--is described by Montessori as being primarily governed by the unconscious needs of the child. The 3 years of Montessori (rather than 2 year-span of Piaget) may be the results of the different populations with which Piaget and Montessori worked. Montessori attributes more abilities to the 3 to 6 year old than does Piaget. Indeed, many of the more advanced exercises in the Children's House Montessori 3-6 classroom with the Sensorial and mathematics materials demand classification and seriation skills which, according to Piaget, should prove difficult for children under 7. Obviously, the various methods used by the Montessori teacher--the isolation of difficulties, the three period lesson, the materials themselves--are effective in teaching children to succeed at these tasks. What is not obvious and is the focus of current research and some controversy in the

Montessori community is what, exactly, the children have learned. That is, have Montessori 5-year-olds (who can perform additions and subtractions with carrying and borrowing correctly) really demonstrated an understanding of place value? The Montessori community is evenly divided on whether this is an important or meaningful question.

Both Montessori and Piaget report a major change in the child at age 6 to 7 years. Their theories come closer together in this --the concrete operational period for Piaget, and the second plane of education for Montessori--and share the idea that the child learns primarily through manipulation of concrete objects.

In addition to their common idea of progress through qualitatively different stages that affect virtually all aspects of a child's thinking, Montessori and Piaget agree that real learning occurs through action--physical manipulation of the environment, rather than passive listening. Also, both are teleological in their ideas about the motivation for learning behavior; the behavior is seen as self-reinforcing, because it facilitates movement toward the goal of development.

RHETA DE VRIES ON PIAGET AND MONTESSORI

The best discussion of the Montessori method from a contemporary Piagetian viewpoint is the chapter on Montessori in Rheta De Vries' *Programs of Early Education: The Constructivist View* (1987 with Lawrence Kohlberg). De Vries reiterates several of the similarities between Piaget and Montessori that were mentioned in previous writings, such as Elkind's (1967) and Chattin-McNichols' (1980). These similarities included:
• The unity of the body and mind; and with this unity, the axiom that the developing organism is not the same as the adult. Further, both saw the progress from childhood to adulthood as a series of qualitatively different stages, undergone in an invariant order.
• The transformation of the child's mental experience through active encounters with the environment. Both saw even very young children as competent and motivated by intrinsic forces, rather than dependent on external rewards.
• A focus on general cognitive development rather than narrow academic skills (against theorists such as Bereiter and Engleman 1966).   Both Montessori and Piaget also see certain kinds of children's actions, especially classifying, seriating, and comparing, as central to this cognitive development.

De Vries goes on to say:

> *Piaget advocated education that is active; Montessori's method is active. Piaget emphasized the importance of experiences with concrete objects, and Montessori's materials are concrete. Piaget stressed the importance of autonomy, and Montessori advocated independence of action and choice. Both emphasized the importance of moral development. Furthermore, in viewing general cognitive as occurring in stages, both agree that this development cannot be taught, and that education must be guided by the way the child thinks and by natural laws of development. (p.263, emphasis in original)*

De Vries goes on to state, however, that it is easy to over-state the degree of similarity between the two. Montessori focused on the development of an educational model; her theoretical understanding of how and why her system worked changed and grew throughout her life, and many of her statements are open to a variety of possible interpretations. Piaget's focus was not on education, and his few general comments in this area are also open to a wide range of possible interpretations.

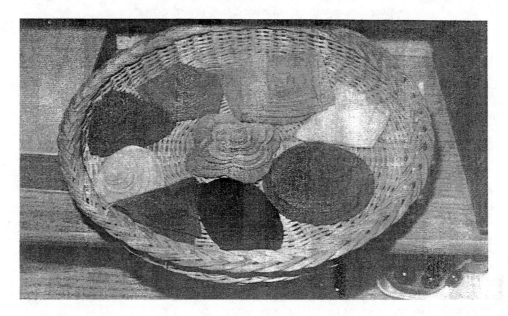

This teacher-made Sensorial material in a 3-6 classroom would engage the child in seriating the felt pieces.

To avoid the possibility in De Vries' book of confusion between the Montessori model and Montessori practices, all discussion is based on Montessori's original writings. This gives her a relatively clear theoretical position to discuss, and is certainly a way to assure that her discussion of Montessori is centered on the main stream of Montessori thought. But it also implies that **practices and our understanding of them have not changed** since Montessori's seminal writing period in the early part of this century. This, I hope, is not entirely correct. Certainly, many Montessori schools have materials in them that were not in early Montessori classes, and the majority of Montessori teacher education programs in the United States require some child development coursework. Our understanding of how and why the Montessori method works continues to grow, fueled especially by developments such as the Teacher's Research Network (see Chapter 15).

In the discussion that follows, I will point out parts of De Vries' discussion in which I think she should examine current practice, rather than Montessori's writings.

De Vries discusses the following areas in which she claims that Montessori theories and practices can be contrasted with constructivist theories:

- exercise of senses vs. exercise of reasoning
- self-correcting vs. open-ended materials
- error-free repetition vs. error-filled experimentation
- work vs. play
- individual vs. collective activity
- obedience vs. autonomy

Let's examine each of these.

Exercise of Senses Vs. Exercise of Reasoning

The first difference De Vries discusses (p. 264 and following) is the focus in Montessori on the "absorbent mind," on the role of the senses in building up knowledge. This part of Montessori's theories echoes the association theories of many early educational philosophers (recall the discussion in the second half of the Sensorial chapter). In her writing about the role of the most basic Sensorial materials, Montessori, especially in her early writings, stressed that the importance of these materials lay in their ability to provide the child with a single clear sensory impression. The child should be taught with a simple lesson--"This is red"-- and a red spool of thread, rather than through a succession of items that have other attributes, such as red trucks, cars, etc.

De Vries says that Montessori's position on the way in which young children learn is more similar to a behaviorist position:

> The external nature of the origin of knowledge which is reflected in the idea of passive sensory absorption is also seen in Montessori's explanation of the sensory process. Like stimulus-response psychologists in the behavioristic tradition, she said that external stimuli act directly upon sense organs, and that the external stimulus activates a motor impulse in a nerve center...
>
> Montessori's theory about the sensory absorption of knowledge as images led her to view the ordinary result of the naturally disordered experience of reality as chaos in the organization of knowledge. She criticized the typical "overstimulating" experience of the young child who must exert great effort to continually correct errors given by the senses. Thus, for Montessori, the educational challenge was to aid the child in organizing

sensations and images. Her goal was to develop an or-
dered mind through regulating the orderliness of experi-
ence." (Pages 264, 265)

De Vries does point out that Montessori described a shift in this model, occurring at approximately three years of age: Montessori called it the move from the unconscious absorbent mind to the conscious absorbent mind. De Vries finds this description of the way children learn and develop to be much more congruent with Piaget's theory than the more passive sensory absorption described for the child from birth to age 3.

Another shift was described by Montessori (and discussed in this book in Chapter 4) at around age six. This "Second Plane of Development" is described by Montessori as/a new level in the child's mental and social growth. De Vries sees this as evidence that Montessori favors a discontinuous model of how children learn, in contrast with Piaget's focus throughout the stages of growth on equilibration.

Self-correcting Vs. Open-ended Materials

De Vries feels that the single-purpose, one right answer nature of the Montessori materials is a practical difference between the Montessori and constructivist classrooms. The constructivist classroom focuses on open-ended materials with many possible right answers. I feel that this position reflects a misunderstanding of what is (or at least what should be) going on in a good Montessori classroom. Even if the discussion is limited to the Sensorial material, surely any good Montessori teacher allows and even encourages the extensions and variations in the use of materials that were discussed in her teacher education program. Wouldn't she be delighted to see a new creative use come from a child, as long as it was not destructive? The brown stair and pink tower are to be used freely, although destructive use and, to a lesser extent, fantasy use are discouraged. Secondly, there are (or, again, there should be) open-ended materials in the Montessori classroom, at the very least in the art area. And lastly, the Montessori program does include some learning that is academic, or in the constructivist terms, cultural, such as learning the names of the numerals, initial sounds, names of the continents, and so on. In these areas, the control of error is provided by the materials rather than having the correction come from the teacher.

The key point here is that while <u>some</u> of the materials, especially those in the Sensorial area like the knobbed cylinders, have one basic way in which they can be used, many other materials can and do get used in a variety of ways. An additional important fact is the number of choices available to a Montessori child, scores of different possible activities. The lower percentage of completely open-ended materials must be seen in this context.

Error-free Repetition Vs. Error-filled Experimentation

Here, De Vries interprets Montessori's observations of children repeating an exercise over and over again differently than Montessorians do. Montessori described this phenomenon and gave it emphasis for two reasons. First, she wanted to stress the powers of concentration of the young child. Secondly, she wanted to stress the internal motivation and process orientation of children, in contrast to the external motivation and product orientation of adults and traditional education. De Vries is concerned that the goal of Montessori teachers is only to produce that repetition; Montessori was saying that this repetition would occur, and that it, like other child-chosen activities, should be respected and not disturbed.

What was more important to Montessori, and thus to Montessori teachers, was the concentration, the attention which a child will give to working on a task that is at just the right level to hold his interest. During some of this period of attention, the child will be making errors and having them corrected by the "control of error," the built-in feedback feature of many Montessori materials. Later, perhaps, she will repeat an activity again and again. If a child were to move directly to error-free repetition, I would predict (and most Montessori teachers would agree with me) that the child was ready to give up that activity soon, and should be introduced to a more challenging one. Of course, with the child's freedom of choice in the classroom, she can go back and repeat exercises again and again. This is a sign to the observant Montessori teacher, often of a need for reassurance, sometimes of an upset in some other aspect of the child's life.

The idea that Montessori children will always be corrected, and thus be prevented from learning from their own errors is a persistent one. The whole notion of the "control of error" revolves around the material, rather than the teacher, providing feedback to the child. (De Vries does admit that Montessori cautions teachers about correcting the child when mistakes are made.) While there is little research on this, a questionnaire study I conducted in 1987 through 1989 examined Montessori teachers' decisions about when to intervene. Over 400 teachers responded, from the U.S., Canada, Haiti, and Trinidad. The most consistent finding of the study (except for the likelihood of intervention when a child was in danger) was the low likelihood reported for intervention when the child has made errors with materials for seriation or classification. On errors of fact, Montessori teachers vary quite a bit in their likelihood of intervention, unlike constructivist teachers, who would typically have no objection to giving correct "cultural" information.

My contention is that quite a bit of error-filled experimentation goes on in Montessori classrooms. In the research section following, this seems to be borne out. Montessori children develop more in their seriating and classifying skills than children in other programs (White, Yussen, and Docherty, 1976). This would not be the case if children were not learning from errors they made.

Work Vs. Play

Montessori's view of the children's free choice of activities in the prepared environment was that this was work, the proper work of the child. Constructivists would call this play, perhaps, but would also value child-chosen activities. More concern from De Vries centers on Montessori's de-emphasis of fantasy, free drawing or painting (unless of real objects), picture puzzles, and so on.

Let's examine these concerns in more detail. Montessori's position on fantasy was primarily an objection to teacher-directed fantasy, as seen in that chapter in this book. The intervention study is important here, although the findings are less broadly supportive of

Montessori: teachers trained by the AMS were significantly less likely to intervene in 11 or 12 specific situations involving fantasy play than those trained by the other large organization, the AMI. Teachers from other training organizations were generally between these two positions. But a criticism based on what Dr. Montessori said misses the point. **All Montessori training organizations advocate art activities in the classroom.** The AMS/ACCESS standards require art, movement, and music methods instruction for all approved courses. It is certainly the case that some, perhaps many, Montessori classrooms could be doing more with art: more different choices, more creative opportunities, and so on. But the same can be said of traditional nursery schools, and of constructivist classrooms--if there were any outside of laboratory school or model program settings.

A more broad problem for the comparison between Montessori and Piaget arises here: there are some 3,000 to 5,000 Montessori classrooms in the U.S. today, with a wide range of teacher preparation, materials, and so on. De Vries has operated a constructivist model laboratory school at the University of Houston for some years; and there are several other model programs in the country. It is difficult to make a comparison between the thousands of diverse Montessori programs, and the very small number of laboratory constructivist schools.

These geometry materials, called the stick box, provide older children with experiences in seriation and classification.

Group games are another area mentioned by De Vries (page 290). There are some of these which are a part of the "orthodox" Montessori classroom, such as the bank game, as well as activities that require more than one child by their nature, such as getting out the million cube, or the tasting bottles. But in general, I would agree with De Vries that far fewer group games such as tag and hide-and-seek occur in   Montessori classrooms than in constructivist classrooms.

Montessori classrooms are certainly not lacking in puzzles. The simpler picture puzzles found in traditional classrooms are often in the 3-6 class at the beginning of the school year, as an activity familiar to most of the new children, and one at which most children can succeed. Later, these puzzles are replaced by more complex puzzles--of a flower, a leaf, or a tree, of continents or countries, and so on. It would be unusual for a Montessori classroom not to have a least ten complex puzzles for the children to work on. (A Montessori teacher's version of Murphy's Law states that the puzzle map of Africa, with its zillions of pieces, is always dumped on the floor by accident just before the end of school on a day when you must leave as early as possible.)

In summary, the distinction of Montessori work and constructivist play may be a real one, at least in some Montessori classrooms. Some Montessori classrooms are rich with art choices, allow fantasy that is not disruptive or dangerous, and offer a number of open-ended materials as well as lots of materials with limited, but more specific uses. Other Montessori classrooms are weaker in art choices, and more limiting of the child's choice when that choice involves fantasy. Whether or not this has long-term consequences is still an unanswered question (see the research section following).   The direction for the "progressive" Montessorians should be to involve their colleagues in open discussion, with the goal of providing what is best for the child.

Individual Vs. Collective Activity

De Vries would agree with Montessori's criticism of the traditional education system as suppressing the social interactions that arise naturally among children. But because of the emphasis in Montessori on individuals interacting with materials, De Vries feels that the constructivist classrooms offer greater opportunities for social interaction--it is a method emphasizing peer interaction. De Vries states:

It would be false to characterize the differences between Montessori and constructivist approaches as a strong contrast between individual vs. collective activity. Montessori's view is compatible with the kind of group feeling, real respect for others, and co-operative interaction we also hold as an aim. (p. 292)

In this case, I feel that perhaps De Vries has been too easy on Montessori schools; there is a need in many classrooms to balance the quiet purposefulness of individuals interacting with their materials with more small group and whole group activities. The research on the effects of Montessori show that verbal-social participation skills, and some other aspects of oral language development are not necessarily (or not consistently) well-developed in Montessori children (see Chapter 14). I think that this may be due to teachers, administrators, and parents attaching a false sense of importance to the Montessori materials themselves--an easy thing to do when you have paid for them! Increasingly, children today come from lives in which very little unstructured peer-play time is allowed them. Children are with other children at ballet, soccer, or Suzuki classes, but these are not play. "Play" at home may be limited to the TV or the video game. If this is the case, then Montessorians must follow the child and allow them to meet their social needs in class.

Obedience Vs. Autonomy

De Vries finds that Montessori and Piaget alike deplored the traditional public school system with its coercive discipline, domination and control of the child's will as a goal, and the idea that the teacher must build the child's mind, rather than the child constructing her mind through experience. But De Vries contrasts Montessori and Piaget's ideas on development in social and moral areas:

> *While Montessori aimed at will as an interior guide, she clearly believed that self-disciplined will meant willing obedience to adults. While believing that character and morality develop through self-discipline rooted in liberty, she outlined methods that seem at least equally rooted in authority.*
>
> *Just as she saw intellectual education from the perspective of sensory psychology, Montessori conceptualized social and moral education in terms of sensory attention and the absorption of order. She believed that customs, morals, religion, and aesthetics are absorbed...*
>
> *Further, she emphasized the importance of directly communicating what is right and what is wrong, as another way of providing the child with order...*
>
> *Montessori did not make a distinction between knowledge as arbitrary or conventional "truths" and sociomoral knowledge requiring cognitive and affective decentering to consider multiple perspectives and construct relations of reciprocity. In contrast with the constructivist view of sociomoral development forged through the fire of interpersonal exchanges in play, Montessori saw sociomoral development in terms of parallel development of will and obedience in work.*
> (page 294)

No one can deny the seminal importance of Piaget's (and later, Kohlberg's) work in the area of the child's moral development. Montessori's theoretical writings in this area are not always consistent or clear. It seems clear that Piaget is correct in his general description of children's increasing decentration[1] and the general role of cognitive development in moral

---

[1] Decentration refers to the process the developing child goes through in becoming increasingly able to take another's viewpoint, and to consider more than one aspect of the situation at a time.

judgements. It is also clear, although in less detail, that children will learn to take others' perspectives from interacting with others. What is not clear is that this is the only way in which they will make progress. Even less clear is exactly how to structure a preschool program so that adults provide exactly the right amount of control to prevent physical and psychological harm, while encouraging the greatest possible degree of autonomy and problem solving among the children.

These girls are interacting socially as they work together on the floor. Many observers don't seem to think such behavior goes on in Montessori classrooms.

The research here is actually stronger in supporting the Montessori program than might be imagined. Stodolsky and Jensen (1969) examined a "permissive," a "school readiness," and a Montessori program by coding episodes of peer interaction. Average numbers of social acts were about the same in each of the three classrooms, and affiliative (social) and cooperative acts were nonsignificantly higher in the Montessori classroom than in the other two. In Mayer's (1973) study of second graders who had been in Montessori, Bank Street, Becker-Engelman, and Weikart cognitive classrooms, the Bank Street and Montessori programs were highest in peer interaction, with no significant differences between these two.

While Montessori classrooms may need to encourage more social interaction, the balance between teacher control and anarchy is easier to write about than to achieve. Classrooms that err on the side of too little control may find negative side effects as well. On the positive side, there are two aspects of Montessori in this area that can be defended.

One is the common practice of including what are called "Grace and Courtesy" lessons in the Practical Life area. This means that very short lessons--from perhaps 15 seconds to a few minutes--are given to children in areas that will help them learn directly the skills needed to get along with others. These range from nose blowing and other aspects of personal hygiene and care, to things like opening and closing a door quietly, and on to the standard repertoire of please, thank you, excuse me, and so on. Many schools extend this with direct teaching of protocols for greeting visitors, offering snacks, table setting, and so on. This may seem like a wonderfully quaint and old-fashioned idea, and unrelated (since it is taught) to the self-constructed knowledge of others that constructivists value. But in fact, we as adults expect these skills in older children and perhaps not all homes are teaching them any more. If we as adults expect these skills, it makes more sense to teach them in short clear lessons than to assume children will somehow absorb them from somewhere. In fact, not only are children able to learn from these lessons, many children delight in them.

While constructivists would downplay the role of these lessons in the child's expanding understanding of social roles and moral behavior, I am not so sure that they are without impact. The rules of politeness have an underlying principle of respect for others. If it is a clear expectation that four-year-olds will say "Excuse me," when they have to walk between two people's closely spaced mats on the floor, most will adapt to that expectation easily. I am not sure that this is "parrot work" and has no impact on the picture of the classroom (and the world) that the child is forming.

A second area that needs examining is Montessori's notion of obedience. Basically, she saw this as a three stage developmental process, with a first stage in which obedience was impossible. (This alone was a step forward in a climate of opinion in which most parents saw any disobedience as willfulness or an attempt to dominate the parents that must be immediately snuffed out.) The second stage is one in which obedience is always possible. The third stage, in which the children obey the adult with joy, is one in which Montessori cautioned the teacher about her immense responsibility in directing the children.

Here, I'm afraid, I not only part company with De Vries in her criticism of this three stage process and the goal of the obedience with joy, but will lose or offend others as well. This notion of obedience is one in which the spiritual side of Montessori and her world view are clearly seen. People who deny the existence of God, feel that it is impossible to enter into a personal relationship with God, or feel that such discussions have no bearing on child development or early education will have trouble understanding Montessori's view on this matter. Such people will not understand how people, including children, can find freedom in obedience to a higher authority. Montessori's point about the third stage of obedience is that the teacher will get such obedience from a child **just to the extent** that she is leading him to his own potential through work. It is more than just a willingness to try what this teacher suggests because she has shown the child interesting things in the past. To the extent that the teacher serves the children's needs, their hunger for development through meaningful activities, to just that extent will she get the joyful obedience Montessori describes. C. S. Lewis defends a theme from the Bible about the husband as head of the family with the observation that what is really said is that the husband is the head to the extent that he is like Christ. The more Christ-like the husband, surely, the less likely he will be to abuse his position as head. This is the model for the Montessori directress--servant leadership.

In this area, I feel compelled to ask the reader to examine Montessori classrooms for herself. Although there are certainly structures--in the environment, the materials, and the teacher's expectations--there is also clearly the goal that children move and act independently. The basics of the environment-- the low, open shelves, the attractive materials-- are enough to encourage most preschool children into independence. It's another, longer story when an older child comes to a Montessori class from a traditional school setting. In my own experience, a period of rigid passivity, waiting for the workbooks or dittos, "yessir, nosir," is followed by a wild and disorganized period in which the newcomer tests the limits of freedom in the classroom. Gradually, in a period usually from 6 weeks to 6 months, the child comes to choose work in the class, to take responsibility for his own learning. Usually the most important force in this transition is the classroom climate, the expectations of the rest of the class that work is worthwhile and interesting. The unfortunate conclusion to all too many of these stories is that the parents are very grateful for the turn around produced in the child and pull him out, back to a "real" school.

Montessori's classroom community--"a family grouping" of ages 3, 4, and 5, with a great deal of free choice, in a context of respect for all--is a very good arena for social and moral development. The Montessori concept of cosmic education, in which each of us is responsible for all of the rest and our planet, provides a clear focus for the support of each child's moral development.

In summary, I feel that I must agree that Dr. Montessori's writings that describe her theory do not compare with the elaborate mathematical models that Piaget and his colleagues have developed over the more than fifty years of research in Geneva and around the world. Montessori's writings are often obscure, and seem even contradictory at times. Her genius lies in the method and materials that she developed, working with children. The rationale that she developed for the success of her methods has some insights, but perhaps also reflects the errors in the psychological and philosophical positions common in those days. If constructivist researchers have shown action, rather than perception, to be the central organizing focus behind the development of knowing in children, the question, it seems to me, is not whether Montessori had guessed this some fifty years ago, but whether Montessori schools should be doing anything differently. In the area of providing materials to work on-- to classify and to seriate, especially-- Montessori classrooms are certainly rich. Despite the criticisms offered by De Vries, Montessori still offers, I feel, the best starting point for the development of the best possible preschool. Those whose orientations are not so exclusively constructivist, such as Bauch and Hsu (1988) have examined the research on Montessori vs. Piagetian perspectives on mathematical learning, and returned a verdict in favor of Montessori. Furthermore, research by Yussen and his colleagues (see below) shows that Montessori preschoolers do better on tests of seriation and classification than children in traditional nursery schools.

RESEARCH ON PIAGETIAN DEVELOPMENT OF MONTESSORI SCHOOL CHILDREN

In his analysis of the concepts and methods of Montessori and Piaget's theories of development, Gardner (1966) has raised the questions of (1) whether the sensori-motor approach of early Montessori training affects the ages at which children move from one Piagetian stage of development to another; and (2) whether the attentional controls developed with Montessori training accelerate the process of decentration. Testing for Piagetian development has its own set of problems, in addition to the general problems associated with research on Montessori, discussed in Chapters 13 and 14.[1]

Kohlberg (1968) reported finding little change in performance on Piagetian tasks of conservation of length and mass, and of transitivity, involving ordering and measuring, among a group of racially integrated low-income and middle-income children participating in a Montessori preschool classroom for one summer. Results of a series of studies by McMorrow, Miezitis, and Rudominer (Miezitis, 1971) confirmed Kohlberg's (1968) findings, using as subjects preschool children of at least normal intelligence from middle- and upper-middle-income families. This series of studies found no significant differences in performance on Piagetian conservation tasks (number, length, and substance) in three groups of children attending (1) an "orthodox" Montessori preschool; (2) a private university-affiliated preschool featuring a child-directed, play-oriented nursery school program; and (3) a regular public kindergarten, with no previous nursery school experience.

In two important new studies in this area, Steven Yussen, at the University of Wisconsin at Madison, has studied the effects of Montessori school experience on areas of Piagetian cognitive development, social cognition, and memory. In his first study, White, Yussen, and Docherty (1976) examined seriation, classification, and conservation skills in Montessori and traditional schools. The groups were further divided into first year and second year students. There were twenty students in each group. The Montessori children were superior in seriation and classification skills, but not in conservation tasks, and there were no differences between the first- and second-year students. The lack of differences in the classification tests was hypothesized to be due to the relatively advanced level of the skills required and the less direct work on this area in the Montessori classroom.

In their 1980 study, Yussen, Mathews, and Knight studied three social cognition tasks: referential communication, speech differentiation, and identifying emotions. There were no differences between the Montessori and traditional nursery school children on any of these tasks. On two tests of memory, there were no differences between the groups on free recall, but the Montessori children were superior on tests in recognition memory. This makes sense in the light of the structure of the three period lesson, in which recognition memory is much more often called for than free recall.

Kohlberg (1968) speculated that the Piaget-based focus upon testing conservation and transitivity might be too narrow for tapping operations of classification and ordering. In addition, he noted that his findings also put in question the adequacy of Montessori's view of cognitive operations as resting directly on sensory experience, a view shared by his protege De Vries. Kohlberg suggested that some additional ordering experiences might be used to supplement the Montessori activities for the development of systems of ordering, number, and conservation.

In research mentioned in her book, De Vries states that when Montessori children and children from a constructivist preschool play a board game without supervision, the Montessori children show significantly more conflict and less conflict resolution (De Vries & Goncu, 1990).

In informal research conducted as a part of the Teacher's Research Network, several teacher-researchers have examined children's understanding of numbers and place value,

---

[1] See Kuhn (1974) for relevant comments on the training for, and testing of, conservation.

with a simple test based on Kamii (1985). Kamii has found that many children as late as second grade fail this test. Teacher-researchers found significant differences favoring Montessori children, when the test was given to children in Montessori and public school programs. The other differences that may exist between the Montessori and public school children, such as socio-economic status, limit the generalizability of these findings. Here is an excellent, important, but simple research project for someone with access to the children in a public Montessori school setting!

In conclusion, research evidence thus far suggests that the general sensory experience and training in Montessori preschools do not affect the acquisition of Piagetian conservation and transitivity, but are more effective than traditional nursery schools for fostering development of seriation and classification skills.

PIAGET IN THE MONTESSORI CLASSROOM

There are some important conclusions for Montessori teachers from an understanding of Piaget's theories. What can Montessori teachers learn from Piaget and from his American followers, such as De Vries?

First, Piaget has indicated some important invariants in human development that should be known to anyone working with young children. Piaget's stages and his ideas of how development occurs--the concept of equilibrium, the idea of constructing knowledge from interaction with the environment, the importance of the social and emotional components of a child's life in his learning-- are all essential for anyone working with young children.

Secondly, Piaget's work provides clear *limits* (rather than goals) for preschool curricula. A science experiment in which one cup of alcohol and one cup of water do not combine to make two cups of mixture, for example, is pointless to a child who does not conserve liquid. Elaborate work with numeration and arithmetic operations seems premature when a child still does not realize that "number" is a system used to determine *more*, rather than length, when he is asked to compare two arrays of objects. The math area is perhaps the one in which Montessori's presentations are most in conflict with what Piagetian theory says the child can meaningfully understand. If second graders are failing a simple test of the understanding of place value, why are we teaching 5-year-olds subtraction with borrowing with four places? Is it that the test being failed is somehow too hard and children really do understand the concept? Is it that Montessori children by virtue of their greater "hands-on" experience are really far ahead in their true understanding of number? Or are we really guilty of pushing too far, too fast, and the children are learning to move objects around in a rote way, without really understanding the concepts underneath? This is an answerable question, one that in my mind is crying out for research.

Lastly, Piaget's idea that active exploration and manipulation of objects are the ways in which children learn seems to validate practices in use in Montessori classrooms for over 70 years. This holds true only if, as Montessori mandated, we actually do allow children to lead us, to let them choose their work from a wide variety offered to them. One way of encouraging development is to induce cognitive conflict. This is brought about by confronting the child with evidence contrary to his non-conserving ideas. The mixed age groups characteristic of Montessori classrooms allow young, non-conserving children to experience this conflict as they work with or observe the older, conserving children.

Summary: In this chapter, we see that Piaget and Montessori, despite different methods and goals, arrive at several similar conclusions about development. Piaget's theories will help teachers understand children, especially some curious limitations of the child on the preoperational and concrete operational stages. The Montessori system, especially if nondestructive exploration with materials is allowed, provides an excellent base for the child to acquire experiences needed to move from one stage to the next. The variety of materials and the mixed age group setting both should facilitate this development. This seems to be true, based on research on seriation and classification, even though Montessori's rationale for the use of the materials, her understanding of the role of the senses, and so on, does not agree with Piaget's.

Rheta De Vries' detailed critique of Montessori from a constructivist viewpoint is discussed; some of her points seem to the author to be well-taken, but many are not, due perhaps to De Vries' reliance on Montessori's writings rather than current classroom practices.

CHAPTER 12
Montessori On Fantasy

Chapter Goals: In this chapter, you will learn:
- Montessori's writings about fantasy play, in comparison to traditional nursery school practices.
- What really goes on in Montessori schools in fantasy play--and what do teachers do to respond?
- What does the research show about Montessori children's use of role play and their creativity?

As we saw in the chapter on the Montessori model, there is a major difference between the most popular forms of preschool--the traditional nursery school--and the next most popular--Montessori schools. An area devoted to fantasy play, called variously the role play, dress-up, or home life area forms an important part of the traditional nursery school, and has no exact counterpart in most Montessori schools. Fantasy play is a major difference between these two programs, despite wide differences among individual schools.

This chapter examines theoretical backing for both sides, clarifies some common misconceptions about Montessori schools in this curriculum area, and makes suggestions for research and practice. In general, this is the area in which there is the largest single disagreement between Montessori and traditional schools, and the area in which Montessori's writings and Montessori practice differ the most. It is also the area in which I have the most discrepant view from the "orthodox" Montessori perspective.

FANTASY PLAY IN TRADITIONAL NURSERY SCHOOLS

The role play area has been accepted as a legitimate part of the curriculum of traditional nursery schools for decades. First of all, it is thought to allow the child to exercise creativity, by using the dress-up material, blocks, furniture, etc., to create an environment of his own devising. Secondly, social roles are practiced in fantasy play. Family roles ("Mommy, Daddy, and Baby") and occupational roles are frequently practiced in this kind of play. The child learns to accommodate his ideas to those of other children, and to play cooperatively.

More recently, the opportunity of the child to engage in fantasy play has been linked to cognitive development. Piaget's description of the development of the semiotic[1] function in the child has led some early childhood educators to link the freedom of the child to engage in symbolic acts such as fantasy play with the development of symbolic reasoning (See, e.g., Lavatelli, 1974). Kohlberg (1968, p. 108) cites unpublished research evidence for the idea that insufficient opportunity for fantasy play may be cause for general cognitive deficit.

---

[1] Related to semantics--the meanings of symbols, especially language.

Others have suggested (Beyer, 1966) that a lack of opportunities for fantasy play might impair social development or creativity in the child.

Although the emphasis on fantasy play was originally in large part a Freudian influence, there seems to be adequate theoretical and practical reasons for its inclusion in traditional nursery schools. Another point to consider is that with the smaller families in today's society, and other social changes, today's children may have less chance to engage in fantasy play with other children (other than at preschool) than in previous generations.

Next, let's examine Montessori's position, bearing in mind the difference between what Dr. Montessori has written and what may be taking place currently in Montessori schools.

MONTESSORI ON FANTASY

Montessori's opposition to fantasy play, in *Spontaneous Activity in Education* (Montessori, 1967) seems to center around representational play structured by the teacher, in the Froebel tradition. She states that imagination is "that spontaneous work of the infant mind by which children attribute desirable characteristics to objects that do not possess them." (p. 256-257) In the same section Montessori criticizes a child who is told that the blocks he has used as horses will now be used to make a village, at the teacher's instigation. She says, "The building of towers and churches with horses brings the mental confusion of the child to its culmination." (page 257)

Montessori's disapproval of this type of fantasy experiences is apparent in her comparison of Froebelian representative fantasy play with the repetition of a child's "baby talk" back to him. (Op. cit., p. 263) She states, "It is one of the careless errors of our day to arrest artificially a stage of development for our amusement..." (Op. cit., pg. 263)

FANTASY PLAY IN MONTESSORI SCHOOLS

The part of the classroom closest to a dress-up area in a Montessori preschool is the Practical Life area. Here children are taught skills having to do with care of their persons (buttoning, zipping, etc.), care of the environment (sweeping, cleaning their tables, etc.), and other skills.

In *The Secret of Childhood,* Montessori (1960, p. 160) indicates how she feels the experiences of children in Montessori preschools differ from those of children in other schools. She apparently feels that toys, rather than scaled-down real implements, can furnish a child with illusions rather than a productive contact with reality. Environments and activities without a particular goal cannot provide the child with an opportunity for real mental concentration.

In *Spontaneous Activity* (p. 264), Montessori states, "It is in living among real possessions of his own ..." that the child will develop to the fullest of all his potentials, including creativity. She strongly criticizes some educators who showed her a model orphanage in which children were pretending to drink tea out of doll-sized cups, when the educators compared this to her exercises of Practical Life.

Despite her criticisms of Froebelian fantasy play for preschoolers, Montessori's method for elementary school includes several sorts of activities involving fantasy play. [1]Montessori was in agreement with the idea of fantasy play, but at an age much later than now suggested by both psychologists and current traditional nursery school practice.

A second part of the differences between Montessori and traditional nursery schools in this area concerns the use of materials, especially the Montessori materials, in the classroom. Each piece of Montessori didactic apparatus has associated with it one or more "presentations," in which a particular way of using the material is demonstrated to the child. Some Montessori teachers will only permit this "correct" use of the apparatus by the child. Other Montessori teachers will permit or encourage the child to find variations on the main theme. That this occurs in many Montessori classrooms is evidenced by the fact that numerous Montessori materials (the latter addition memorization charts, for example) were first devised by Montessori children and later adopted as valid variations by Montessori teachers and the manufacturers of Montessori materials.

Some Montessori teachers will insist that the child demonstrate his knowledge of the "correct" use of a piece of material before allowing the child to experiment. Other teachers will allow any non-destructive use of the materials. What actually happens in both these areas of intervention, and in fantasy play in the Montessori classroom is the subject of two studies.

FANTASY PLAY--HOW COMMON IS IT IN MONTESSORI SCHOOLS?

One of the most important studies on what actually goes on in fantasy play in Montessori schools remains unpublished as of the date of this book. In a study in conjunction with the Teacher's Research Network, undertaken in 1986 and 1987, Martha Torrence studied 97 AMS affiliated Montessori preschools with a questionnaire on fantasy play. This study has limitations in its generalizability due to the restriction of the sample to AMS schools (although teachers were from several training traditions), and to the fact that there was no attempt to see if the responding schools differed in any way from those who did not choose to respond. Finally, these are questionnaire data, which have not been verified by on-

---

[1] *The Montessori Elementary Material* (reprinted 1967, p. 183) lists several groups of interpretive readings. These range from simple sentences describing a single action to paragraphs portraying a complex series of actions and speech. The child is to read and interpret these actions to a group or the whole class, similar to the game of charades. *Science in the Montessori Classroom* is a film from the early 1940's showing the London elementary classroom of Dr. Claude Claremont. Claremont, the translator of *The Absorbent Mind,* was an early adherent of Montessori's, whose classroom would certainly represent orthodoxy in the Montessori method. A box of costumes and a small stage were available in the classroom for the children's use as a regular part of the classroom materials.

site visits. Social desirability may have influenced the responses. Despite these limitations, this study remains our only glimpse into the issues around fantasy in Montessori schools today.

Figure 12-1

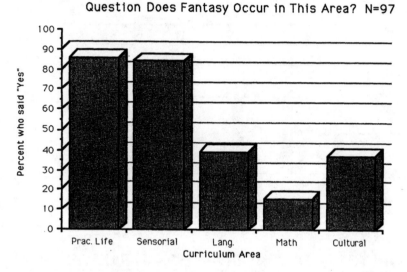

The most important finding is shown in Figure 12-1: The majority of the 97 schools responding did report that they had fantasy play occurring. It appears to happen much more frequently in the Practical Life and Sensorial areas than elsewhere.

Figure 12-2 shows how common various non-Montessori items (frequently used for fantasy play in traditional nursery schools) are in the sample of Montessori schools. In another interesting aspect of the study, Torrance compared the presence of these sorts of materials in schools that were half-day only vs. those that were full-day or child care. In almost every area, the presence of activities such as use of blocks or fantasy play with clay was related to the length of day. So, at least in this sample, the programs with children in them for longer periods of time are more likely to have the more traditional materials used for role play and fantasy play. Finally, Torrance assessed whether the teachers felt that their training programs had prepared them well enough for the issues of fantasy they faced in Montessori schools. Over 45% said that they felt they had not been well-prepared: a strong message to which training program directors need to respond.

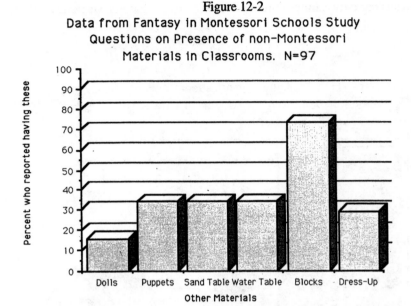

Figure 12-2
Data from Fantasy in Montessori Schools Study
Questions on Presence of non-Montessori
Materials in Classrooms. N=97

MONTESSORI TEACHERS' INTERVENTION IN FANTASY PLAY

In the intervention study that I conducted, several of the questions dealt with teachers' intervention in fantasy situations. For example, the graph below shows the teachers' responses to three situations that I have called "OK" fantasy, in that the three situations are usually covered and legitimatized in Montessori training programs. The three questions are:

- "A child playing the banker in the Bank Game with the golden beads begins to call out softly,"Money! Get your golden money here! I'm the Banker! See me now for changing money!"
- "The child is using the Farm, but rather than applying the labels, she is making each animal move and make its characteristic sounds, such as 'Moo!'"
- "A child makes several constructions with the geometric solids, calling them a silo, a church, and so on."

As you can see from Figure 12-3, there is a good deal of variability in teachers' responses. This is not too surprising when you consider that the sample includes Caribbean and North American Montessori teachers from a wide variety of training traditions. But, in general, there is a tendency to let most of these fantasy behaviors go on; the frequencies of the responses on the left side are higher than those on the right side. The intermediate score of "sometimes" means simply that the teacher would take individual differences into account in deciding when to intervene.

Figure 12-3

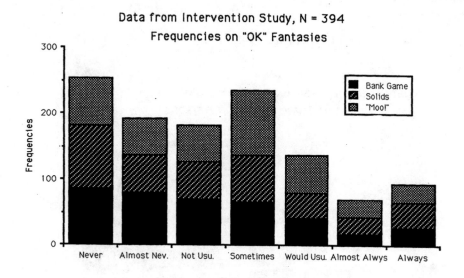

Data from Intervention Study, N = 394
Frequencies on "OK" Fantasies

In Figure 12-4, the three questions were:
- "The child has created an enclosure ('a corral') with the pieces of the long red rods. Some of the smaller rods ('the cattle') are enclosed within."
- "A child has placed the counters from the cards and counters exercise into two groups of 'men' and is preparing to have one group attack another."
- " A child has laid out several of the color sequences from the third box of color tablets. 'This is my beauty parlor,' she says. 'Show me what color you would like your nails done.'"

As you can see, two of these questions show the same general pattern as the last three questions. On making a "corral" and on playing beauty parlor with the color tablets, teachers are both quite variable in their responses, and generally lenient. In the case of the use of counters preparing to "attack," however, it is quite a different story. This item had one of the highest likelihoods of intervention of any, almost as high as questions concerning danger to the children. It's not clear whether the teachers felt that this would lead to noise or disruption, or even danger, or whether this was seen as a gross misuse of materials. In any case, this warlike fantasy would be stopped by almost all teachers.

In Figure 12-5, six questions on fantasy have been grouped together, since they all show similar patterns. The questions include a child claiming to be president of Brazil (because of a flag on her desk), a child tasting the tasting bottles and proclaiming "Good wine!", a child who has constructed the "Fortress of Solitude" out of the broad stair and cube tower, a child who states that she will live in a castle she has just painted, a child playing baker with a rice-pouring activity, and a child who claims a plasticene snake is real. As can be seen, teachers are quite unlikely to intervene (at least in their self-report on themselves) in any of these situations.

Figure 12-4

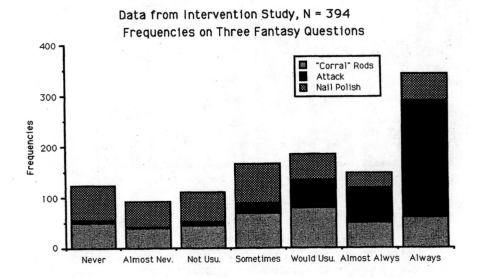

Data from Intervention Study, N = 394
Frequencies on Three Fantasy Questions

In general, then, with the exception of the likely intervention in the planned war with the counters, Montessori teachers seem to be reporting that they do allow fantasy activities to continue. The fantasies mentioned in most training programs are the most likely to be sanctioned. Finally, many training programs need to improve their coverage of this important topic.

Montessori was concerned with the child's contact with reality. Her emphasis was on real activities, on learning the right way to use the Montessori materials, and not encouraging creative dramatic play until after the child is six. Montessori schools, however, report that fantasy play does occur, and most teachers do not intervene in situations such as the ones described above.

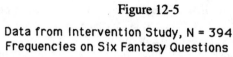

Figure 12-5

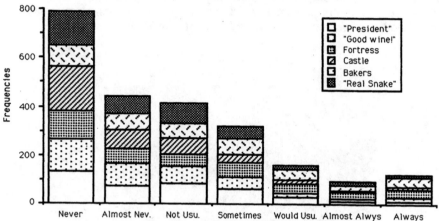

RESEARCH EVIDENCE ON CREATIVITY

Few studies have compared Montessori and traditional nursery school children in a way that allows the difference in the amount of fantasy play in the two programs to be evaluated for its effects. Despite the wide variations in individual programs in both traditional and Montessori classrooms, it is safe to assume that the average Montessori classroom provides fewer opportunities for fantasy play than the average traditional nursery school classroom. If this is true, then perhaps children in Montessori classrooms will show less creativity than those in other classrooms. Despite the difficulty of measuring something as hard to pin down as creativity, some researchers have attempted to look for differences between Montessori and non-Montessori preschoolers.

Dreyer and Rigler (1969) were the first to compare the creativity of Montessori and traditional nursery school children. The two programs are not described in detail, leaving the question of the representatives of the two classrooms, and thus the generalizability of the study, open. Their study compared 14 pairs of 5-year-old white middle class children of above average intelligence attending either a Montessori preschool or a traditional nursery school.

The children were matched on numerous variables, including age, sex, IQ, exposure to the program, and family attitude toward preschool, family values, and family structure. As a measure of creativity, Dreyer and Rigler employed the Torrance Picture Construction Test, a subtest of the Torrance Tests of Creative Thinking. In this nonverbal response test, the child is presented with a blank sheet of paper, a piece of red gummed paper in the shape of a jelly bean, and a pencil. The child is then asked to think up and draw a picture in which the colored paper is an integral part. Performance is assessed by a summed score which takes into account degree of originality, elaboration, activity, and title accuracy. Dreyer and Rigler found that the traditional nursery school children performed significantly better than the Montessori children, although the Montessori children completed the test more quickly. On measures of general cognitive development, the Montessori children were superior.

Puppet theater in a Montessori elementary classroom.

Brophy and Choquette (1973) conducted a study with Montessori children to test the hypothesis that teacher instruction in the "correct" use of the Montessori materials inhibits the children's ability to generate other possible uses for that equipment. This is a measure of divergent production of ideas, a variable often used to measure creativity. Subjects were 31 matched pairs of four- and five-year-olds from middle class homes, attending either of two Montessori or two traditional nursery schools. Creativity was measured by the number of uses that each child could generate for two pieces of Montessori materials and two items familiar to the children (a stuffed toy and a fork). Responses were scored for fluency, flexibility, originality, and elaboration, following Yamamoto's (1964) scoring guidelines. The analyses revealed that Montessori children were superior to traditional nursery school children for both the familiar items and the Montessori apparatus, in terms of the number of uses generated and most of the other measures.

It appears that nonverbal creativity is more affected by the absence of fantasy play than verbal creativity. What about the effects of this curriculum area on general cognitive development? Reviews of research by Miezitis (1974) and Chattin-McNichols (1981) show no consistent advantage of one program over the other. A recent study by Miller and Dyer, (1974) however, shows some differences.

Miller and Dyer's study did not use a matching design, but randomly assigned children to preschool treatment groups. Socioeconomic status, race, age, and family intactness were controlled for. Montessori children showed small but significant advantages over nursery school children in measures of curiosity and some measures of cognitive development. More importantly, Montessori children's gains were, overall, the most lasting.

Again, this research does not speak directly to the effects of fantasy play in the classroom. Even in a well-designed study like Miller and Dyer's, there are too many differences between the two programs to attribute the differences in effects to the presence or absence of fantasy play. It is possible to design a research study that would address the question of the effects of fantasy play. A simple four-classroom design, in which two Montessori and two traditional classes are tested, could be used. One of each of the programs should encourage fantasy play in the usual ways. Children could be tested after a period of exposure to these classrooms on measures of verbal and nonverbal creativity, cognitive development, and the development of symbolic reasoning.

Summary: Fantasy play is included in the curricula of many traditional nursery schools because it is thought to foster creativity and the development of imagination in children. Some early childhood educators have linked fantasy play to the development of symbolic reasoning in the child. Montessori was against teacher-directed representative fantasy play in the Froebelian tradition. She also thought that play with unrealistic toys would lead to problems, such as an inability to distinguish fantasy from reality. This last contention does not seem to have been born out, considering the thousands of children who have had these kinds of experiences in nursery schools.

Research has shown slight advantages in general cognitive development for Montessori children, and slight disadvantages in nonverbal creativity. Research could be done to answer the question of the effects of fantasy play in both programs. The research so far does show that Montessori teachers see fantasy in their classrooms, and that many kinds are reported to be allowed to continue.

Teachers and parents will have to weigh the meagre research evidence and consider whether or not fantasy play might be a worthwhile addition to Montessori classrooms. Montessori school teachers should consider ways in which this kind of activity could be included in the program without detracting from the other areas.

CHAPTER 13
What Actually Happens In Montessori Classrooms: Process Research

Chapter Goals: In this chapter, you will learn:
- The methods used in the most important studies done on Montessori children.
- How do Montessori preschool and elementary school children spend their time in classrooms?
- What are the research findings relating to role play, socialization, and other social development areas for Montessori children?

This chapter begins the discussion of the research that has been done on Montessori so far. First, the most important studies done will be described. The rest of this chapter will focus on process research, the study of what actually goes on in Montessori preschool and elementary classrooms.

THE MILLER AND DYER STUDY

The single most important recent research study of the effects of the Montessori preschools is Miller and Dyer (1975). The study took place in several phases. First, the sample (N = 248) was randomly assigned to one of four preschool treatments.

The sample was composed of approximately 98 percent black children, with mean family incomes of approximately $3,000 (in 1968). There were four school sites, and four replications of each program (Bereiter-Engelmann, traditional, DARCEE, and Montessori), except the Montessori program, for which there were only two replications.

The Bereiter-Engelmann (BE) program is a heavily didactic program with a behavioral orientation; it is the antecedent of the DISTAR program. The DARCEE program is another new program, with some direct teaching and some time for children to use cognitively oriented materials. The TRAD program was based on the usual nursery school practices, and represents a typical HeadStart program.

One of the very few flaws of the Miller and Dyer study was that only two Montessori classrooms were studied. This was because "none of the 22 HeadStart teachers available was qualified for Montessori training," (p.17); two individuals, therefore, were recruited. These teachers substantially differed from the other teachers in age, experience, educational background, race, IQ, and personality variables. Perhaps more importantly, these women, with less experience than the other teachers, were in a summer eight-week training program. The year of Montessori teaching on which the study is based was their internship year, but they were without an experienced head teacher in the classroom as is the usual practice.

In addition to the inexperience of the teachers in contrast to that of the teachers in other programs, it must be remembered that the Montessori program is designed as a three-year program, for the child from ages three to six, not for a single year, as was the case in this study. For these reasons, the results of this study must be interpreted as representing the lower bounds of the effects of Montessori preschool experience.

Figure 13-1

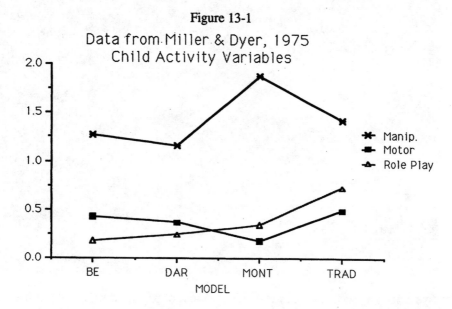

Miller and Dyer first conducted an examination of the different philosophies of the four models, by having the teachers report their agreement with a list of statements derived from each model. This part of their study showed that teachers from the four models did have differing views of the goals and means of preschool education. Next, consultants rated the classrooms on a variety of measures to determine the extent to which the classrooms could be judged to represent the models. Finally, both live and videotaped observations were conducted. This thorough job of assessing the programs, rather than assuming that a program labelled "Montessori" would be an adequate model, is one of the exemplary features of this study.[1]

The four programs are shown on Child Activity Variables in Figure 13-1. The Montessori program, as might have been predicted from Montessori's writings, shows the

---

[1] See, e.g., Carta and Greenwood (1989) on the vagueness of the independent variable in studies in early childhood education.

highest incidence of manipulation of materials. Large motor activities are, however, the least frequent in MONT classrooms. Somewhat surprisingly, MONT is second-ranked (after TRAD) in the amount of role play. Perhaps the fact that the most common comparison is between Montessori and traditional nursery schools has led to the over-generalization that Montessori classrooms are low in role playing. (Another source would be the common confusion on Montessori's own thoughts on this area.) In comparison with academic preschools, Montessori children are, at least in this study, engaging in more role playing. This area--the frequency of role play--is addressed later in summarizing Torrence's (1988) work.

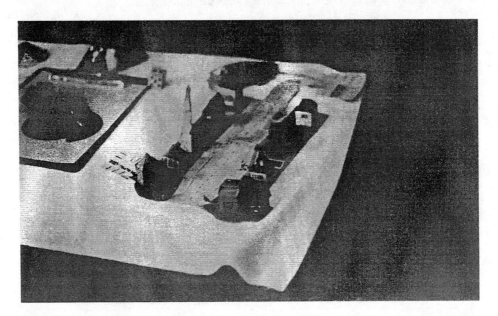

Creative activities, such as constructing a village out of paper, are an important part of both the 3-6 and elementary environments.

Figure 13-2 shows verbal child activities. Again, clear program differences, predictable from the models, can be seen. The BE program has large amounts of verbal recitation, the MONT program moderately large amounts, and low amounts of recitation were recorded for DAR and TRAD. Despite the perception of little social behavior in the Montessori classroom, in fact MONT students are the highest (virtually tied with TRAD) on the amount of conversation recorded. This finding is made more clear in the light of Back's (1977) findings, discussed later.

Figure 13-2

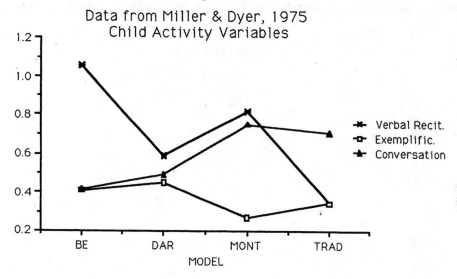

Data from Miller & Dyer, 1975
Child Activity Variables

Figure 13-3

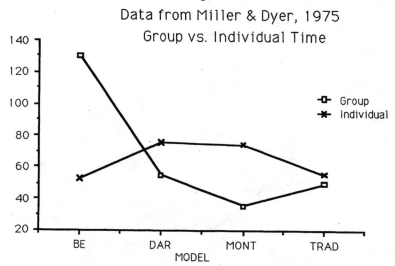

Data from Miller & Dyer, 1975
Group vs. Individual Time

Figure 13-3 shows that BE has by far the most group time, and MONT the least. DAR and MONT share first place in the amount of time alone. In examining teacher behavior, Figure 13-4 shows that BE has by far the highest amount of asking behaviors, and MONT the least, while MONT is the highest in giving information. MONT is the only group in which more giving than asking occurs. Figure 13-5 shows that the behaviorally oriented BE program has large amounts of positive and negative reinforcement occurring.

Surprisingly, at least in terms of common perceptions of Montessori, MONT teachers were providing more positive reinforcement than TRAD teachers, and less negative reinforcement.

Figure 13-4

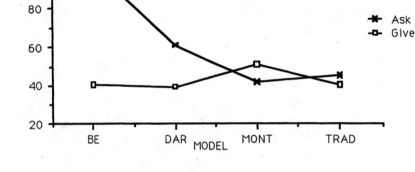

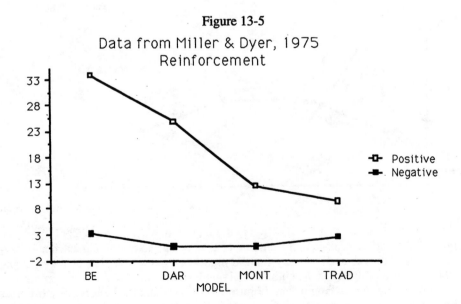

Figure 13-5

In other findings, TRAD was found to be the highest on conduct control, and MONT dramatically lower than other programs in the amount of language imitation requested. (BE was the highest.)

Overall, the observation data from the Miller and Dyer study paint a complex picture. In most areas, Montessori classrooms are as Dr. Montessori described them decades ago: The children work with materials, often individually. The teachers very seldom give large group lessons. Little conduct control is needed from the teachers. But in two areas, these findings contradict the common view of Montessori: role play is not absent, but at a moderate level, in comparison with the other three programs; and conversations are going on at a fairly high rate. This second area, social interactions, was studied in more detail by Back (1977), Reuter and Yunik (1973), by Wirtz (1976), and by Baines and Snortum (1973).[1]

Two children working in parallel at a Montessori school.

SOCIAL INTERACTIONS IN MONTESSORI CLASSROOMS

Back (1977) compared classrooms at each of three schools representing British Infant School and at three more representing Montessori. Her findings in the areas of outcome are presented later. Her observational measures shed some light on social behaviors:

---

[1]Related studies of interest include: Berger (1970), Berliner (1974), Bridges (1927), Foster (1972), Karlson (1972), and Reuter (1973).

> *...British Infant subjects were more likely to engage in social activity (i.e., game playing, conversation, and social interaction) than Montessori subjects (p 25)... (p.83)*
>
> *...of all the variables in the study, the one that best discriminated the two groups was Prepare and/or Clean Up[1]...*
>
> *...[Also differentiating the groups were] Requests Cognitive Information, Seeks Proximity to Adults, and Offers Cognitive Information to Peer. These behaviors characterized the Montessori Ss. (p. 122)*
>
> *...These categories [Seeks Attention and Seeks Attention from Adult] were more characteristic of the British Infant group. (p.122, 123)*
>
> *...The finding that Montessori Ss were high on Ratio of Peer to Adult Interactions appears to be in contradiction with the ANOVA result that the British Infant Ss were more likely to engage in social activity. It should be noted , however, that Social Activity refers to types of activities, while the Ratio of Peer to Adult category refers to persons with whom the child interacts. Thus, Montessori children had a high ratio of peer interaction even though their activity was less play-oriented. (My emphasis.) Apparently, they were more likely to work together in non-social situations. The criticism cited by Miezitis (1972) that Montessori education isolates children from each other was not supported by the findings of this study. Rather, the results tend to support Montessori's (1967) view that work with materials leads to increased self-confidence which eventually results in mature social interaction with children. (page 123)*

These findings are interesting to compare with Reuter and Yunik's 1973 findings. These researchers compared a Montessori preschool with a token economy laboratory preschool and a parent cooperative preschool using traditional nursery school methods. Contrary to their hypotheses, Reuter and Yunik found that it was the token economy classroom that spent the least time in social interaction (16.5%), with the Montessori children spending 25%. The parent cooperative group was not significantly different from either of the other two groups. Also, social interaction increased with age. This finding is confirmed, with some interesting twists, by Wirtz (1976).

Wirtz's study used time-sampling observations to see if there were differences in the amounts of social interaction occurring in the four curriculum areas in the Montessori classroom. Sex and age differences were also examined. As can be seen in Figure 13-6, there are both age and area differences in the uses of the materials. It seems surprising to me that the use of the language area and especially the math area would decrease with age, and that the Practical Life area would increase. While I strongly believe that 5-year-olds should

---

[1] This variable was higher for the Montessori group.

be actively involved in Practical Life activities, my observations and discussions with teachers across the country lead me to think that many classrooms do not offer challenging activities for the older Montessori children. Despite my suspicions, it did not appear to be the case that a greater amount of socialization was going on in the Practical Life area: in Figure 13-7, the rates of social interaction by children using the materials and those "off-task" can be seen.

The only sex difference was that boys interacted significantly more in the math area than girls. Keep this finding in mind in relation to the long-term sex differences in math achievement by Miller and her colleagues, which are reported in Chapter 14.

Figure 13-6

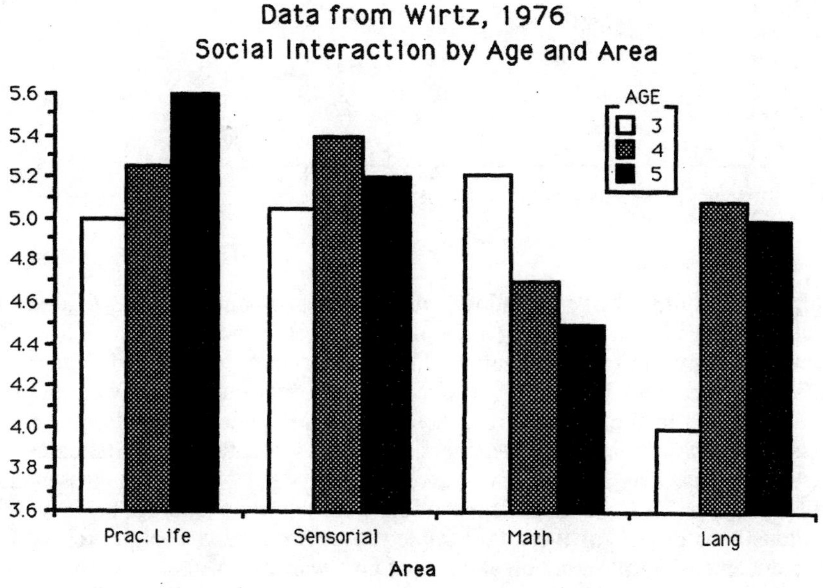

Data from Wirtz, 1976
Social Interaction by Age and Area

Baines and Snortum (1973) examined the behavior of children in a traditional public elementary school and a Montessori elementary classroom, using time sampling methods similar to those of Wirtz. Montessori children (N=8) spent the largest percentage of time (44%) in self-directed study. The traditional school children spent over 90% of their time under direct supervision of the teacher. One of the most interesting findings from Baines and Snortum is that the Montessori children spent sizable amounts of time teaching each other (and being taught).

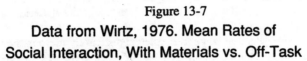

Figure 13-7

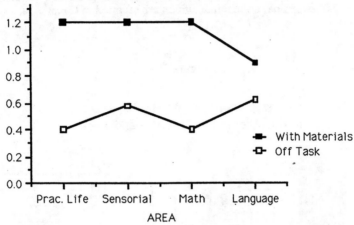

Feldman's (1983) work examined physical movement in the 3-6 and 12-15 Montessori classrooms in Ohio, finding very similar rates of movement. Feltin (1987) documented what occurred in four elementary classes in her dissertation titled, "Independent Learning in Four Montessori Elementary Classrooms." All four classrooms were in private, tuition-charging schools in the Seattle area, thus limiting the generalizability of the study. All four classrooms had experienced teachers with AMS elementary certificates. The observation data are based on six morning observations in each of the four classes during October and November. The age ranges for the four classes were 5-8, 5-10, 8-10, and 9-11. Years of previous Montessori for the total sample ranged from zero to eight years. In the observation of students, the following breakdown of time was observed.

(Percentage of total behaviors shown as decimals, from Feltin, 1983)	
Working Alone **(68 percent)**	
Visual evidence of checklist	.04
with pencil/paper	.34
with manipulatives	.28
aimless	.02
Other Activity Alone **(21 percent)**	
organizing desk/work space	.03
choosing/gathering material	.07

correcting work	.02
misusing materials	.00
being distracted	.03
cleaning up; putting away	.04
leaving the room	.02
Working With Peers (13 percent)	
interactive	.04
parallel	.03
verbal	.02
non-verbal	.04
Talking With Peers (13 percent)	
student-initiated	.04
peer-initiated	.03
sharing ideas activities	.02
seeking help	.00
assisting another	.01
disagreeing	.00
conversing	.03
Talking With Teacher (32 percent)	
teacher-initiated	.04
student-initiated	.06
with assistant	.03
verbal	.07
nonverbal	.02
management	.04
instructional	.05
personal	.01

(147 percent of total time)

The total individual student observed behaviors is over 100 percent since some activities were occurring simultaneously, such as verbal student-initiated instructional interaction with the teacher. Again, the pattern seen here is the familiar one: Montessori children appear to be spending their time as Montessori predicted, moving independently, doing work, talking with each other about both work and social topics, and requiring relatively little conduct control.

Summary: The Montessori environments studied so far have revealed that students are spending relatively little time in whole group instruction. Rather, they move about the classroom, choose their work, work individually, and talk with each other. They do spend significant amounts of time conversing, but a relatively high portion of this is either related to school work or actual peer teaching. Lack of similarity in observation instruments obscures the extent to which this is true at different age levels.

It was seen that more and better research into the processes of Montessori environments is needed. This will become even more clear when the effectiveness of these environments is discussed in the following chapter.

Lastly, some of the ideas about what goes on in Montessori classrooms--such as little social interaction and role play--must be be carefully reexamined. More research is needed here in particular, to examine the extent and depth of role play at various age levels, and to examine social interactions in even greater detail.

CHAPTER 14
The Effects Of Montessori School Experience

Chapter Goals: In this chapter, you will learn:
- What are some of the weaknesses in currently available outcome research on Montessori?
- What are the research findings on the effects of Montessori experience on cognitive, academic, motor development and other areas?
- What are the most important directions for research on Montessori in the future?

This chapter reviews what has been learned about the effects of Montessori schooling on children. Process research, the study of what goes on during the school day, has been covered in the previous chapter; this chapter will be concerned with outcome research. The pattern of results reported and the methodological criticisms offered will, I hope, stimulate more and better research into the effectiveness of Montessori schools. One of the bright spots in the picture of the Montessori movement is the Teacher's Research Network, which is discussed in the final chapter.

In an attempt to clarify and organize a large number of studies, the results are presented in several sections: (1) general verbal intelligence; (2) perceptual, motor, and performance IQ development; (3) academic achievement and school readiness; (4) attention, concentration, resistance to distraction, and impulsiveness; and (5) creativity and motivational factors. A section on methodology and suggestions for future research conclude the chapter.

DESCRIPTIONS OF MAJOR STUDIES

Di Lorenzo (1969) studied the effects of a year prekindergarten school experience on 1,807 low-income children. Again, the majority of the children studied were black. The study was a true experimental design, with stratified random assignment, in eight school districts in New York. Four of the programs were described as early childhood oriented, four as cognitively oriented. Of the four cognitively oriented programs, one (Mt. Vernon) was a Montessori program. The type of training of the teacher and the orientation of the Montessori program were not specified; talking typewriters were used as a supplement to the traditional Montessori curriculum. Three waves of children were tested on measures including the Stanford-Binet IQ test, the Peabody Picture Vocabulary Test, the Illinois Test of Psycholinguistic Abilities, the Learner Self-Concept Test, and the Metropolitan Readiness Test, at the beginning and end of prekindergarten, kindergarten, and first grade years.

The Sands School Project (Banta 1969) was conducted in Cincinnati with 72 black children from lower-middle and lower socioeconomic status (SES) families. These children were placed into four groups: Montessori preschool/Montessori primary school, Montessori preschool/open-classroom primary school, HeadStart/conventional public school, and a no pre-school/conventional school group. Banta (1969) evaluated these children between the ages of five and six on the Cincinnati Autonomy Battery, which includes tests of cognitive style, performance IQ, curiosity, and impulse control. Follow-up studies (Gross, Green, and Clapp 1973; Sciarra and Dorsey 1974) examined 13 similar measures at the end of the second year, interviews with the parents on their feelings about the project at the end of the third year, and achievement test results for the next three years.

Karnes (1969, Karnes, Shwedel, Williams, 1983) compared the effects of five different nine-month nursery school programs (including one Montessori program) for four-year-old black and white children from low-income homes. Her study was followed up, and presents some interesting summary data on the overall effectiveness of various models of preschool education in helping low-income children succeed in public schools.

GENERAL VERBAL INTELLIGENCE

Kohlberg (1968) has reported finding no significant overall changes using alternate forms of the Stanford-Binet intelligence test among children in a Montessori summer Head-Start program enrolling black low-income and white middle-income children. In a year-long Montessori program, however, ten low-income black children studied showed a mean Stanford-Binet IQ increase of 17 points between October and January. The children of average IQ on the first testing increased as much as the children of low IQ. A group of middle-income children in the same class showed a mean increase of 10 IQ points.

Using 14 matched pairs of middle-income children of above-average IQ, Dreyer and Rigler (1969) found that those in a traditional nursery school obtained higher scores on the Peabody Picture Vocabulary Test than those in a Montessori nursery school.

Pendergast (1969) administered the Peabody Picture Vocabulary Test twice, seven months apart, to three groups of upper-middle-income children attending (1) a Montessori nursery school; (2) a conventional nursery school; and (3) no preschool. There were approximately 40 children in each group. There were no significant differences among the groups on Peabody Picture Vocabulary Test performance. The author concluded that the enriched upper-middle-income environment tended to outweigh any effects of special training, and therefore the school programs may have contributed little to the children's developmental needs.

Di Lorenzo (1969) compared the effects of eight, year-long prekindergarten programs longitudinally, as described previously. Post-tests at the end of one year and follow-up testing at the end of kindergarten indicated that pupils in the four cognitively oriented programs, one of which was a Montessori program, surpassed those in the four traditional nursery school programs on Stanford-Binet and Peabody Picture Vocabulary Test scores. The Montessori program (N = 177) was found to be associated with modest but significant gains in Stanford-Binet IQ.

Karnes (1969; Karnes, Shwedel, Williams, 1983) compared the effects of five different nine-month nursery school programs (including one Montessori program) for four-year-old black and white children from low-income homes. She reported that the Montessori program produced lower gains in Stanford-Binet IQ scores than the Karnes Ameliorative Program, which included development of perceptual, attentional, conceptual, and language skills, self-concept and achievement motivation. There were no significant differences among the five groups in Peabody Picture Vocabulary Test gain scores. In a follow-up investigation with the five groups at the end of one year of public school attendance, Karnes found that the Montessori children, particular those on the low IQ range, made continuing IQ gains, suggesting that the program was relatively effective in establishing improved intellectual functioning with children who had initially indicated limited potential. This finding takes on more significance in the light of the long-term effects of Montessori preschool experience reported in the follow-up studies of the Miller and Dyer research (Miller and Bizzell, 1982, 1984). Karnes' long-term follow-up (1985) is also important here.

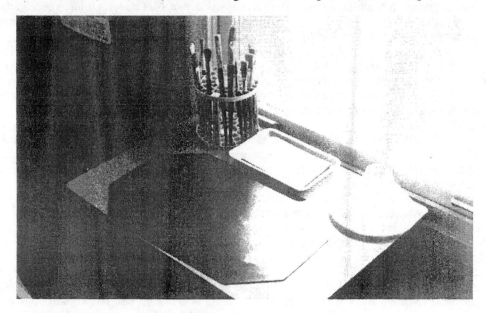

A table near a window set up for painting.

Stodolsky and Karlson (1972) investigated changes in performance on the Stanford-Binet intelligence test over an eight-month span among 29 low-income and 29 middle-income preschool children who were in their first, second, and third years of attendance in a private Montessori school. They found that all the children in their first year of preschool showed a statistically significant gain in Stanford-Binet IQ from pretest to post-test. Children in their second and third years of preschool, however, did not show significant IQ gains.

Stodolsky and Karlson present several possible explanations for these findings. One possible explanation is that gains after first school exposure are due more to rapport and test practice effects than to cognitive growth. Alternatively, the curriculum may not be sufficiently powerful to do more than has been accomplished in the first year of schooling to boost test performance. Additionally, the failure to see change in subsequent years of preschooling on a measure like the Stanford-Binet may be a function of its gross quality; measures sensitive to specific areas emphasized in the curriculum might be necessary to tap the effects of the program.

Fleege, Black, and Rackauskas (1967) matched a group of 21 children from a Montessori classroom with another 21 from a non-Montessori preschool on variables including age, sex, IQ, birth order, SES, and parental education. The two groups were compared on standardized tests (Peabody Picture Vocabulary Test, SRA Primary Mental Abilities) and on ratings by the teacher in eight areas of competence. A second phase compared achievement test scores and teacher ratings of children in elementary grades who had had Montessori, other preschool, or no-preschool experience. In the comparison between the two matched groups, a complex analysis showed superiority of Montessori children on a verbal ability factor. The comparison of teacher ratings showed "no particular adjustment problems peculiar to Montessori trained children." (Fleege, Black, and Rackauskas 1967, p. 54)

Miller and Dyer (1975) also studied changes on several measures of general verbal intelligence after one year of Montessori preschool. Stanford-Binet scores averaged across the whole group rose from two to ten points. The average of the two Montessori classes was a larger gain than the DARCEE or control groups' average gain and slightly less than the gains for the Bereiter-Engelmann or traditional nursery school groups at the end of the preschool year.

Changes from fall to spring on the Peabody Picture Vocabulary Test favored the Montessori group over the traditional nursery school group slightly, and were significantly higher than the control group. Bereiter-Engelmann and DARCEE classrooms gained slightly more than the Montessori classrooms.

The Parallel Sentence Production and Expressive Vocabulary Inventory tests (Stern 1969) were administered to provide a more direct assessment of language skills, especially the mastery of standard English, by this sample. Bereiter-Engelmann classes scored highest, followed by DARCEE, Montessori, traditional, and controls, in that order.

A most interesting finding is the results of Stanford-Binet testing at the end of kindergarten and first and second grades. **The Montessori classrooms, one in Work Spend (a behavior analysis Follow Through program) and one in a regular Louisville elementary school, showed the least decline in IQ scores and had the highest IQ scores at the end of the project.** The high score of the control group was explained by Miller and Dyer as a possible artifact of the background characteristics of the control group, in particular a higher likelihood of family intactness than the experimental groups.

Later follow-up by Miller and Bizzell (1983, 1985) and Karnes (Karnes, Shwedel, Williams, 1983) indicates that this trend continues, at least until the children are in tenth grade. The Montessori group retained its superiority on Stanford-Binet test scores over the other programs at a follow-up testing. The most significant effects are on math scores for males. Differential drop-out rates or other artifacts do not account for this difference. This raises a most interesting question: What aspects of the one year Montessori program could be affecting math scores in 10th graders? Clearly, content taught to the four year olds is not relevant. Among the most likely mediating variables are self-esteem, self-confidence, or attitudinal changes.

The Sands School Project tested black, lower SES children on a subtest of the Wechsler Preschool Skills Inventory that required them to repeat sentences back to the examiner. Nonsignificant differences favored the Montessori preschool and primary group and the Montessori preschool/ open-classroom group next; the no-preschool group had the lowest scores.

In conclusion, these findings suggest that Montessori preschool, over a period of approximately one year, has positive short-term effects upon general intelligence, as measured by tests that are heavily based on verbal performance, such as the Stanford-Binet. The Montessori program compares favorably with traditional preschools, and is less effective (in short-term effects) than academic programs such as Bereiter-Engelmann or the Karnes Ameliorative Program. Gains, however, appear to be more resistant to decline over time; this may be due to changes in distractibility, or other attitudinal or motivational characteristics.

PERCEPTUAL, MOTOR, AND PERFORMANCE IQ DEVELOPMENT

Pendergast (1969) administered the Frostig Developmental Tests of Visual Perception twice, seven months apart, to upper-middle-income children (1) in a Montessori nursery school; (2) in a conventional nursery school; and (3) to children with no preschool experience. This study was done in order to evaluate eye-hand coordination and visual perception skills. Pendergast found that the Montessori children showed significantly greater gains in eye-hand coordination than those who attended the conventional nursery school. In figure-ground perception and position in space skills, there were nonsignificant gains in favor of the Montessori children.

Berger (1969, in Miezitis 1971) conducted a longitudinal comparative assessment of 93 black and Puerto Rican three- and four-year-olds enrolled in HeadStart Montessori programs and conventional preschool programs. On an experimental test battery of perceptual-conceptual functioning, significant differences in favor of the Montessori children were found only on the perceptual measures, and the pro-Montessori trend was most salient for the poor perceptual achievers.

Stodolsky and Karlson (1972) examined changes in scores on selected performance scales of both the Wechsler Preschool and Primary Scale of intelligence and the Merrill-Palmer Scale of Mental Tests, among 29 low-income and 29 middle-income preschool children. These children were in their first, second, and third years of attendance in a private Montessori nursery school. Results indicated that, in general, the Montessori curriculum appeared to be effective over a period of two years in nurturing continuing development in children in the areas of visual-motor integration, matching and sorting skills, and psychomotor skills.

The Sands School Project (Banta 1969) tested children with preschool and primary Montessori experience against control groups with and without a non-Montessori preschool year. The Montessori/Montessori group, Montessori/open classroom group, control with preschool group, and the no-preschool group finished in this order on all tests. The difference in the scores was significant at $p < .01$ for a test that involved matching two appropriate objects out of three objects. Scores on Banta's (1970) Early Childhood Embedded Figures Test (ECEFT) were significantly different in the order given above at p. .01.

No significant program or experimental versus control group differences on the ECEFT (Banta, 1970) were found by Miller and Dyer (1975).

In conclusion, the evidence suggests that the Montessori method is effective in nurturing development in the areas of visual-motor coordination and integration, matching appropriate objects, and visual-perceptual ability, but of uncertain effectiveness in developing the ability to disembed figures from their contexts. This cognitive style may not be affected by the Montessori school experience; or only some Montessori children's experience may have an impact on figure-ground perception. This is an area for future research, as is the whole question of the relationship of Montessori school experience and cognitive styles.

ACADEMIC ACHIEVEMENT AND SCHOOL READINESS

Bereiter (1967) conducted an experimental comparison of the effects of the Montessori method (N = 17) and of the Bereiter-Engelmann method of direct verbal instruction (N = 18) among upper-middle-income children ranging in age from three years, ten months to four years, ten months. The children given the Bereiter-Engelmann training were drawn from the waiting list of the Montessori school, and thus were assumed to be similar to the Montessori group in SES and other home background factors. The Montessori group had attended school one full year whereas the direct verbal instruction group had not. Montessori "instruction," in Bereiter's terms, was for two hours daily and included training in verbal reasoning, reading, arithmetic, printing, and experimental science. The measure of academic achievement employed was the Wide Range Achievement Test, administered six weeks after the beginning of instruction and again at the end of the school year. Results showed that the direct verbal instruction group performed significantly better than the Montessori-trained group in reading, spelling, and arithmetic. This echoes the short-term effectiveness of the Bereiter-Engelmann program found in Miller and Dyer (1975). It's unfortunate that Bereiter did not follow up this study to see if long-term results would also favor his program.

In Di Lorenzo's (1969) study it was found that children attending highly structured, cognitively oriented language prekindergarten programs--including one Montessori classroom--performed better on the Metropolitan Readiness Test at the end of kindergarten than children in traditional nursery school programs. The children in the cognitive programs also performed better on the Metropolitan Achievement Test at the end of first grade.

Karnes (1969) found that four-year-olds attending a Karnes Ameliorative Program (development of perceptual, attention, conceptual, and language skills, self-concept, and achievement motivation) or a Direct Verbal Instruction program (Bereiter-Engelmann) showed higher gains on the Metropolitan Number Readiness Test than a group of children attending a Montessori program.

Figure 14-1

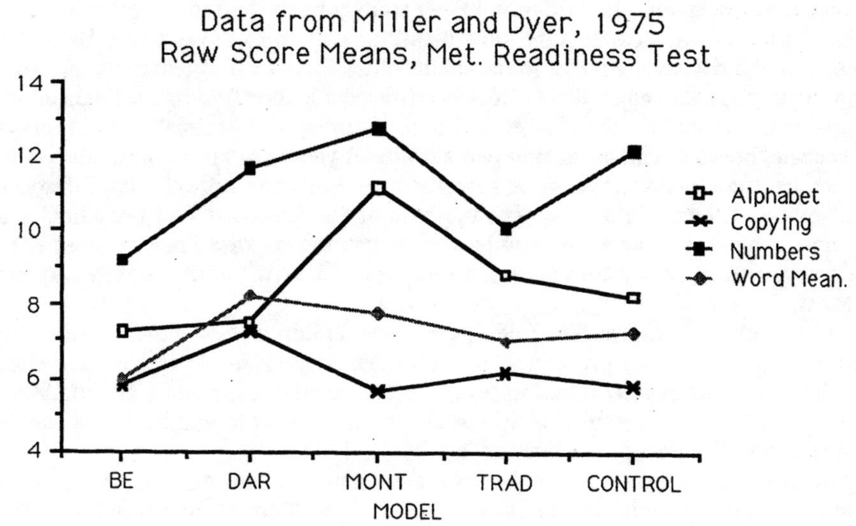

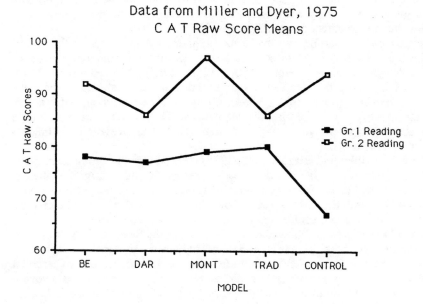

Data from Miller and Dyer, 1975
Raw Score Means, Met. Readiness Test
14
12
10
8
6
4
BE
DAR
MONT
TRAD
CONTROL
MODEL
Alphabet
Copying
Numbers
Word Mean.

Figure 14-2

Data from Miller and Dyer, 1975
C A T Raw Score Means
100
90
80
70
60
C A T Raw Scores
BE
DAR
MONT
TRAD
CONTROL
MODEL
Gr. 1 Reading
Gr. 2 Reading

The more recently published long-term follow-up of Karnes' research (1985) is very important, since it is, along with the Miller and Dyer study, one of the few long-term studies of the effects of Montessori. The results show a similar pattern to those found by Miller, with the exception of a delayed decrease in the scores of the Bereiter-Englemann and Karnes programs in the early school years. This difference from the Miller findings reflects an important difference in the studies: the Karnes and Bereiter preschool groups (but not others) were given special "booster" classes during two additional years. Karnes comments on the "sleeper" effect that the Montessori program seems to have, and offers attentional differences as a possible reason. Overall, in a composite measure of the effects of four preschool programs on a wide range of measures, the **Montessori program was rated as the most effective in producing long-term school success, ahead of the Karnes and behaviorally oriented programs.**

Fleege, Black, and Rackauskas (1967) compared children (N = 124) in public and private school from Montessori preschool, non-Montessori preschool, and no-preschool background. Teachers rated the children in several areas on an experimental questionnaire. Montessori children were rated significantly superior on interest in learning, independence, interpersonal relations, leadership, and learning ability.

Figure 14-1 shows the results of the program versus control group comparisons in the Miller and Dyer (1975) study for scores on subtests of the Metropolitan Readiness Test. The Montessori children appear superior to the other groups in tests of numbers and alphabet knowledge, similar to controls in a test of copying, and intermediate in a test of word meanings. On the California Achievement Test administered at the end of grades one and two, an interesting pattern emerges. The preschool vs. control difference was the only significant one at the end of grade one. But by grade two, the MONT and Control groups have risen dramatically, in relation to the others' scores (Figure 14-2).

Montessori children, particularly males, had higher reading scores at the end of grade two, as shown in Figure 14-2. Montessori theorized that there are sensitive periods for several areas of development, among them reading. Elliott (1967) reviewed a series of research studies on reading and concluded that "...current research has substantiated the value of an earlier start in reading" (earlier than grade 1), placing it between the age of 4 and 5, which is within the sensitive period theorized by Montessori. Thus, most reading principles involving the sensitive period are similar and consistent with current research findings of contemporary reading specialists.

The follow-up (Miller and Bizzell, 1983, 1985) showed that the Montessori group maintained statistically significant differences in reading and math, and nonsignificant superiority on all other tests. Miller and Bizzell elaborately analyzed the drop-out patterns among the groups and other possible spurious causes of this result, and concluded that the Montessori program itself was responsible for the achievement test superiority.

Sciarra and Dorsey (1974) followed up the children in the Sands School Project on the Montessori Achievement Test. This is an important study as it represents one of the few reported empirical studies on the effects of Montessori elementary school experience. Because the children ranged in age from eight to almost ten years, age was used as a covariate to adjust the scores. The use of analysis of covariance (see Cronbach et al. 1977), the small number of subjects, and the possibility of differential attrition by groups all suggest caution in the interpretation of the results. The authors conclude that continued experience in this Montessori system increases the benefits of preschool exposure. This is interesting in the context of the Miller and Dyer (1975) findings. Perhaps the most important conclusion from this area is that the effects of Montessori elementary school should be investigated in more detail.

Dawson, in an unpublished Master's thesis (1988), examined the academic performance of public elementary Montessori school students by race. This revealing study showed that the Montessori magnet schools in Houston were extremely effective for children of all races, but especially for Hispanics. In all cases, class means for achievement were above district norms. This was the case even though another magnet program for gifted students "siphoned off" some of the brightest students. (Dawson, 1988)

Figure 14-3

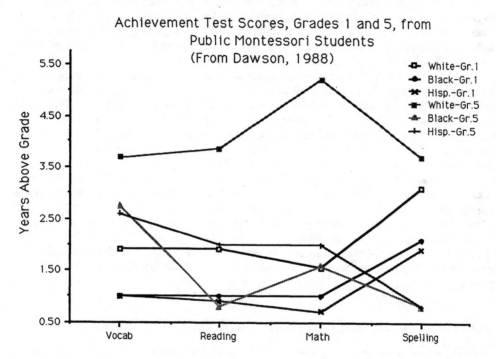

Achievement Test Scores, Grades 1 and 5, from Public Montessori Students (From Dawson, 1988)

Duax (1989) examined the performance of children in a Milwaukee public Montessori program. His findings were very similar to Dawson's: 84% of the graduates are above the 50th percentile on achievement as measured by standardized tests. More importantly, to my mind, is the fact that only one student did not score at or above the average score.

In addition, his teacher survey data showed that Montessori graduates in middle school had higher scores on the following:

- "use basic skills necessary to survive in middle school"
- " be responsible and can be counted on"
- " show enthusiasm for class topics"
- " be individualistic and not afraid to be different"
- " exhibit multicultural awareness"

Takacs and Clifford (1988) report on a sample of graduates from the Cleveland public Montessori program. In the Reading subtest of the California Achievement Test, the Montessori group had higher scores: 62nd percentile vs. 48th percentile for a matched comparison group. On a teacher survey form, again several significant differences were found in areas such as Pursuit of a Task beyond the Minimum.

In an intriguing study, graduates of the Franciscan Earth school in Portland, Oregon, were asked about their occupational choice: Montessori graduates preferred investigative jobs (such as botanist or computer programmer) rather than social jobs (teacher, social worker). (Glenn, 1989) This study also reported that Montessori graduates were, "more guarded in response, more critical of others, and less freely expressive," on the Children's Personality Questionnaire. All results were in the normal range.

A most important final area of research that needs continued investigation is whether the Montessori environment has any impact on the understanding of math concepts, such as subtraction. Working from Kamii's researches in this area (1985), Baker (1988), and a variety of Teacher's Research Network members have attacked this problem, with some findings indicating a difference, and others not. Instrumentation is clearly an issue here. The entire nature of the Montessori math curriculum area and the role of manipulatives in general can be investigated here. See also Bauch and Hsu, 1988.

In conclusion, studies that have focused on the effects of Montessori training upon measures of academic achievement and school readiness suggest that preschool programs that emphasize direct training in academic areas and in language skills produce greater gains on these types of measures than Montessori programs; but in turn, Montessori training appears to produce greater gain on these types of measures than traditional nursery schools. The gains produced by Montessori preschools are less likely to deteriorate over time than those of other programs, and may not fade out at all if the Montessori program is continued beyond preschool.

ATTENTION, CONCENTRATION, DISTRACTIBILITY, AND IMPULSIVITY

In summarizing his observations on Montessori, Gardner (1966) has noted that the development of attentional controls seems to be particularly encouraged in the Montessori environment, and has called for research in this area.

Judge (1974) compared four Montessori classrooms, four classrooms using the *Science-A-Process Approach* method, and two classrooms described as non-Montessori/non-*Science-A-Process Approach*, on the Science Process Instrument, which tests competence in observation. Montessori children did not differ from the *Science-A-Process-Approach* group, although both differed from the two control classrooms. The Montessori classrooms showed large variability due to the teacher factor. The Montessori school experience, then, was found to be as effective as a program specifically designed to increase observational skills.

Kohlberg (1968) has reported finding an increase in ratings of distractibility in the test situation in a permissive classroom, as compared to students receiving Montessori experience during summer-long preschool intervention programs. A drop in IQ was found to be correlated with increased distractibility; behavioral observations in the classroom supported the distractibility rating data. In the year-long programs, he found that an IQ increase shown by low-income children receiving Montessori preschool training was matched by an increase in ability to attend.

McCormick and Schnobrich (1971) administered, as an addition to the regular Montessori training, a seven-month program of perceptual-motor training which stressed control of impulsiveness and development of attentional skills to 25 children ranging in age from three to five years attending a morning Montessori preschool. The children in the afternoon Montessori preschool class, not receiving the special training program, were the controls. Measures of attention, administered pre- and post-preschool, were the auditory-vocal sequencing and the visual-motor sequencing subtests of the Illinois Test of Psycholinguistic Ability. Results showed greater gains on both measures for the group receiving the training. The authors concluded that perceptual-motor training can improve the ability to concentrate visually and auditorily, and that this training would be a useful addition to the present Montessori curriculum because "Montessori training itself does not seem to result in such improvement." (McCormick and Schnobrich, 1971)

In a series of studies, McMorrow, Miezitis, and Rudominer (Miezitis 1971) found that middle- and upper-income children attending either a child-centered, play-oriented nursery school or a regular public kindergarten were more impulsive, as measured by Kagan's Matching Familiar Figures Test, than a matched group of children attending a Montessori nursery school. The children (N = 80) in the study, ranging in age from five to six years, were matched for age, sex, and SES, and were of at least average intelligence.

Berger (1969, in Miezitis 1971) in a longitudinal assessment of 93 black and Puerto Rican three- and four-year olds enrolled in HeadStart Montessori programs and conventional preschool programs, found that motor impulse control scores from the Cincinnati Autonomy Test Battery consistently favored the Montessori children.

Banta (1969) found nonsignificant differences that favored control groups over the Montessori preschool groups on the "Draw-a-Line Slowly" test of impulse control, the only negative finding in the original assessment of the Sands School Project.

Miller and Dyer (1975) made use of Banta's (1970) Replacement Puzzle Test, in which each child is rated on items that can be summed to produce scores on aggression, verbal-social participation, timidity, independence, and achievement motivation. Also, the Face Sheet of the Stanford-Binet and the Face Sheet of the Preschool Inventory were used. In these, the tester rates the child on factors that may influence performance, such as motivation, confidence, etc.

On the aggression and verbal-social participation ratings of the Behavior Inventory administered after one year, the Montessori program (along with the Bereiter-Engelmann program) produced lower gains than DARCEE. Bereiter-Engelmann, DARCEE, and Montessori programs reduced the aggression rating more than the traditional program. Comparison to the control groups during this first year were not made. DARCEE and, to a lesser extent, the traditional program were favored over Montessori on verbal-social participation. For both of these variables, differences favored all groups over controls.

Montessori classrooms were consistently first or second highest in aggression ratings, with a high score representing low aggression. Overall, Montessori children were less distractible, more persistent, more verbal-social, but not consistently less aggressive than controls. Montessori programs did not differ significantly from the other preschool programs in fostering persistence, resistance to distraction, but Montessori programs were less successful than traditional and DARCEE at fostering verbal-social participation. This finding offers partial support for my hypothesized explanation for the lower Peabody Picture Vocabulary Test scores of Montessori children. Bereiter-Engelmann and Montessori programs are more successful than DARCEE and traditional at reducing aggression, however (Miller and Dyer 1975).

The Face Sheet ratings for preschool indicate that Montessori children were rated intermediate between Bereiter-Engelmann and DARCEE children on achievement motivation and other factors affecting their ability to score at their potential.

In summary, the limited amount of research to date on the effects of Montessori preschool experience on the development of attention suggests that Montessori preschool experience is effective in increasing children's ability to pay prolonged attention to school-related tasks. This increase in attention may be a major factor accounting for the observed positive effects of Montessori preschool training on performance on intelligence tests of the Stanford-Binet type. There is also evidence (McCormick and Schnobrich 1971) suggesting that perceptual-motor training, stressing control of impulsiveness and development of attentional skills, added to the regular Montessori preschool curriculum can increase the effects of Montessori experience on the ability to concentrate visually and auditorily.

Resistance to distraction and persistence, as measured by Banta's (1970) Replacement Puzzle Test, are increased more by the other preschool programs studied, although Montessori children perform better than controls. Montessori children are less able to inhibit a motor response, such as drawing a line slowly, than control groups with Head-Start or no-preschool experience. Similar results were obtained for Behavior Inventory scores on ambition and verbal-social participation, with Montessori faring slightly better than DARCEE and traditional programs in reducing rated aggression.

CREATIVITY AND MOTIVATIONAL FACTORS

One area of controversy surrounding the Montessori method is the extent to which it might affect the young child's creativity. The concern is based on the observation that the method requires the teacher to demonstrate the correct way to use classroom materials.

In a series of studies by McMorrow, Miezitis, and Rudominer (Miezitis 1971), performance on measures of divergent thinking (Torrance Toy Dog and Kangas Action-Agent tasks) was compared among five- to six-year-old middle- and upper-income children attending three different types of nursery school: (1) an "orthodox" Montessori program; (2) a child-directed, play-oriented nursery school; and (3) a regular public kindergarten. The children (N = 80) were matched for age, sex, and SES, and were at least normal in intelligence. No significant differences were found among the three groups on divergent thinking.

Dreyer and Rigler (1969) compared 14 matched pairs of five-year-old middle-income children of above average IQ attending a Montessori and a traditional nursery school. As a measure of creativity they employed the Torrance Picture Construction Test, a nonverbal task of the Minnesota Test of Creative Thinking. This test was described in Chapter 12. Dreyer and Rigler (1969) found that the traditional nursery school children performed significantly better than the Montessori children on this nonverbal measure of creativity.

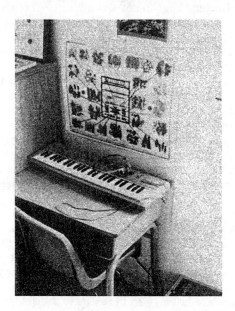

Synthesizer in a Montessori elementary classroom.

Brophy and Choquette (1973) conducted a study with Montessori children to test the hypothesis that teacher instruction in the correct use of classroom equipment inhibits children's ability to generate other uses for that same equipment. Subjects were 31 matched pairs of four- and five-year-old, suburban, upper-middle-income white children from two Montessori preschools and two traditional nursery schools. Measures of creativity were four adaptations of the Unusual Uses Test from Torrance's Minnesota Tests of Creative Thinking and Writing. Children were given a stuffed toy dog, a fork, a triangular wooden shape used to fit into the Montessori geometric cabinet apparatus, and a Montessori button frame, and asked to tell as many different uses of these items as they could.

Responses were scored for fluency, flexibility, originality, and elaboration, following Yamamoto's (1964) scoring guidelines. The analyses revealed no signs of reduced ability on the part of Montessori children to produce verbal responses regarding divergent uses for objects: a majority of the significant comparisons favored Montessori children.

Banta (1969) found significant differences favoring the Montessori preschool/Montessori primary group, and the Montessori preschool/open classroom group over the two control groups on a measure of task initiation, on manipulation of the curiosity box, and on verbalizations made while exploring the box. Dog and Bone test scores are designed to measure divergent production, a variable often assessed as an important aspect of creativity. Banta (1969) reports significant differences on this test favoring the two Montessori groups over the no-preschool control group.

Both Curiosity Box and Dog and Bone test scores were also reported by Miller and Dyer (1954) for preschool through second grade. DARCEE and Montessori were significantly higher than the Bereiter-Engelmann and traditional programs on the Dog and Bone test of divergent production after one year of preschool. Over all four testing periods, DARCEE children had, on the average, higher scores than Montessori, and Bereiter-Engelmann children the lowest. On the Curiosity Box measure, Montessori children had the highest score at the end of grade two.

This area is difficult to summarize due to the wide variability in the methods used to assess creativity, in addition to the usual problems encountered in trying to make generalizations from several studies. Montessori children do less well than traditional nursery school children on the Torrance Tests of Creative Thinking, which test originality, elaboration, activity, and title accuracy in a drawing. On several tests of divergent production, across several samples, Montessori children are superior to control groups and most other preschool programs. Verbal creativity, while not as widely assessed, seems to be developed to the same or greater extent in Montessori children as in children attending other preschool programs.

Summary: This chapter reviewed the research on the effects of Montessori school experience on children in several areas. The Montessori method cannot be considered to have received a complete or detailed evaluation by the research undertaken to this point. In general, however, it was found that the Montessori program performs as well as most preschool programs in most areas, such as school readiness, and intelligence. Direct-instruction programs produce faster gains in academic subjects, which, however, seem to be much less long lasting than Montessori program gains.

Special programs, with a focus in one area, such as language, Piagetian development, or perceptual development can produce better scores in these areas in most cases. This is not surprising, given the wide range of learning that should be going on and the close match between content and test in these studies.

Vocabulary recognition, and ratings of verbal-social participation are areas in which programs other than Montessori produce higher gains.

In the development of attentional strategies, general intelligence, achievement in academic areas, and especially in maintaining these gains, the Montessori method performs better than most programs studied. Evidence also indicates that a continuation of Montessori experience beyond preschool would consolidate the gains made; the need of research to examine this possibility is seen as the strongest conclusion to be drawn from the research evidence presently available.

Limitations of the research on Montessori are of two kinds: those shared with other research on early childhood education programs, and those unique to Montessori. In the first group are problems such as small sample size, short-term rather than longitudinal designs, confounding of teacher and method by using a single teacher to represent a model, confounding of the effects of a model with the effects of parent selection, and so on. The selection of inappropriate measures, the use of only part of an instrument (thus invalidating any information on the reliability and validity of the instrument) and other instrumentation problems are also of concern. Although other research may also suffer from the confusion between programs and the model they supposedly represent, this has been a major source of confusion in the research on Montessori. What is needed is a clear and objective way to assess whether a given classroom is within the bounds of typical Montessori practices. At the very least, researchers must specify in more detail the teacher and environment of the Montessori classrooms they study.

Unique to Montessori research are the problem(s) of designing research studies that address the goals of Montessori education. Much more work needs to be done in this area. The Teacher's Research Network has begun to address this need.

CHAPTER 15
New Trends In Montessori Education

Chapter Goals: In this chapter, you will learn:
- The areas in which the Montessori movement is growing and changing in the U.S. today, including:
- Montessori and religious instruction.
- Montessori in the public schools.
- Montessori programs serving infants, toddlers, and older children.
- Montessori groups making strides toward increased links with other professional groups.
- The Teacher's Research Network.

One of the primary points I have tried to make in this book is that the Montessori movement in the United States has never been static. Right from the beginning, Montessori here in America has been a collage of good and bad schools and training programs, dedication on the part of many Montessorians and eagerness for a quick buck by a few. This diversity continues today; there are certainly things going on today under the wide umbrella of the Montessori movement that would have most Europeans (although perhaps not Maria herself) shaking their heads. In this chapter, I will try to describe some of the most important trends in Montessori education today.

MONTESSORI AND RELIGION

Although (as we learned in Chapter 2) there are no necessary links between Montessori and Catholicism or even Christianity, there are some historical links. Montessori came from a Catholic Italian background; some of the new schools that were started were in church buildings. This influence is still evident in the American movement today: the most influential of the second American wave of schools in the late fifties was the Whitby School in Greenwich, Connecticut. Although a private rather than an archdiocesan school, Whitby is a Catholic school. The majority of the universities with Montessori teacher education programs as a part of the regular, on-campus offerings, are Catholic. It's safe to say, then, that a large number of the people who knew about Montessori in this country were Catholics.

In the mid-eighties, a new group of Montessorians began meeting, then began to organize and conduct training sessions, bringing over experts from Italy. What made this group unique was that they were mostly already trained Montessorians, and the training they were getting concerned the setting up of special areas, often in homes rather than in schools, for the aiding of the spiritual development of young children.

The new movement to use Montessori principles to aid the spiritual development of the child came from the same sort of parent who was dissatisfied with the education their child was receiving at the local parochial school. They felt that memorization of the catechism was not the ideal way to aid a child in her spiritual development. This feeling runs deep, since many people have felt that in some ways young children are less sinful than adults, and that a religious education that stresses the sinfulness of man too much (rather than the infinite love of God) is not the best possible program. Then, too, people were concerned about a religious education program that focused almost entirely on memorization of content.

With these concerns, the work that had been carried on in Italy on the spiritual development of young children, primarily by Dr. Sofia Cavaletti, sparked a great interest. People began, perhaps, by reading Dr. Cavaletti's book, *The Religious Potential of the Child*, and then by going on to a little known book of essays by Montessori and others, edited by E.M. Standing, *The Child in the Church*. Despite its now-quaint, pre-Vatican II perspective, this hard-to-find book continues to sell.

People began to travel to Rome to see Dr. Cavaletti's work, and to be trained by her on the setting up of an "atrium" in their own communities. The term "atrium" is used for the learning area, relating back to a quote from Montessori that children should work and learn about God and His love in a room that was an atrium or entry hall to the church.

One of the most influential people in this area is Dr. Jerome Berryman of Houston. His atrium for children attracted observers from all over the country. Dr. Berryman began to write about his work, and to speak around the country. Dr. Cavaletti and Gianna Gobbi, a close associate, were prevailed on to come to the U.S. to describe the materials and activities used in the atria in Rome. Soon, an organization was formed, and a newsletter was started. The group chose the name of <u>The Catechisis of the Good Shepherd</u> for itself.

The name comes from the lesson on the Good Shepherd, one of several key phrases or themes that run through the work in the atria; another is the Lord as the Light of the World. To my mind, one of the most striking proofs of the effectiveness of the atria and the work of the catechists is the artworks produced by the children as a regular part of their time in the environment. The art reveals the effectiveness of what goes on in communicating essential concepts to young children, and also the success of the activities and stories at touching the imaginations and the hearts of the children.

This movement is still growing, and it's hard to predict where it will end. Very active chapters exist in the Washington D.C., and St. Paul areas, with active groups in most other large urban areas. Training workshops for catechists are held almost every summer, with the latest attention being focussed on working with the elementary aged child. One challenge still to be met is the seeming indifference of the majority of those directly involved in religious education out in the parishes. In most areas, there are sympathizers with the new groups and their ways--but the majority of Catholic religious education is carried on with traditional means and content.

MONTESSORI IN THE PUBLIC SCHOOLS

One of the most common ways in which Montessori is attacked is to contrast the poor children in the first Casa dei Bambini in the worker's slum in Rome with the well-fed, fashionably dressed young children in a typical suburban Montessori school. The fact that it is not the fault of Montessorians that there are so few opportunities for lower income families to send their children to Montessori schools never seems to be considered. It is not the Montessorians who make decisions about programs in public schools, or programs in Head-Start. Sometimes, however, it is not always educational bureaucrats who make all these decisions, either. So it is that in 1989, some 100 public school districts in the United States, and at least 4 in Canada, have Montessori programs of some type.

The programs in public schools are a diverse lot. Some are new; the oldest go back to the early 1970's. Almost all were started by grass-roots pressure from the parents, rather than teachers or administrators. One of the most common ways in which a Montessori program got started was as a magnet school, to help a school district comply with Federal desegregation requirements.

Magnet schools continue to enjoy popularity as an adjunct to or an alternative to bussing programs. A popular type of program, which will attract middle-class white parents and their children, is begun at an inner city school. The middle-class parents volunteer to have their children attend the program, and racial balance is achieved. A wide variety of models have been proposed and tried as magnet programs. Montessori and open-classroom programs are two that have proven their "salability" to parents over the years.

The public Montessori programs may or may not get funding over and above what the regular programs get. Montessori programs in public schools have almost always relied on very active parent groups for support in areas such as fundraising for buying materials, making materials, in-classroom help, and so on.

The availability of students in public Montessori programs is also a great boon for those of us interested in research on the effectiveness of the Montessori method. The achievement tests and any other tests given the students are sometimes made available to researchers, and provide us with a means for comparing achievement between those in the Montessori program and other students in the district. The achievement tests are not a particularly good test of what the Montessori method is all about, of course, but the information they provide allows for some standard of comparison, and no parent is truly disinterested in reading and math scores. The comparison of Montessori and other students in the public schools has to be made with caution, because the parents or the child have selected the Montessori program. It cannot be assumed that the families who have selected the Montessori program differ on no other variables, and that achievement test scores are thus due only to the model. But there is one great advantage to examining these scores: the public school data will contain information on children from a wide range of racial and socioeconomic backgrounds. Far too much of the research on Montessori has focussed on the almost exclusively middle-class world of private Montessori schools. These considerations make the findings of researchers like Dawson, whose study of achievement in the Houston public Montessori schools was presented in the last chapter, especially important.

Public Montessori programs are not without their problems. Many of these surface during the period of the development of the Montessori program. For example, the

Montessori model requires three-year age spans, beginning in elementary school, with classes usually of 6-, 7-,and 8-year-olds, a "6 to 9" class. Public schools work with one-year age spans, and have the 5-year-olds in kindergarten, usually for one-half day, as the typical entry point. Many schools opt for compromises, such as two-year age spans, or a 5-, 6-, and 7-year-old class. Some of these modifications are successful, some are not. Another area for problems is in the materials and curriculum. Montessori classrooms typically require a very large classroom materials budget at start-up, but fewer costs over the ensuing years--fewer workbooks and other consumables, for instance. Getting the funding for this within a tight school budget may require outside funding, entry into the world of research accountancy, or both.

Another problem is in the admission criteria: elementary Montessori classrooms work very differently when the percentage of children with experience in 3-6 Montessori falls below about 60%--some would say 80%. Having wrestled with this problem as a teacher as well as a supposed expert, I know that it comes down to a matter of expectations developed in a good 3-6 classroom, expectations about completing a cycle of work, and taking responsibility for one's one work. Some children without Montessori preschool experience adapt easily to the expectations in the Montessori elementary classroom and some do not. Some sit passively at their desks, awaiting a ditto page or workbook that never comes. Some, quite literally, climb the walls. When this represents 2, 3, or even 6 of your class, the teacher can focus extra attention, use older children as tutors and guides, and so on. When it represents half the class or a majority, orthodox Montessori elementary practices just can't be conducted, at least not early in the school year.

Yet in a public program, one cannot restrict enrollments to only those who could have afforded private Montessori preschool. Many sorts of admission criteria are in use at the many school districts; it's not clear that any of them are perfectly satisfactory. There are also cases in which some of the middle-class parents are not happy with the public school environment, and the children are returned to the private setting. But by and large, Montessori programs are successful magnets in both attracting and retaining "customers" and in educating students well, as shown by the achievement test data.

Other problems sometimes come about when the administrators don't see a clear match between district learning objectives and the materials and activities offered the students in the public Montessori program. Part of the problem is that only a tiny percentage of the administrators of public Montessori programs--either principals or district level supervisors-- have any extensive background in Montessori themselves.

Perhaps the biggest problem in starting and maintaining a high quality public program is the scarcity of good Montessori elementary teachers. To teach in a public program, the teacher must have both state teaching certification and Montessori elementary teacher training. Practically, this means that either a state certified teacher must become so enamored of Montessori that she takes either a year or at least a summer[1] to study Montessori,

---

[1] The AMI programs require either two summers or one school year off, away from teaching and salary. The AMS programs require a summer of intense study followed by an internship teaching year. Although the preferred model is a year under an experienced master teacher, exemptions for a self-directed internship are routinely granted. The rationale is that many of the graduates are already experienced teachers and that there are too few experienced teachers available. Certainly the financial differences between working as a teacher and working as an

or that a Montessori elementary teacher takes a year off and pays a university to become a state certified teacher. In either case, the teacher is paying twice and certainly having to sit through some of the same content. Even with the salaries that public schools can offer, and benefits packages often totally lacking at private Montessori schools, public programs often have a hard time filling positions. This usually results in teachers working in Montessori programs without the combination of full elementary Montessori certification or state credentials.

Two new sources of up-to-date and clear information on public Montessori schools have now become available. One is a short brochure describing public Montessori programs from a new resource group called The Montessori Public Schools Consortium, representing AMI, AMS, and NAMTA. The second is a newsletter called *Public School Montessorian.*

SERVING OTHER POPULATIONS

One way in which Montessori continues to expand is in broadening the age range that is served. Montessori training programs to train adults to work with infants or toddlers are now available in several locations. AMI programs exist in Mexico City and Houston, and AMS programs in New York, Chicago, and Texas, with others planned. This is a critical area for Montessori now. As increasing numbers of families seek out-of-home care for their children, more and more infant and toddler centers are opened. The level of training of staff in these centers is quite variable. The compensation to infant and toddler teachers is often low enough to contribute to substantial turnover of staff during the course of the year. While this is potentially harmful to a child's sense of security at any age, high rates of teacher turnover have the potential for significant negative impact on young children. The fact that people are willing to undertake the long, demanding, and relatively expensive Montessori training for this level is a very positive sign.

At the other end of the age span, much work is going on to develop and strengthen Montessori secondary education. Two schools--a public Montessori magnet in Dallas, and a private Montessori school near Washington DC-- have expanded their schools to include teacher education at this level.[1] Another Texan (Dr. Elizabeth Coe, a member of the AMS Board) has worked to develop a stronger Montessori middle school model.

Finally, there is some hope that Montessori is finally beginning to lose its position of isolation. Links are beginning to be made between Montessorians and some of their natural allies on the American education scene. For example, Montessori schools have quite a lot in

aide come into this as well.   Other training programs vary in their requirements. My 1981 study found the overwhelming majority of the public Montessori teachers to be AMS trained, rather than AMI.

[1] The Dallas public schools have the public 7th and 8th grades; training is done through the Dallas Montessori Teacher Programs, P.O. Box 2423, Dallas, TX 75221. The Barrie Day School in Silver Springs, Maryland, is a Montessori high school; training is done by the Institute for Advanced Montessori Studies, 2400 Bel Pre Rd., P.O. Box 6158 Silver Springs, MD 20906.

common with alternative educators. A new publication, *The Holistic Education Review*, has an article about Montessori--but also articles on peace education, open classroom methods, and so on. The *Public School Montessorian* newsletter is another example of a bridge-building attempt, an attempt to de-mystify Montessori and make the good things that Montessori has to offer available to more children.

Attempts by Montessorians in developed countries to reach out to the children and adults in the Third World are another hopeful sign. The Comite Hispañio de AMS has been a clearinghouse for information on Montessori in Spanish for many years now. They (individually and as an organization) have visited many schools in Latin America, offering consulting and workshops. This little-known work has led to a great deal of good. Other outreach activities have had positive results as well. The AMS affiliated Montessori Teacher Education Center[1] of the San Francisco Bay area has begun a special program to give Montessori training to day care providers who are migrant farm workers.

The work of Peter Hesse, a West German manufacturer of artists' paints, is another example. As a frequent traveler, he had visited a number of Caribbean countries, and been impressed with the Montessori preschools he saw in the more developed of the countries, such as Trinidad. He began a foundation that gave money to start Montessori preschools in Haiti, a nation with tremendous disadvantages in economic and educational resources. After the third school was set up, the foundation paid for Caribbean experts to begin a training program. Now the schools, still growing in number, can be staffed with native Haitians. The latest project is the opening of a factory for the local manufacture of the basic Sensorial and other Montessori materials. The machine tools, paints, and so on were still awaiting customs clearance when we spoke last, but here is clearly an example of what one man can do to make a difference in children's lives.

NEW EVIDENCE OF PROFESSIONALISM

The last new trend I will comment on is the new feeling of professionalism in the Montessori movement in the U.S. today. One piece of evidence is the progress Montessori has made in its relationship with the National Association for the Education of Young Children, the professional early childhood education organization in the U.S. In the 70's, there were very few mentions of Montessori in the national conventions of this organization. In the 80's, Montessori began to be seen in the pre-conference workshops, and in the festival of organizations that precedes the sessions. Montessori groups began to become more organized in submitting proposals for speakers at these conferences. Now, there is a Montessori track at the national conference, with good attendance. Some state level organizations are beginning to follow the national and offer something for Montessorians, and allow others to see what is going on in the Montessori movement. Also, Montessori is much more frequently mentioned in articles in *Young Children* now than in the past.

Another example is the attempts of the American Montessori Society to create a federally recognized accreditation model for its teacher education model. The Accreditation

---

[1] 16292 Foothill Blvd., San Leandro, CA 94578.

Council for Childhood Education Specialist Schools (ACCESS) has been the body in charge of accreditation decisions for the AMS for some years now. This organization works very much like regional accrediting bodies for schools or like the accreditation process that colleges or universities undergo.

A program that desires ACCESS accreditation prepares a proposal following the ACCESS guidelines. The proposal is a formal, complex document that specifies how the program will comply with all of the requirements. In addition to requirements about clarity and truth in advertising, nondiscrimination, and so on, the proposal lists the curriculum and number of hours in each content area, and the experience and educational attainments of the faculty. This proposal is screened, and feedback given to the authors. After a successful screening, the process continues, with an on-site visit to verify that the program behaves as its proposal claimed it did, and a review by a separate Commission on Accreditation. The process is tedious and expensive, but it represents a fair way to ensure that training programs will be fairly evaluated and will produce graduates who meet certain minimum standards.

So far, federal recognition of Montessori teacher education programs has not been forthcoming, but this effort continues.

THE TEACHER'S RESEARCH NETWORK

The TRN is described in detail in my article in *Young Children* in July, 1989. The basic idea is to gather working teachers together for an intensive week of work on the basics of research design. The teachers also work late into the evenings at a library (in our case, at the University of Oklahoma) on the previous research done on their topic. The goal is that each teacher leave the first session with a research project ready for field testing. This occurs during the rest of the school year, and data collection typically takes place during the following school year. The teachers return the next summer to perform statistical analysis and write up their results.

So far, we have had three groups of teachers attend. Most were able to collect data, and returned to analyze it, write about it, and share it with their fellow teacher-researchers. The teachers often report that they are better teachers, more careful observers, and more articulate spokespersons for what they do as a result of their TRN experience.

Summary: In this chapter, several trends in Montessori education were presented. There is a new interest in using Montessori ideas to foster children's spiritual development, primarily from Catholic and Episcopalian religious educators. There has been a rapid expansion of public Montessori programs, and a rapid development of Montessori teacher education programs at the Infant and Toddler and Secondary levels to serve the new schools for children at these age levels. There has been considerable progress in some Montessori organizations towards a professional model of accreditation for Montessori teacher education. Along with this, there has been increased communication between the Montessori and traditional early childhood education communities. The Teacher's Research Network is seen by the author as a good example of a new direction for growth for Montessori educators.

This is an exciting time for the Montessori movement in the United States. We are working hard to make programs the best they can be, and expanding what we can do to reach other children. We are reaching out to the mainstream of American education, sharing what we have as Montessorians. We are in a position to actualize Dr. Montessori's dream of providing an education that will meet the needs of every child.

REFERENCES

Ascheim, S. Materials for the Open Classroom. New York: Dell Press, 1975.

Baines, M., and Snortum, J. "A Time-Sampling Analysis of Montessori Versus Traditional Classroom Interaction." *Journal of Educational Research* , Vol. 66, 1973.

Baker, K. The interpretation of subtraction held by children in the Association Montessori Internationale curriculum. Unpublished Master's thesis, University of Maryland, 1988.

Banta, T. J. "Research on Montessori and the Disadvantaged." In *Montessori and the Special Child,* ed. R. C. Orem. New York: Putnam, 1969.

Banta, T. J. Tests for the Evaluation of Early Childhood Education: The Cincinnati Autonomy Test Battery (CATB). In *Cognitive Studies*, ed. J. Hellmuth. New York: Brunner/Mazel, 1970.

Bauch, J., and Hsu, H. Montessori: Right or Wrong About Number Concepts? *Arithmetic Teacher,* 1988.

Bereiter, C. *Acceleration of Intellectual Development in Early Childhood.* Washington, D.C.: Department of Health, Education and Welfare, U.S. Office of Education, Bureau of Research, 1967.

Bereiter, C. and Engelman, S. *Teaching Disadvantaged Children in the Preschool.* Englewood Cliffs, NJ: Prentice-Hall, 1966.

Berger, B. A comparative investigation of Montessori and traditional pre-kindergarten practices. *American Montessori Society Bulletin*, Vol. 8, No. 2, 1970.

Berliner, M. Montessori and social development. *The Educational Forum,* Vol. 38, 1974.

Black, S. A Comparison of Cognitive and Social Development in British Infant and Montessori Preschools. Unpublished doctoral dissertation, Temple University, 1977.

Blumenthal, A. Language and Psychology. New York: John Wiley & Sons, Inc. 1970.

Boehnlein, M. Montessori Research: Analysis in Retrospect. Special Edition of the *North American Montessori Teachers' Association Journal*, Vol. 13, No. 3, Summer, 1988.

Boehnlein, M. The NAMTA Montessori Bibliography. Special Edition of the *North American Montessori Teachers' Association Journal*, Vol. 10, No. 2, Summer, 1985.

Bower, T. C. *Development in Infancy.* San Francisco: W. H. Freeman and Company, 1974.

Bower, T. C. Human Development. San Francisco: W. H. Freeman, 1979.

Bridges, K. Occupational interests of three year old children. *The Pedagogical Seminary*, Vol. 34, 1927.

Brophy, J. , and Choquette, J. Divergent Production in Montessori Children. Paper presented at the Biennial Meeting of the Society for Research in Child Development, Philadelphia, March, 1973.

Brown, R., Layden, C. B. Bellugi, U. The Child's Grammar From I to III. Paper read at 1967 Minnesota Symposium on Child Psychology. Minneapolis, 1967.

Carta, J., and Greenwood, C. Establishing the Integrity of the Independent Variable in Early Intervention Programs. Early Education and Development Vol. 1, No. 2, 1989.

Cazden, C. Some Questions for Research in Early Childhood Education. In *Preschool Programs for the Disadvantaged*, ed. J.C. Stanley. Baltimore: Johns Hopkins University Press, 1972.

Chattin-McNichols, J. and Loeffler, M. Teachers as Researchers: The First Cycle of the Teacher's Research Network *Young Children* Vol. 44, No. 5, 1989.

Chattin-McNichols, J. Piaget in the Montessori Classroom. *American Montessori Society Constructive Triangle* , 1980.

Chattin-McNichols, J. The Effects of Montessori School Experience. *Young Children* Vol. 36, 1981.

Chomsky, N. Aspects of the Theory of Syntax Cambridge, Mass: M. I. T. Press, 1965.

Cossu, G., Shankweiler, D., Lieberman, I., Katz, L., and Tola, G. Awareness of phonological segments and reading ability in Italian children. Applied Psycholinguistics, Vol. 9, 1988.

Cronbach, L.; Ragosa, D.; Floden, R.; and Price, G. Analysis of Covariance in Non-randomized Experiments: Parameters Affecting Bias. Unpublished manuscript, Stanford Evaluation Consortium, September 1977.

Dawson, M. A Comparative Analysis of the Standardized Test Scores of Students Enrolled in HISD Montessori Magnet and Traditional Elementary Classrooms. Unpublished Master's thesis, Texas Southern University, 1988.

De Vries, R. *Programs in Early Education: A Constructivist View* New York: Longman, 1987.

DeVries, R., and Goncu, C. Interpersonal relations in four-year-old dyads from constructivist and Montessori classrooms. Cited in DeVries (1987).

De Vries, R. with Kohlberg, L. *Programs of Early Education: The Constructivist View.* New York: Longman, 1987.

DiLorenzo, L., et al. *Pre-Kindergarten Programs for Educationally Disadvantaged Children.* New York State Education Department, 1969.

Dreyer, A. S., and Rigler, D. Cognitive Performance in Montessori and Nursery School Children. *Journal of Educational Research* Vol. 67, 1969.

Duax, T. Preliminary Report on the Educational Effectiveness of a Montessori School in the Public Sector *North American Montessori Teachers' Quarterly*, Vol. 14, No. 2, 1989.

Durkin, D. A classroom-observation study of reading instruction in kindergarten. Early Childhood Research Quarterly. Vol. 2, 1987.

Ehri, L. and Wilce, L. The influence of orthography on readers' conceptualization of the phonemic structure of words. Applied Psycholinguistics, Vol, 1, 1980.

Elkind, D. Piaget and Montessori. *Harvard Educational Review.* Fall, 1967.

Elliot, L. Montessori's Reading Principles Involving Sensitive Period Methods Compared to Reading Principles of Contemporary Reading Specialists. *Reading Teacher* Vol. 21, 1967.

Feldman, D. ...And Bodies Must Move. Unpublished research paper, Xavier University (Ohio), 1983.

Feltin, P. Independent Learning in Four Montessori Elementary Classrooms. Unpublished doctoral dissertation, Seattle University, 1987.

Flavell, J. *Cognitive Development* (2nd Ed.) Englewood Cliffs, NJ: Prentice-Hall, 1985.

Flavell, J. On cognitive development. *Child Development*, **53**,1-10,1982.

Fleege, U.; Black, M.; Rackauskas, J. *Montessori Preschool Education Project 5-1061.* Grant No 0E3-10-127. Washington, D.C.: Office of Education, 1967.

Forman, G. E., and Kuschner, D. S. *The Child's Construction of Knowledge.* Monterey, California: Brooks/Cole Publishing Company, 1977.

Foster, L. Some criticisms of the Montessori method examined. *The American Montessori Society Bulletin*, Vol. 11, 1973.

Furth, H. G. *Piaget and Knowledge.* Englewood Cliffs, NJ: Prentice-Hall, 1969.

Furth, H. G. *Piaget for Teachers*. Englewood Cliffs, NJ: Prentice-Hall, 1970.

Gardner, R. W. A Psychologist Looks at Montessori.: *Elementary School Journal* , **67**, 1966.

Ginsberg, H., and Opper, S. *Piaget's Theory of Intellectual Development*. Englewood Cliffs, NJ: Prentice-Hall, 1969.

Glenn, C. A Comparison of Lower and Upper Elementary Montessori Students with a Public School Sample. *North American Montessori Teachers' Quarterly*, Vol. 14, No. 2, 1989.

Goldman, A. & Levine, M. A developmental study of object sorting. *Child Development*, **34**, 1963.

Goodlad, J.; Klein, M.; and Novotney, J. *Early Schooling in the United States*. New York: McGraw-Hill, 1973.

Gross, R. ; Green, B.; and Clapp, D. The Sands School Project *American Montessori Society Bulletin* Vol. 11, No. 1, 1973.

Jensen, M., and Hanson, B. Helping Young Children Learn to Read: What Research Says to Teachers. Young Children, Vol. 36, No. 1, November, 1980.

Judge, J. A Comparison of Preschool Children in Observational Tasks from Two Programs: Montessori and Science-A-Process Approach. Unpublished doctoral dissertation, University of Texas at Austin, 1974.

Kahn, D. *Montessori Public School Consortium Special Report 1988*. Available from the Consortium, 2859 Scarborough Road, Cleveland Heights, OH 44118.

Kamii, C. An application of Piaget's theory to the conceptualization of preschool curriculum. In R. K. Parker (Ed.), *Conceptualization of Preschool Curricula*. Boston: Allyn & Bacon, 1976.

Kamii, C. *Young Children Reinvent Arithmetic*. New York: Teachers College Press, 1985.

Kamii, C., and Radin, N. A framework for preschool curriculum based on some Piagetian concepts. In I. J. Athey and D. O. Rubadeau (Eds.), *Educational Implications of Piaget's Theory*. Waltham, MA: Ginn-Blaisdell, 1970.

Karlson, A. A naturalistic method for identifying behavioral aspects of cognitive acquisition in young children participating in preschool programs. Unpublished dissertation, University of Chicago, 1972.

Karnes, M. "Research and Development Project on Preschool Disadvantaged Children." Washington, D.C.: U. S. Office of Education, 1969.

Karnes, M., Shwedel, A., and Williams, M. A Comparison of Five Approaches for Educating Young Children from Low-Income Homes in *As the Twig is Bent*. The Consortium for Longitudinal Studies (Ed.) Hillsdale, NJ: Lawrence Erlbaum Associates, 1983.

Klein, R. Multivariate Comparison of Two Model Preschool Programs. *Psychological Reports* Vol. 40, 1977.

Kohlberg, L. "Montessori with the Culturally Disadvantaged" A Cognitive-Developmental Interpretation and Some Research Findings. In *Early Education*, ed. R. D. Hess and R. M. Baer. Chicago: Aldine, 1968.

Kuhn, D. Inducing development experimentally: Comments on a research paradigm. *Developmental Psychology,* **10**, 1974.

Lanaro, P. Classification development in the Montessori classroom. *American Montessori Society Constructive Triangle*, 1984.

Lavatelli, C. *Piaget's Theory Applied to an Early Education Curriculum*. Boston: American Science and Engineering, 1970.

Lowery, l. *Learning About Learning: Classification Abilities*, Berkeley: University of California at Berkeley, 1981.

Mann, V. Phonological awareness: The role of reading experience. Cognition, Vol. 24, 1986.

Mayer, R Describing Children's Experiences in Theoretically Different Classrooms: An Observational Assessment of Four Early Education Curriculum Models. Unpublished Doctoral Dissertation, Harvard University, University Microfilms International, 1973.

McCandless, B., and Trotter, R., Children: Behavior and Development. New York: Holt, Rinehart, and Winston, 1977.

McCormick, C., and Schnobrich, J. Perceptual-Motor Training and Improvement in Concentration in a Montessori Preschool. *Perceptual and Motor Skills 32* (1971): 71-77.

Miezitis, S. Cognitive Style, Exploratory Behavior, and Verbal Fluency in Montessori and Non-Montessori Trained Preschoolers. Ontario Institute for Studies in Education, 1971.

Miezitis, S. The Montessori method: Some recent research. *American Montessori Society Bulletin*. Vol. 10, No. 2, 1972.

Miezitis, S. The Montessori method: Some recent research. *Interchange*, **2,** 1971.

Miller, L. and Bizzell, R. Long-Term Effects of Four Preschool Programs: Ninth- and Tenth-Grade Results. Child Development, Vol. 55, No. 4, 1985.

Miller, L. and Bizzell, R. Long-Term Effects of Four Preschool Programs: Sixth-, Seventh-, and Eighth-Grades. Child Development, Vol. 54, No. 3, 1983.

Miller, L., and Dyer, L. Four Preschool Programs: Their Dimensions and Effects. *Monographs of the Society for Research in Child Development* (1975): 162.

Montessori, M. From Childhood to Adolescence. New York: Shocken, 1975.

Montessori, M. The Absorbent Mind. New York: Dell, 1967.

Mussen P., Conger J., and Kagan, J. Child Development and Personality. New York: Harper and Row, 1969.

Pendergast, R. "Pre-Reading Skills Developed in Montessori and Conventional Nursery Schools. " *Elementary School Journal* Vol. 70 (1969).

Piaget, J. *Play, Dreams and Imitation in Childhood.* New York: Norton (Originally published 1945) 1962.

Piaget, J. *The Child's Conception of Number.* New York: Humanities Press, 1952.

Piaget, J. *The Moral Judgement of the Child* . New York: Free Press (Originally published 1932) 1965.

Piaget, J., and Inhelder, B. *The Child's Conception of Space* . London: Routledge and Kegan Paul, 1963.

Piaget, J., Inhelder, B., and Szeminska, A. *The Child's Conception of Geometry.* New York: Basic Books, 1960.

Reuter, J. A comparative study of social interaction in a Montessori preschool. *American Montessori Society Bulletin*, Vol. 12, No.1, 1974.

Reuter, J. and Yunik, G. Social interaction in nursery schools. *Developmental Psychology* Vol. 9, 1973.

Rudominer, R. Self-Reliance, Initiative, and Mastery of Montessori and Non-Montessori Trained Preschool Children. Unpublished Master's thesis, University of Toronto, 1970.

Schickedanz, J. The place of Specific Skills in Preschool and Kindergarten. In Strickland, D., and Morrow, L. (Eds.) Emerging Literacy: Young Children Learn to Read and Write. Newark, Delaware: International Reading Association, 1989.

Schmid, J., and Black, K. An Observational Study of the Choice and Use of Toys by Montessori and Non-Montessori Preschoolers. In *Evaluations of Educational Outcomes, Proceedings of the National Conference on the Evaluation of Montessori and Open Classrooms*, ed. S. Makhick and J. Henner. American Montessori Society, 1977.

Sciarra, D., and Dorsey, A. Six Year Follow-Up Study of Montessori Education. *American Montessori Society Bulletin* 12, No. 4, 1974.

Slobin, D. Psycholinguistics, Glenview, Illinois: Scott, Foresman, and Co., 1971

Slobin, D. "Universals of Grammatical Development in Children" in Advances in Psycholinguistics Ed. G. B. Flores D'Arcais and W. J. M. Levet, 1970, North Holland Publishing Co. Amsterdam.

Starr, R., and Banta, T. Manual for the Uses of Didactic Materials Schedule. University of Cincinnati, 1966.

Stern, C. Evaluating Language Curricula for Preschool Children. *Monographs of the Society for Research in Child Development* Vol. 33, No. 8, 1968.

Stodolsky, S. and Jensen, J. Final Report: Ancona Montessori Research Project for Culturally Disadvantaged Children. Submitted to the Office of Economic Opportunity, 1969.

Stodolsky, S., and Karlson, A. Differential Outcomes of a Montessori Curriculum. *Elementary School Journal*, 1972.

Strickland, D., and Morrow, L. (Eds.) Emerging Literacy: Young Children Learn to Read and Write. Newark, Delaware: International Reading Association, 1989.

Takacs, C. and Clifford, A. Performance of Montessori Graduates in Public School Classrooms. *North American Montessori Teachers' Quarterly*, Vol. 14, No. 1, 1988.

Teal. W., and Sulzby. E. Emergent Literacy: New Perspectives. In Strickland, D., and Morrow, L. (Eds.) Emerging Literacy: Young Children Learn to Read and Write. Newark, Delaware: International Reading Association, 1989.

Torrance, E. P. *Guiding Creative Talent*. Englewood Cliffs, N. J.: Prentice-Hall, 1962.

Torrence, M. Fantasy in American Montessori Schools. Unpublished research project of the Teacher's Research Network, 1985.

Villegas, A., and Biwer, P. Parent Involvement in a Montessori Program: The Denver Public School Experience. *North American Montessori Teachers' Quarterly*, Vol. 13, No. 1, 1987.

Vygotsky, L. S. Thought and Language (Reprinted 1962) Cambridge, MA: MIT Press, 1934.

Weikart, D. P. *Ypsilanti Preschool Curriculum Demonstration Project.* Ypsilanti, Mich.: High-Scope Educational Research Foundation, 1969.

White, J. , Yussen, S., and Docherty, E. Performance of Montessori and Traditionally Schooled Nursery Children on Tasks of Seriation, Classification, and Conservation. *Contemporary Educational Psychology,* **1**, 1976.

Wirtz, P. Social Behavior Related to Material Settings in the Montessori Preschool Environment. Unpublished doctoral dissertation, George Peabody College for Teachers, 1976.

Yamamoto, K. "Experimental Scoring Manuals for Minnesota Test of Creative Thinking and Writing." Kent, Ohio: Kent State University Bureau of Educational Research, 1964.

Yussen, S., Mathews, S., and Knight, J. Performance of Montessori and Traditionally Schooled Nursery Children on Social Cognitive Tasks and Memory Problems. *Contemporary Educational Psychology,* **5**, 1980.

APPENDIX: MONTESSORI TERMS

(These are from the lectures given during Montessori training, as well as from Montessori's writings. The language is kept as close as possible to the original Italian, even though this makes the English sound somewhat strange. These definitions were first used at the Santa Monica Montessori Institute, in Santa Monica, California.)

ADAPTATION

The process of the response of the individual to the environment; this process results in the individual's construction of himself. All parts of the individual's psyche must be properly adapted to his environment. Then, and only then, will the mature adult feel serene and satisfied with his own situation. For living beings, being correctly adapted is very important; without proper adaptation, grave physical and psychological difficulties will occur. An adapted person has had harmonious, appropriate development.

DEVELOPMENT

The process by which each being is brought from conception to adulthood, first on a physical, then on a psychological level. Each person's development is due to an unconscious power. Each person is guided, even pushed, toward development by a vital force. The philosopher Bergson called this force "elan vitale." Dr. Montessori used a term borrowed from philosopher Sir Percy Nunn, horme´. This is from the Greek: 'opμε" (life). This force, in Montessori's thought, is similar to the force that is pushing or driving all of the world toward its teleological end in the philosophy of the French Jesuit Pierre Teilhard de Chardin. Horme´ is assisted in its work by another force, mneme, "memory."

EDUCATION

For Montessori, education must include all phases of an individual's life, and the focus must be on the individual, not on the utilitarian needs of the society. Education must correspond to the individual's developmental needs, and should assist the adaptive process he undergoes in relation to all phases of his environment.

HORME´

The leading force of the great intelligence that is pushing all matter, living and nonliving, toward its final goals.[1] Montessori gives examples of horme´; it is seen in the force that unites two separate substances to form a new compound; out of a limited number of elements, every known compound in the universe is formed, including those that live. The universal unconscious intelligence, guided and pushed by horme´, is the intelligence that organizes this. Another example is the force that joins the molecules in a substance; each

---

[1]Final in the sense of *telos* or goal-end, not merely to the end of life in death. Montessori on occasion described this force as "unconscious"; it is unclear whether she meant that the force acted on us at a level below our consciousness, or that the force itself was unconscious. It is also unclear what the relationship of this force (in Montessori's thought) might be to the source of the similar push in Chardin's thought, the Christian God.

phase change (from liquid to gas or solid to liquid) occurs at a specific pressure and temperature. If the conditions are not fulfilled, the change will not occur. In biology, an example of horme' is the gene pattern carried in each cell of every organism. Using this pattern, the unconscious intelligence, guided and pushed by horme', directs the amazing task of the organization and construction of an entirely new creature, which is nevertheless a duplicate based on the genes of both parents. Only death can stop horme'.

Horme' extends over a vast field. Human beings can be compelled to act against their wills, for example, with hypnotism. There are in the universe unconscious forces that can overcome our wills. Some of these things are let free especially when crowds gather. People will do things in groups or mobs that they would not think of doing as individuals. Certain actions of children are the result of powerful forces acting on them, independent of their wills. Often a child, asked the reason he has done something, will reply, "I don't know."

Montessori says that we must work to defend the child against the negative aspects of types of these forces. The human being must be understood from birth, and his conscious will developed. This is what education should do, and it is one of the most important aims of the new education.

Horme' is the force that powers the spontaneous work of the children in the Children's House; it is what makes them repeat an exercise until they are satisfied. In small children, this drive or push is on the unconscious level, like the drive to eat. In older children, it becomes a voluntary factor. This vital force can be either a conscious or an unconscious biological force; the unconscious part is much greater.

MNEME

This is a hereditary memory, an unconscious memory reproducing the past and preserving all the experiences of the beings before us. [2] *All living beings have this, both plant and animal life. This memory of race exists in every being, and allows each being to reproduce his kind and repeat the same ways of living. For example, each species of bird builds a different kind of nest, but within one species, the nests will be the same.*

There are two kinds of mneme: one, the physical kind, all life has: plant, animal, and man. This allows them to reproduce their kind.

Then there is psychic mneme, which is different for animals and man, and plant life has none. In animals, this is called instinct. It is the same from generation to generation for the most part, but it is not absolute or completely rigid. Instinct can be modified according to the conditions of the environment. That is, animals always reproduce their own species, but unless there is a possibility of adaption, a species is bound to die. As an example, take the dinosaurs; they were huge and powerful, but they could not adapt to the coming of the cold with the Ice Age. So, they died out and were replaced by the more adaptable mammals.

This possibility of adaptation of instincts is comparable to the adaptability of man through his genes. Human genes, dominant and recessive, are always combining to produce new phenotypes, new expressions. If the environment changes, some of the recessive genes

---

[2] Note: Compare to Jung's idea of the "collective unconscious."

that now produce occasional changes in humans that are not important or even a handicap, could become essential for survival.

Plants are also adaptable because of the <u>mneme</u> they possess. In all cases, adaptation is much easier in the developing being than in the adult.

In man's psychic embryo, there are no instincts comparable to those of the animals. There are instincts in man, in the physical embryo, concerning heartbeat, digestion, and other lower functions, but there are none in the psychic embryo. The beings that have instincts are helped by them, but they are limited. They can only adapt to a limited degree to any new environment. Take the lion as an example: although he can adapt to life in a cage, he could not adapt to the temperature of a fairly cold climate such as Bergamo (Italy), without outside help from man. He is limited to a certain range of latitudes on the globe. Man can, and does, make his dwellings anywhere on earth, from deserts to within the Arctic Circle.

Instead of instincts, man has potentialities, which Montessori called <u>nebulae</u>. Man is born free.

<u>NEBULAE</u>

In space before the creation of the stars, there existed vast quantities of a substance that was to form the stars, hydrogen. Dr. Montessori pictured this invisible hydrogen floating in infinite space filled with what she called horme´. It was this horme´ that caused the particles of hydrogen to coalesce into swirling masses: the nebulae. The nebulae, pushed by the universal unconscious intelligence of horme´, would sometimes break off and condense further to form a star, and, later, planets. This was the picture Montessori had of the development of "instincts" in the psychic embryo of man from the potentialities he is born with. For this reason, she called these potentialities <u>nebulae</u>. These <u>nebulae</u> are indistinct, indefinite, but there, waiting for the right moment to go into action.

For example, a child is not born with a predetermined language, but with the potential to learn any language. This potential exists in the child, driving him to learn the language of those around him; he is responding to his environment. When the language is incarnated, the potential will disappear. The child will know the language. Never again will he be able to learn any language so easily, and he will never be as fluent in another tongue as he is in his own.

Man is not born with instincts, but with these <u>nebulae</u>, making him able to form his own instincts; making him able to have almost infinite acquisitions and learnings. Man has endless possibilities for adaptation and development. Man is born free, but through the experiences of his life, he builds his own instincts. He builds a special attitude towards life. When he is an adult, this instinct works in him like the instincts of the animals work in them. Therefore, it is important how this attitude toward life is built.

This instinct, adaptation to life, that man builds in himself from childhood through adolescence to adulthood, is a very strong force and can become something frightening. Through this adaptation, men can become fanatical if their environment or their adaptation is wrong. A man can become a religious, political, national, or idealistic fanatic. Why is this instinct built in the wrong way? Because the directions given by the environment are wrong, or because of a lack of coordination. There are other dangers besides fanaticism. People can be dangerous, unbalanced. These maladapted people don't have the behavior to fit the world they live in.

These <u>nebulae</u> are mysterious potentialities. Just as the genes in the germinative cell direct the formation of complex organs in the physical embryo, the <u>nebulae</u> direct the construction of the psychic embryo after birth. The <u>nebulae</u> are helped in this job by the powers of the <u>subconscious</u>.

<u>SUBCONSCIOUS</u>

The <u>subconscious</u> is the collection of all the experiences amassed by an individual from his birth onwards. These build the attitude toward life of every organism, making it able to adapt to a changing environment. It is a very strong force in the human psyche.

Some, but not all, of these experiences laid down in the subconscious come "to light" in the conscious mind.[3] The passage from the subconscious to the conscious does not take place suddenly. The human psyche can be compared to a huge house, with consciousness on the upper levels, and a huge dark cellar where the subconscious lives. The cellar is also like a furnace in the house of the mind, and there is always work going on there.

The subconscious is also like a great factory that works 24 hours a day, never resting or sleeping. In fact, when the conscious mind rests in what we call sleep, the subconscious is at its most active, It becomes the sole master of the psyche. Often the subconscious will prepare answers to problems we have had during the day while we are asleep. There are proverbs in many languages that tell us to sleep before making a decision. In Italian, "Night brings good advice," and in English, "Sleep on it" are two examples.

Maria Montessori compared the subconscious to a large room in which are stored all the experiences of a lifetime, but the experiences are stored in a mixed-up way. To make it worse, the room is dark. When the consciousness looks for an answer, a flashlight searches in the room, and what is needed can sometimes be located and carried up to the conscious mind.

Freud and other psychologists are certain that this subconscious exists, but little is known about how it works in the brain. The activity in the subconscious is thought to be produced by engrams. These are traces or after-effects of every experience. The important thing is that these traces are not merely stored, like letters in a mail room. They work, they interact with each other, and because of this work, light emerges into our conscious mind.

Dr. Montessori illustrates this with the example of a child learning to speak. The actual appearance of speech will seem to us to be quite sudden; one day the child will speak. But this is not really something sudden; this is really the result of a very long period of activity in the subconscious. It starts when the child is 2 or 3 months old and is fixated on the lips of the people who are speaking to him. Through sight and hearing, he absorbs the movement of the lips and the sound he hears; these are deposited on the subconscious. At a certain point, the explosion takes place.

The engrams were likened by Montessori to worms working in a piece of earth; through their constant activity they make the soil fertile for plants to grow. The engrams are always working to prepare the mind for what must be learned next.

---

[3] Again, a comparison to Jung comes to mind here.

Things experienced in early childhood and forgotten are still at work inside the subconscious. These experiences are still there in the subconscious and can be called back in psychoanalysis.

The subconscious is much more important than the conscious. In the past, psychologists thought that only the conscious mind was important, and that everything we learned, we learned through the conscious association of ideas. The engrams, however, are powerful, always working, and they allow us to learn a great deal that could never be learned with the conscious mind.

When we hear the phrase, "That person is learned or cultured," we do not mean that he remembers everything that he has ever known or experienced. (The Italian educato is difficult to translate; perhaps genteel would be a better word.) But his subconscious remembers these things and he is thus intelligent; his subconscious is rich in all the experiences of his life. This is one of the bases of the Montessori method; not a keeping of knowledge in the conscious mind, it is based rather on the possibility of continuous, varied, and repeated experiences and the storage and interrelations of these experiences in the subconscious mind.

INDEX